ATTRIBUTE-VALUE LOGIC AND THE THEORY OF GRAMMAR

CSLI
Lecture Notes
Number 16

ATTRIBUTE-VALUE LOGIC AND THE THEORY OF GRAMMAR

Mark Johnson

CSLI
CENTER FOR THE STUDY
OF LANGUAGE
AND INFORMATION

CSLI was founded early in 1983 by researchers from Stanford University, SRI International, and Xerox PARC to further research and development of integrated theories of language, information, and computation. CSLI headquarters and the publication offices are located at the Stanford site.

CSLI/SRI International
333 Ravenswood Avenue
Menlo Park, CA 94025

CSLI/Stanford
Ventura Hall
Stanford, CA 94305

CSLI/Xerox PARC
3333 Coyote Hill Road
Palo Alto, CA 94304

Printed in the United States
94 93 92 91 90 89 88   5 4 3 2 1

Library of Congress Cataloging-in-Publication Data

Johnson, Mark, 1957 June 17–
Attribute-value logic and the theory of grammar / Mark Johnson.
p. cm. – (CSLI lecture notes ; no. 16)
Bibliography: p.
Includes index.
1. Grammar, Comparative and general. 2. Language and logic.
3. Computational linguistics. I. Title. II. Series.
P151.J67 1988
415–dc19   88–25120
CIP

ISBN 0–937073–37–7
ISBN 0–937073–36–9 (pbk.)

To my parents
and
Katherine

Contents

Acknowledgements

Thanks are due to my advisor, Stanley Peters, the other members of my thesis committee, Paul Kiparsky and Fernando Pereira, and to Jon Barwise, Ivan Sag and Lauri Karttunen. They made many suggestions, most of them good, and most of which I followed. Both the form and the content of this work are heavily influenced by them.

I have some rather specific debts to acknowledge. Jon Barwise gave me a crash course on compactness that lead to the proof in Section 2.6. Annie Zaenen helped me through the Dutch Double Infinitive Construction, and provided me with much of the data that appears in Chapter 4. Ron Kaplan convinced me (via a series of terse but frequent electronic mail messages) that I should regard attribute-value descriptions simply as descriptions rather than 'partial objects', providing me with perhaps the central theme of this work. Yes, you were right Ron, it does all work out rather simply this way.

A special thanks to Ewan Klein and Bill Rounds for reading and commenting on an earlier draft of this work. As always, their comments were both insightful and encouraging.

This work was supported by CSLI and a grant from the System Development Foundation. They provided me with a stimulating and pleasant place to actually get it all done. Thanks also to my colleagues at CSLI and the Linguistics Department at Stanford University, and especially to Stephen Neale, Trip McCrossin and Pete Ludlow for putting up with me during the final months involved in getting this written. I also would like to thank the members of the Foundations of Grammar group at CSLI. I learnt much from that group, both individually and collectively. Martin Kay was especially generous with his time and suggestions, and much of this book is influenced by his approach.

Chapter 1

Introduction

This book studies attribute-value structures and their use in attribute-value based theories of grammar, such as Lexical-Functional Grammar (Bresnan and Kaplan 1982), Head-driven Phrase Structure Grammar (Pollard and Sag 1987, Sag and Pollard 1987), and Categorial Unification Grammar (Karttunen 1986). I abstract away from the details of these theories to characterize attribute-value structures in a simple and precise way, and then investigate the implications of this characterization. Thus this work differs from most linguistic research in that I am concerned not with a particular linguistic theory, but with an entire class of linguistic theories constructed from essentially the same formal devices. This work is also unusual in emphasizing the investigation of how the 'knowledge of language' that an attribute-value grammar represents can be put to use.

In the next chapter I formally define attribute-value structures and develop a language $\mathcal{A}$ for their description. This language extends previous work in this area by treating negation and disjunction in a purely classical fashion. To show that the problem of determining whether there exists an attribute-value structure satisfying a particular description is decidable, I develop a logic of this language and present an algorithm based on this logic capable of determining whether a given description is satisfiable. By investigating the properties of this logic I characterize the set of attribute-value structures that a formula of $\mathcal{A}$ describes, and use these results to relate the work presented here to earlier studies of attribute-value structures.

Chapter 3 examines one way in which a theory of grammar can use attribute-value structures. In this sort of attribute-value grammar, a linguistic structure is a pair consisting of a constituent structure tree and an attribute-value structure, and a grammar is a pair consisting of a finite set of lexical entries and a finite set of syntactic rules. I then show that if an attribute-value based theory of grammar is defined such that any finite tree is a possible constituent structure, then the universal recognition problem for these theories is undecidable. On the other hand, I show that if the set of constituent structure trees is restricted by requiring each tree to satisfy the Off-line Parsability Constraint, then the universal recognition problem for these theories of grammar is decidable.

In chapter 4 I turn from the formal details of attribute-value structures and consider one aspect of their linguistic application. It turns out that the attribute-value framework only weakly constrains the substantive analyses of particular linguistic phenomena; it does not even determine the nature of the representation of grammatical relations in these theories. I investigate two different ways in which grammatical relations might be represented in attribute-value based theories, which I call the direct and the hierarchical encodings. I show that in an attribute-value based theory using the direct encoding of grammatical relations, an analysis of the Dutch Double Infinitive Construction based on that of Bresnan *et al.* (1982) requires constituent structures that violate the Off-line Parsability Constraint, while a similar analysis expressed in a theory that uses the hierarchical encoding of grammatical relations does not require such structures.

1.1 Attribute-Value Grammar and the Theory of Language

As mentioned above, the orientation of the material presented here differs significantly from most linguistic work. In this section I try to explain the rationale for this difference in orientation, and why the results of this work are relevant to the study of language as a whole.

Chomsky (1986, p. 3) lists the following three questions as the basic questions that arise in the study of language.

(1a) What constitutes knowledge of language?

(1b) How is knowledge of language acquired?

(1c) How is knowledge of language put to use?

Answers to all of these questions have been given in attribute-value based theories of grammar. Most of the work on attribute-value based formalisms can be viewed as attempting to define exactly what constitutes knowledge of language. Pinker (1982) describes one way in which a grammar from a particular attribute-value based theory, LFG, might be acquired. In these two aspects then, work in attribute-value based theories of grammar parallels that of work in other modern theories of grammar, such as Government and Binding Theory (Chomsky 1981).

However, the attribute-value framework differs from most other approaches to the theory of grammar in that there exist general, straight-forward mechanisms by which the "knowledge of language" that a particular grammar represents can be "put to use." There are practical computational algorithms which, when given an arbitrary attribute-value grammar, are capable of parsing the language generated by that grammar.[1] While these algorithms are not intended as psychologically realistic models of language processing, such models can be developed from them (e.g., Ford, Bresnan and Kaplan 1982).

More importantly, the existence of these algorithms shows us that the knowledge of language represented by a grammar from an attribute-value theory is of a kind that can in principle be used by a computational device capable of solving some of the problems faced by a real language user. If we assume that processing a natural language involves solving the parsing problem for that language, then their existence shows at least that this problem is in fact soluble, even if it turns out that humans do not use these algorithms. Clearly this provides only a preliminary account of the use of knowledge of language, which needs to be refined in many different ways. Nonetheless, the attribute-value framework can provide, at a fairly abstract level, the outline of an answer to Chomsky's third question (1c) regarding the nature of language use.

Understanding in a formally precise way the relationship between attribute-value grammars and their parsing algorithms is one of the goals of this book. I accomplish this by abstracting away from the details of particular linguistic theories, proposing a general formalization of an attribute-value based theory of grammar, and proving that with certain additional assumptions, the universal recognition problem for such grammars is decidable. Thus this work is relevant to the study of language because it demonstrates, in a fairly abstract way, that the knowledge of language represented by an attribute-value grammar

---

[1] In the terminology of Aho, Sethi and Ullman (1986) these algorithms are *parser-generators*, i.e. devices which, when given a grammar, generate a parser for the strings that that grammar generates.

of the kind described in Chapter 3 can in fact be used by a computational process.

More specifically, attribute-value based theories of grammar typically use some apparatus to associate strings with descriptions of attribute-value structures in the manner described in Chapter 3. From a computational point of view, an attractive feature of such theories is that a language processing need only consist of two computationally simple components: one associating a string with a description of an attribute-value structure, and another that 'reads off' the required information from this description. The major formal accomplishment of this book–the treatment of how information about an attribute-value structure can be determined from its description–is thus an important step in providing a principled answer to Chomsky's third question.

It is important to note the difference between the parsing algorithms for attribute-value grammars discussed here and many other models of natural language processing, such as the Marcus parser (Marcus 1979). Unlike the attribute-value parsing algorithms just mentioned, parsers such as the Marcus parser do not use the (competence) grammar of the language directly, but require a set of specialized (usually hand-coded) instructions to direct the parsing operation. While such processing models may provide an explanation for certain processing phenomena such as 'Garden Path' effects, until the relationship between the (competence) grammar of a language and the specialized instructions required by the parser is determined and shown to be computationally realizable, these models cannot be viewed as providing an answer to Chomsky's third question.[2]

1.2 An Example of an Attribute-Value Grammar

Attribute-value based theories of grammar are distinguished from other theories of grammar by both the nature of the linguistic structures they use, and the types of formal devices that are employed in a grammar to describe them. In this section I informally discuss an attribute-value grammar fragment. There is no universally accepted formulation of attribute-value grammar, so I present the fragment in the formalism developed in Chapter 3.[3]

---

[2] For further discussion, see Stabler (1984).

[3] For an introduction to attribute-value grammars based on a different approach, see Shieber (1986).

A linguistic structure of an attribute-value based theory of grammar is called an annotated constituent structure. It consists of a constituent structure tree, an attribute-value structure, and an association of the nodes in the constituent structure tree with elements of the attribute-value structure.

A constituent structure tree is a labelled, oriented tree similar to context-free grammar derivation trees, except that the lexical forms do not appear as separate nodes of the constituent structure tree, but appear as annotations on the terminal nodes of the constituent structure tree.

An attribute-value structure consists of a set of entities called the attribute-value elements. There are two kinds of elements in an attribute-value structure; the atomic or constant elements, which have no internal structure, and the complex elements, which have a hierarchical internal structure defined by their attributes and the corresponding values. The value of an attribute of a complex element may be any other element of the attribute-value structure, including another complex element. It is not necessary that all attributes of a complex element have a value, and it is also allowed that an element may be the value of two or more attributes of an element.

A typical annotated constituent structure that might be generated by an attribute-value grammar is depicted in Figure 1.

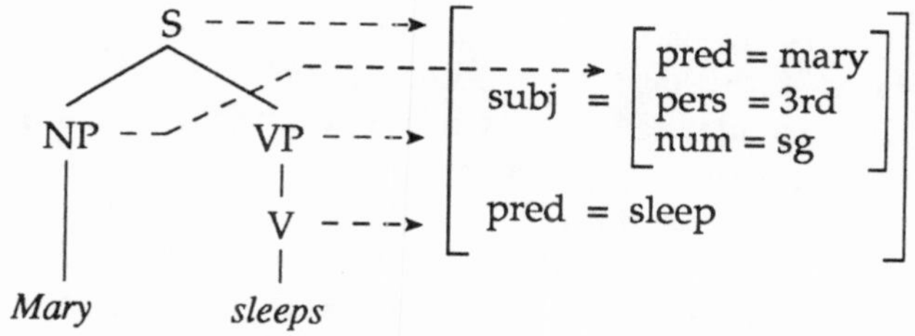

Figure 1 A typical annotated constituent structure

The terminal string or the yield of the annotated constituent structure depicted in Figure 1 is *Mary sleeps.* The attribute-value structure that forms part of the annotated constituent structure is depicted in matrix form. The constant elements of that attribute-value structure are *mary, 3rd, sg* and *sleep.*[4] All of the constituents in the constituent

[4] As I show in the next chapter, it is convenient to treat the attributes of an attribute-value structure as constant elements as well. If this is done, then the constant elements of the attribute-value structure would include *pred, pers, num* and *subj* as well.

structure tree are associated with complex elements. The NP is associated with a complex element that has values for the three attributes *pred, pers* and *num*. The value of the *pred* attribute is the constant element *mary*, the value of the *pers* attribute is the constant element *3rd*, and the value of the *num* attribute is the constant element *sg*. The S, VP and V constituents are all associated with the same complex element. That element has values for the two attributes *subj* and *pred*. The value of the *pred* attribute is the constant element *sleep*, while the value of the *subj* element is the complex element that is associated with the NP constituent.

An attribute-value grammar does not directly assign attribute-value elements to nodes of the constituent structure tree, but merely requires that the elements associated with constituents meet certain conditions, or alternatively, satisfy certain constraints. The grammar can thus be viewed as a set of *licensing principles* for the nodes of the constituent structure tree. An annotated constituent structure tree is generated by a grammar if and only if every node in that tree is licensed. Terminal nodes are licensed by lexical entries, and non-terminal nodes are licensed by syntactic rules. A single lexical entry or syntactic rule can license any number of nodes in an annotated constituent structure (including zero), so the size of an annotated constituent structure is not bounded by the size of the lexicon or the number of syntactic rules.

A lexical entry licenses a terminal node if and only if (i) the lexical form associated with that terminal node matches the form in the lexical entry, (ii) the syntactic category of the terminal node is the same as the syntactic category as the lexical entry, and (iii) the attribute-value element associated with the terminal node satisfies the requirements of the lexical entry. These requirements are stated as an open formula containing the distinguished variable x, and they are satisfied if the formula is true when x denotes the attribute-value element associated with the terminal node.

Two sample lexical entries are given below.

(2a)	*Mary*	NP	$x(\text{num}) = \text{sg} \wedge$ $x(\text{pers}) = \text{3rd} \wedge$ $x(\text{pred}) = \text{mary}.$
(2b)	*sleeps*	V	$x(\text{subj})(\text{num}) = \text{sg} \wedge$ $x(\text{subj})(\text{pers}) = \text{3rd} \wedge$ $x(\text{pred}) = \text{sleep}.$

The lexical entry (2a) licenses any terminal node with a lexical form *mary* and a syntactic category NP, so long as the attribute-value element associated with that terminal node has (at least) the three attributes *num, pers* and *pred,* and moreover the value of the *num* attribute is the constant element *sg,* the value of the *pers* attribute is the constant element *3rd,* and the value of the *pred* attribute is the constant element *mary.* Thus this lexical entry licenses the NP node of the annotated constituent structure depicted in Figure 1.

The lexical entry (2b) is more complicated. It licenses any terminal node with a lexical form *sleeps* and syntactic category V, so long as the attribute-value element it is associated with has (at least) the two attribute *subj* and *pred* with values meeting the following conditions. The value of the *pred* attribute must be the atomic constant *sleep,* and the value of the *subj* attribute must itself be a complex element which has (at least) the two attributes *pers* and *num,* where the value of the *pers* attribute must be *3rd,* and the value of the *num* attribute must be *sg.* Thus this lexical entry licenses the V node of the annotated constituent structure depicted in Figure 1.

A syntactic rule licenses a non-terminal node if and only if the syntactic categories of that node and its daughter nodes match the those specified in the syntactic rule, and the attribute-value elements associated with the node and its daughters satisfy the requirements of the syntactic rule. If the rule licenses $n \geq 1$ daughter nodes, the requirements on the attribute-value elements associated with these nodes are stated as an open formula containing the $n + 1$ distinguished variables $x, x_1, \ldots, x_n$, and they are satisfied if the formula is true when x denotes the attribute-value element associated with the node being licensed, and each x_i denotes the attribute-value element associated with the ith daughter of the node being licensed.

Three sample syntactic rules are presented in (4).

(4a) S → NP VP $\quad x = x_2 \wedge x(\text{subj}) = x_1.$

(4b) VP → V $\quad x = x_1.$

(4c) VP → V NP $\quad x = x_1 \wedge x(\text{obj}) = x_2.$

The syntactic rule in (4a) states that an S node can have an NP node and a VP node as its daughters (in that order) if the attribute-value element associated with the S node is the element associated with the VP node, and the value of the *subj* attribute of element associated with the S node is the element associated with the NP node.

This rule thus licenses the S node of the annotated constituent structure depicted in Figure 1.

All of the grammar is specified in this manner. Structure modification (in the form of transformations or principles such as 'Move-α') does not occur. Furthermore, because the syntactic rules are capable of stating constraints only between the attribute-value structures assigned to a node and its immediate daughters, there is a very strong locality restriction on the primitive interactions that can be specified by the grammar. Longer distance interactions must thus be reduced to a series of strictly local ones using the sort of feature-passing techniques made famous by the 'slash category' analyses of GPSG (Gazdar *et al.*, 1986).

To conclude this section, I compare the attribute-value formalism just presented with the grammar formalism for Lexical-Functional Grammars developed by Kaplan and Bresnan (1982). Although it may not be apparent, the attribute-value formalism just described is closely related to the LFG grammar formalism. LFG lexical entries and syntactic rules differ mainly in typographical detail from the lexical entries and syntactic rules presented above. LFG lexical entries are virtually notational equivalents of the lexical entries presented above, with the symbol '↑' taking the place of the variable x.

LFG syntactic rules differ more markedly from the syntactic rules presented above. The constraints on the attribute-value elements associated with the node licensed by the rule and the elements associated with its daughters do not constitute a separate component of the rule, as in the format described above, but rather are expressed as 'equational annotations' are 'attached' to individual daughter constituents of the phrase structure rule. Informally speaking, within any annotation attached to a daughter constituent the symbol '↑' denotes the attribute-value element associated with the node being licensed, while '↓' denotes the element associated with the daughter constituent in question.

The LFG lexical entries and grammar rules given in (5) and (6) license the same annotated constituent structures as the lexical entries and grammar rules of (2) and (4) do.

(5a)	*sleeps*	V	(↑ subj num) = sg
			(↑ subj pers) = 3rd
			(↑ pred) = sleep
(5b)	*John*	NP	(↑ num) = sg
			(↑ pers) = 3rd
			(↑ pred) = john.

(6a) S → NP VP
$(\uparrow \text{subj}) = \downarrow$ $\uparrow = \downarrow$

(6b) VP → V
$\uparrow = \downarrow$

(6c) VP → V NP
$\uparrow = \downarrow$ $(\uparrow \text{obj}) = \downarrow$

The two grammar formalisms do differ in terms of the types of constraints that they can concisely express. For example, the LFG formalism allows the abbreviation of the syntactic rules (6b) and (6c) to (7), something which the formalism described above does not allow.

(7) VP → V (NP)
$\uparrow = \downarrow$ $(\uparrow \text{obj}) = \downarrow$

On the other hand, the LFG syntactic rule format only allows constraints that mention the attribute-value elements associated with the node being licensed and one of its daughter constituents. Thus constraints that hold between the attribute-value elements associated with two different daughter constituents, such as the one shown in (8), must be re-expressed in a different way.

(8) VP → V NP $x_1(\text{subcat})(\text{first}) = x_2 \wedge$
$x_1(\text{subcat})(\text{rest}) = x$.

The two rule formalisms are equivalent in the sense that it is always possible to 'translate' a grammar written in one formalism into a grammar with written in the other that generates the same strings and assigns the same constituent structures to those strings. On the other hand, the 'translation' may have the property of being exponentially larger than the original;[5] thus a grammar that appears linguistically motivated and insightful when written in one formalism can sometimes only be translated into a relatively unperspicuous grammar in the other.

1.3 Previous Work on Attribute-Value Grammar

In this section I attempt to place the material in this book in the context of the on-going work on the attribute-value based approach to grammar.

---

[5] For example, an LFG rule with n optional daughter constituents would be translated into 2^n distinct grammar rules in the format proposed here.

Kaplan and Bresnan's (1982) Lexical-Functional Grammar provides the basis for much of the subsequent development of the attribute-value approach, including the material presented in this book. Kaplan and Bresnan introduced attribute-value structures as the *f*-structures of LFG, devised formulae for their description called *f*-descriptions, and used these formulae as constraints that appear in lexical entries and syntactic rules on the attribute-value elements associated with syntactic constituents in essentially the same way as in Chapter 3. Kaplan and Bresnan (1982) also recognized the importance of the Off-line Parsability Constraint in ensuring the decidability of the parsing problem for Lexical Functional Grammars.

Kay's (1979) notion of 'unification', and his Functional Unification Grammar that was based on it, inspired much of the work in the attribute-value based approach to grammar outside of LFG theory. In contrast to LFG and the approach taken in this book, Kay directly assigns attribute-value structures to lexical entries and syntactic rules to represent the 'linguistic information' they contain. 'Unification' is an operation applied to two attribute-value structures that yields another attribute-value structure that 'contains' all of the 'information' present in both of the input attribute-value structures. At a conceptual level at least, the 'linguistic information' associated with a linguistic structure constructed by the application of syntactic rules to various lexical forms is simply the 'unification' of the 'linguistic information' (i.e., the attribute-value structures) associated with each of the lexical entries and syntactic rules involved in its construction.[6]

Kay's work initiated a line of research that I call the 'unification view' of attribute-value grammar. Shieber (1986) contains an excellent introduction to this way of viewing attribute-value grammar. In Shieber's formulation, lexical entries specify directly the attribute-value structures associated with terminal constituent structure nodes, and syntactic rules map constituent structure *n*–tuples, together with their associated attribute-value structures, to new constituent structures associated with attribute-value structures.

The 'unification view' is attractive in that it suggests that language processing is simply 'information collection', i.e., the unification of the attribute-value structures associated with the lexical entries and syntactic rules used in the construction of a linguistic structure. Nonetheless, attempts to extend the attribute-value framework under this view to include disjunction or negation (e.g., Karttunen 1985) have proved to be problematic: it is not clear what a 'disjunctive

---

[6] This ignores some of the complexities in the FUG treatment of constituent structure.

attribute-value structure' is, nor how one could prove that a particular formulation of 'disjunctive attribute value structures' (and unification over such structures) is correct.

Rather than introducing disjunction into the attribute-value structures themselves, Kasper and Rounds (1986) deal with disjunction in the attribute-value framework by devising a language for describing attribute-value structures that included disjunctive descriptions. Moshier and Rounds (1987) subsequently extended the Kasper and Rounds (1986) system to include negation in the same fashion. In both Kasper and Rounds (1986) and Moshier and Rounds (1987) the language for describing attribute-value structures is developed as a logical system, and in both cases the authors provide a complete set of logical equivalences for their languages. I follow Kasper and Rounds (1986) and Moshier and Rounds (1987) in devising a specialized language for describing attribute-value structures, and then studying the logic of that language.

The success of the Kasper and Rounds (1986) and the Moshier and Rounds (1987) treatments of disjunction and negation suggests that the distinction between attribute-value structures and their descriptions originally made by Kaplan and Bresnan (1982) and abandoned by Kay (1979) is an important one. Indeed, it is the fundamental distinction made in the treatment of attribute-value structures presented in the following chapters.

The treatment of attribute-value structures presented here differs from Moshier and Rounds (1987) in that negation is interpreted classically rather than intuitionistically. Kapser and Rounds (1986) and Moshier and Rounds (1987) devised their languages to understand monotonic instantiation of record structures, and use the 'succession relation' of intuitionistic logic (Fitting 1969) to model the accretion of information in such structures. Their approach might be appropriate for modelling the changing 'information state' of a language user over time.

The language I develop in the next chapter differs from those of Kasper and Rounds (1986) and Moshier and Rounds (1987) in that its formulae are interpreted as descriptions of an attribute-value structure that does not 'change' over time. This is consistent with the formulation of attribute-value grammar presented in Chapter 3, in which the 'generates' relation relates grammars to linguistic structures (as totally instantiated objects). This formulation is in turn itself ultimately grounded in the structuralist view of language implicit in this version of attribute-value grammar. That is, in contrast with the view which focuses on the informational states of the language user, this formulation of attribute-value grammar views a linguistic structure as a complete object whose identity is determined by the constraints of the grammar and the utterance. In this system partiality is located in the relationship between descriptions and linguistic structures, not in the structures themselves.

Thus the language for describing attribute-value structures presented in the next chapter is one in which the propositional connectives have a purely classical interpretation. In this system attribute-value structures play only one role: they are defined in order to give a semantics for the language that describes them. None of the algorithms given in the following chapters actually constructs an attribute-value structure: instead, they operate on descriptions of attribute-value structures to determine the existence and the properties of those structures. The clean separation between attribute-value structures and the language for their description results in a system with a relatively simple structure, and in which important formal results, such as the decidability of the satisfiability problem, are easy to obtain.

Chapter 2

Attribute-Value Structures

In this chapter I investigate in detail the properties of attribute-value structures. I present a language called $\mathcal{A}$ for describing attribute-value structures, and then axiomatize the valid formulae of that language to give a logic that I call AVL (for 'Attribute-Value Logic'). The results of this chapter are used in the next chapter, where I explain how attribute-value structures and descriptions of them can be used in a theory of grammar.

In the first section I enumerate the fundamental properties of attribute-value structures, and then present a definition that captures them. This definition is deliberately broad, allowing attribute-value structures that some theorists might wish to exclude, so I discuss a number of restrictions that could be imposed on attribute-value structures, showing in each case what the consequences of the restriction would be.

In the second section I present the formal language $\mathcal{A}$ for describing attribute-value structures, specifying its syntax and semantics precisely. In the third section I study the logic of that language, giving axioms and rules of inference by means of which all and only the valid formulae of the language can be proven.

In the fourth section I prove that this axiomatization is sound, and in the fifth section I prove that it is complete. In this section I also present algorithms for determining the satisfiability and validity of formulae, demonstrating that these problems are decidable. These decidability results are important because, as I show in the next chapter, one way of processing an attribute-value grammar involves determining the satisfiability of attribute-value formulae.

In the sixth section I prove that the language is compact, and in the seventh section I investigate the effects that the restrictions on attribute-value structures discussed at the beginning of the chapter have on the satisfiability and validity of formulae of $\mathcal{A}$. In the eighth section I examine the expressive power of this language, and characterize the sets of attribute-value structures that formulae of this language can describe.

In the ninth section I examine the relationship between the language $\mathcal{A}$ and the quantifier-free first-order languages with equality and function symbols. I show that the satisfiability problem for formulae of $\mathcal{A}$ is $\mathcal{NP}$-complete by providing a polynomial reduction to the satisfiability problem for the quantifier-free first-order languages with equality and function symbols, and a polynomial reduction of the satisfiability problem for the propositional calculus to the satisfiability problem for $\mathcal{A}$.

I end this chapter with a discussion of the major difference between my treatment of attribute-value structures and the usual one: I do not treat attribute-value structures as 'partial' entities, contrary to most formulations of attribute-value grammar (see, e.g., Shieber 1986). Rather, the relationship between attribute-value models and the formulae that describe them is the same as the relationship that holds between models and formulae in standard model-theoretic treatments of logics.

The treatment developed here of attribute-value structures and the logic of the language for their description is very similar to standard treatments of first-order model theory. The overall layout of my presentation is loosely based on Andrews' (1986) presentation of first-order logic. I indicate in the text where material is directly drawn from this or other works. Most of this chapter focuses on determining the properties of the language for describing attribute-value structures, building on earlier work of Kaplan and Bresnan (1982), Pereira and Shieber (1984), Karttunen (1985), Kasper and Rounds (1986), Shieber (1986), Kasper (1987), Moshier and Rounds (1987), and Pereira (1987). The work presented here extends these earlier treatments in treating negation classically and in allowing the use of attributes as values.

This work has its roots in the work of Pereira and Shieber (1984), who emphasize the need for an explicit semantics for a grammar formalism. The use of logic as a tool for explaining disjunction and negation in an attribute-value formalism was introduced by Kasper and Rounds (1986) and Moshier and Rounds (1987). The work presented here primarily differs from these treatments in that it does not view partiality or unification as defining properties of attribute-value structures.[7] In this respect I follow the pioneering work of Kaplan and Bresnan (1982), who also view attribute-value formulae as descriptions which a particular attribute-value structure may or may not satisfy.[8]

It is important to recognize that this work is not intended as the presentation of a theory of grammar. According to the generative account of language, a theory of language includes a specification of at least three things: (i) the class of possible grammars, where a grammar of a language characterizes knowledge of that language, (ii) the class of possible linguistic structures, where a linguistic structure characterizes linguistic knowledge of an utterance, and (iii) the 'generates' relation, which identifies the possible linguistic structures with respect to a particular grammar.

Characterizing the class of possible human languages is not one of the goals of the work presented in this chapter or the following one. I am not concerned with specifying the notion of 'possible linguistic structure' or 'possible grammar of a human language'. Rather, these chapters provide a foundation of formal devices that can be used in the specification of a particular theory of grammar.

These chapters nevertheless do address the question of how the knowledge of language that a grammar represents can be put to use in language processing. I do this by showing that any grammar in any theory formulated in the attribute-value framework can in principle be used in language processing. In the next chapter I show that the recognition problem for such an attribute-value based grammar may involve determining whether certain descriptions of attribute-value structures are satisfiable; i.e., whether there exist attribute-value structures that meet these descriptions. In this chapter I provide algorithms for actually determining whether arbitrary descriptions of attribute-value structures are satisfiable, thus confirming that this problem is soluble.

Whether humans processing language actually manipulate attribute-value descriptions in the manner described in this chapter is an open question, but this work shows that these problems are soluble, and thus provides a preliminary account of one way in which knowledge of language might be used in language processing.

---

7 This is why I use the term 'attribute-value based approach to grammar' rather than 'unification-based approach to grammar'. For a different perspective, see Shieber (1986).

8 My presentation of attribute-value structures differs from that of Kaplan and Bresnan (1982) in that the satisfiability of negated formulae is defined classically, rather than with respect to a 'minimal model'.

2.1 Attribute-Value Structures

In this section I present a formal definition of an attribute-value structure. To justify this definition, I informally review the use of attribute-value structures in an attribute-value based theory of grammar and describe what I view as the important properties of attribute-value structures.

2.1.1 The Use of Attribute-Value Structures

In an attribute-value based theory of grammar certain structural properties of utterances are represented by attribute-value structures. More precisely, a linguistic structure consists of a labelled, ordered tree, an attribute-value structure, and an association of each node in the tree with an element in the attribute-value structure. An example is shown in Figure 1.

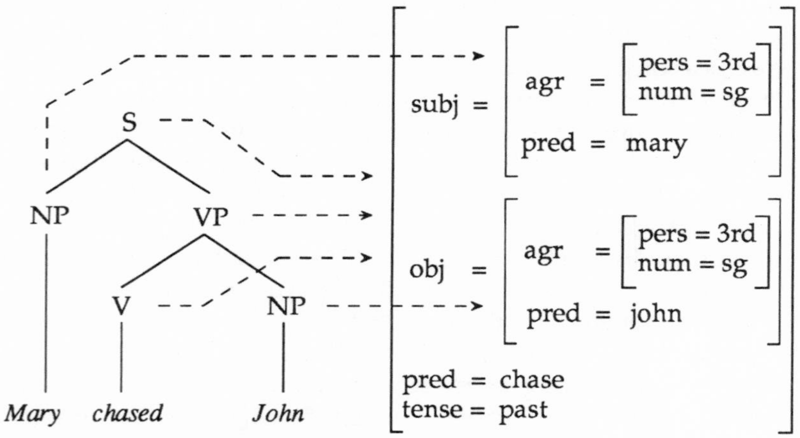

Figure 1 An attribute-value structure used as part of a linguistic structure

Attribute-value structures are employed for various purposes and given different names in the several attribute-value based theories. For example, they are called *f*-structures in LFG, feature matrices in GPSG, and functional structures in FUG. Despite the diversity of uses to which they are put, the attribute-value structures employed in these theories have a great deal in common.

2.1.2 The Important Properties of Attribute-Value Structures

To motivate the formal definition given below, I now identify what I view as the three central characteristics of attribute-value structures. These are:

(1a) The elements of an attribute-value structure are either atomic constants with no internal structure, or else are complex elements with a hierarchical internal structure.

(1b) The internal structure of an element is defined by its attributes and their values. The value of an attribute may be any element, either atomic or complex; thus the hierarchical internal structure of a complex element is determined by its attributes and their values.

(1c) An element may be the value of two or more attributes of an element, or the value of attributes of two or more elements; i.e., values may be 'shared'.

The attribute-value elements associated with each of the constituents of Figure 1 is a complex element. These are the three distinct elements to which the arrows point. The values *3rd, sg* and *mary* are atomic, or constant, elements in the attribute-value structure in Figure 1, while *subj, agr* and *pred* are attributes of that attribute-value structure, which are also atomic, or constant, elements. The values of the *subj* and *obj* attributes of the element assigned to the clause as a whole are complex attribute-value structures with their own internal structure, while the value of the *pred* and *tense* attributes are atomic constants.

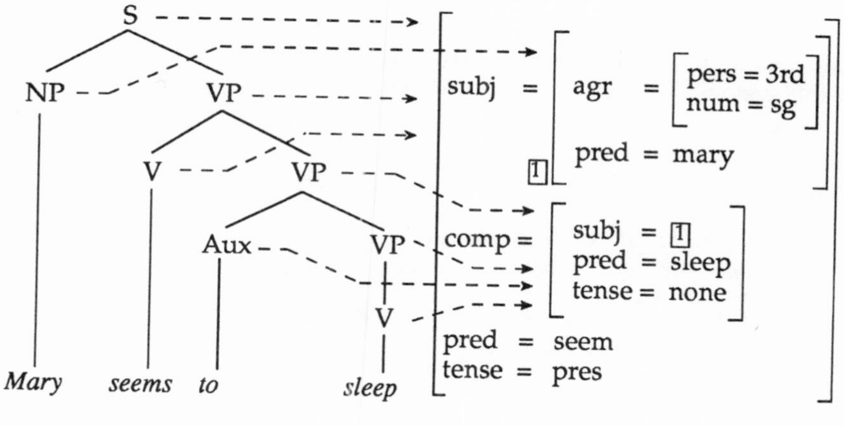

Figure 2 Using 'shared values' in an analysis of Subject-Raising

The 'sharing' of values in an attribute-value structure is useful in analyzing phenomena such as 'Raising to Subject' in terms of a single element that is simultaneously the value of two attributes, as shown in Figure 2.

The boxed index '$\boxed{1}$' in Figure 2 is used to indicate that the same entity is the value of both the *subj* attribute of the whole structure and of the *subj* attribute of the element associated with infinitival phrase *to sleep*.

2.1.3 A Definition of Attribute-Value Structures

Attribute-value structures can be defined in a variety of different ways. Some of the proposals in the literature are: elements from an informational domain (Pereira and Shieber 1984), directed acyclic graphs or 'dags' (Shieber 1986), elements from a space of finite functions (Kaplan and Bresnan 1982), and deterministic automata (Kasper and Rounds 1986).

I abstract away from the particulars of each of these definitions, and define attribute-value structures as follows:

Definition 1: *An* ATTRIBUTE-VALUE STRUCTURE *A is a triple $A = \langle F,C,\delta \rangle$, where F is a set, C is a subset of F, and δ is a partial function from $F \times F$ into F such that $1(c,f)$ is undefined for all $c \in C$ and $f \in F$. The set F is called the set of* ATTRIBUTE-VALUE ELEMENTS *of A, and the set C is called the set of* CONSTANT ELEMENTS *of A. The class of attribute-value structures is called* AVS.

Intuitively, $\delta(f,a)$ is the value associated with attribute a in the attribute-value element f. In this system attributes are themselves attribute-value elements. The constant elements are special attribute-value elements that have no attributes; they form the atomic entities of the system. δ is a partial function because it need not be the case that every attribute has a value for a given attribute-value element. It does not actually matter what the elements of F are; the partial function δ captures the structure of how attributes take values in A.

Example 1: *The attribute-value structure depicted in Figure 1 can be formally modeled as the attribute-value structure $\langle F,C,\delta \rangle$ below:*

(i) F = *{subj, obj, pred, tense, agr, mary, john, 3rd, sg, chase, past, pers, num, a, b, c, d, e}*

(ii) $C = F - \{a, b, c, d, e\}$

(iii) $\delta(a,subj) = b$ $\delta(a,obj) = c$ $\delta(a,pred) = chase$
$\delta(a,tense) = past$ $\delta(b,pred) = mary$ $\delta(b,agr) = d$
$\delta(c,pred) = john$ $\delta(c,agr) = e$ $\delta(d,num) = sg$
$\delta(d,pers) = 3rd$ $\delta(e,num) = sg$ $\delta(e,pers) = 3rd$

The formal definition of an attribute-value structure just given is deliberately very broad because it is designed to encompass every structure that might be regarded as an attribute-value structure. A particular linguistic theory might regard many of the structures in *AVS* as impossible linguistic structures. Below I identify three restrictions on the class *AVS* that a particular linguistic theory might impose; in a later section I discuss the effects of imposing these restrictions.

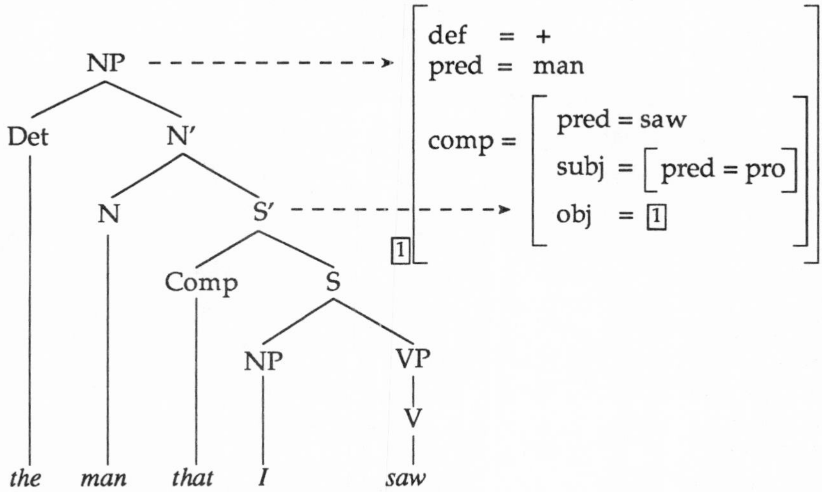

Figure 3 Using cyclic structures to describe 'filler-gap' dependencies in relative clauses.

This definition differs from some other formulations of attribute-value structures (e.g., Kasper and Rounds 1986) in allowing cyclic structures. Cyclic attribute-value structures are investigated in detail later in this chapter, but they can be characterized informally as structures that contain an element such that the value obtained by following some sequence of attributes from that element is that element itself. Cyclic attribute-value structures might be used to describe the 'filler-gap' dependencies of relative clauses, where the attribute-value structure of the whole relative clause would also appear in the position of the 'gap', as shown in the example in Figure 3.[9]

The structure shown in Figure 3 sketches how a cyclic structure might be used to describe the 'filler-gap' relationship between the relative clause as a whole and the gap in the embedded clause.

Another difference between the definition of attribute-value structures just given and most earlier proposals is that while the earlier proposals permit any element to be a value only, this definition permits any element to be an attribute (i.e., this definition identifies the set of elements with the set of attributes).[10] Although a distinction between attributes and elements is built into most definitions of attribute-value structures, it turns out that it is formally unnecessary, and we obtain a more general notion of attribute-value structure if it is not made.

In fact, we must allow attributes to be values if we are to have attribute-value structures of the sort LFG requires with rules of the form:

$$
\begin{array}{lllll}
(2) & \mathrm{VP} \rightarrow & \mathrm{V} & (\quad \mathrm{NP} \quad) & \mathrm{PP}^{*} \\
 & & \uparrow = \downarrow & (\uparrow \mathrm{obj}) = \downarrow) & (\uparrow (\downarrow \mathrm{pcase}) = \downarrow)
\end{array}
$$

The term '$(\downarrow$ pcase$)$' denotes the value *f* of the *pcase* attribute of the element associated with the PP constituent, and the formula '$(\uparrow (\downarrow$ pcase$) = \downarrow)$' says that the attribute *f* of the element associated with the VP constituent has as its value the element associated with the PP (Kaplan and Bresnan 1982, p. 197). The rule (2) generates linguistic structures such as the one in Figure 4. In this structure, the value of the *pcase* attribute of the element associated with the PP *in the bed* is the constant element *in*, which is the grammatical function that this constituent fills in the clause as a whole.

Using attributes as values is important to the LFG analysis of prepositional phrases. In this analysis the value of the *pcase* attribute identifies the grammatical relation that a prepositional phrase bears in the clause as a whole, and since the grammatical relation that a constituent bears in a clause is identified by which attribute of the clause's feature structure the constituent's feature structure appears as the

[9] If one assumed that conditions on anaphora are stated as attribute-value structure constraints, such cyclic structures might be motivated by the presence of the reflexive in relative clause examples such as *The pictures of himself that John painted last year are on display in the gallery.*

[10] As I discuss momentarily, Kaplan and Bresnan (1982) use attribute-value structures in which the same constant element functions as both an attribute and a value. The work here generalizes their use of attributes as values by allowing any element to be both an attribute and a value.

value of, it is necessary that the value of the *pcase* attribute be able to function itself as an attribute.

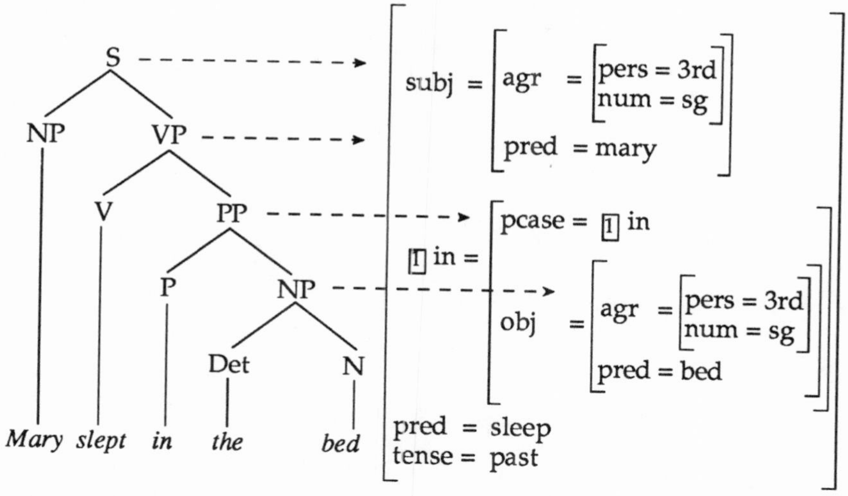

Figure 4 A structure involving the use of attributes as values

2.1.4 Depicting Attribute-Value Structures

Attribute-value structures can be depicted in several ways. The two most common are the *matrix* representation and the *directed graph* representation. All of the attribute-value structures shown so far, including the attribute-value structure of Figure 1, have been depicted in matrix representation. The attribute-value structure of Example 1 of Section 2.1.3 is depicted in directed graph representation in Figure 5.

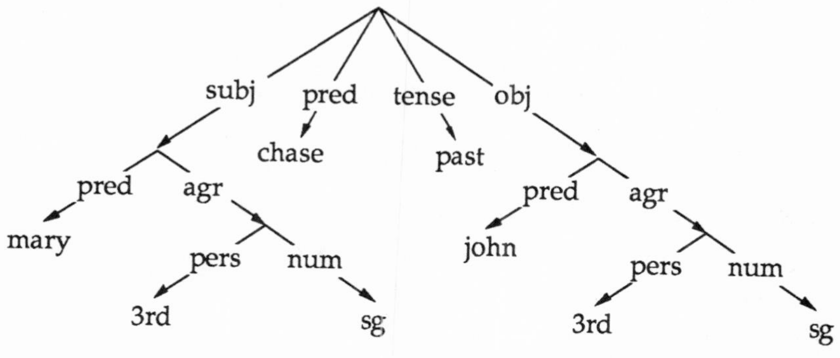

Figure 5 An attribute-value structure in directed graph form

$$\left[\begin{array}{l} \text{subj} = \left[\begin{array}{l} \boxed{2}\,\text{agr} = \left[\begin{array}{l}\boxed{3}\,\text{pers} = \boxed{5}\,\text{3rd}\\ \boxed{4}\,\text{num} = \boxed{6}\,\text{sg}\end{array}\right]\\ \boxed{1}\,\text{pred} = \text{mary}\end{array}\right] \\ \\ \text{obj} = \left[\begin{array}{l} \boxed{2}\,\text{agr} = \left[\begin{array}{l}\boxed{3}\,\text{pers} = \boxed{5}\,\text{3rd}\\ \boxed{4}\,\text{num} = \boxed{6}\,\text{sg}\end{array}\right]\\ \boxed{1}\,\text{pred} = \text{john}\end{array}\right] \\ \\ \boxed{1}\,\text{pred} = \text{chase} \\ \text{tense} = \text{past} \end{array}\right]$$

Figure 6 The value sharing in Example 1

Note that according to the definition of attribute-value structure given above, each constant element appears only once in an attribute-value structure.[11] This means that in fact there is much more 'value sharing' in the actual attribute-value structure than is indicated in the depictions shown above. In Figure 6, I indicate in matrix form all of the shared structure in the attribute-value structure of Example 1 of Section 2.1.3.

In general it is extremely inconvenient to coindex all of the shared constant elements as in Figure 6, and I adopt the following convention for representing attribute-value structures using the matrix or directed graph representations:

(i) multiple occurrences of orthographically identical atomic constants denote the same constant element,

(ii) multiple occurrences of orthographically isomorphic complex elements denote different elements, and

(iii) coindexing is used to identify shared complex values.

2.1.5 Restricting the Class of Attribute-Value Structures

The definition of attribute-value structure given above was deliberately very broad, and allows structures that particular linguistic theo-

11 In this formulation constants are attribute-value elements. This contrasts with the definition of attribute-value structures given by Kasper and Rounds (1986), in which constants are labels for attribute-value elements.

ries may not regard as a possible linguistic structure. Though I am not attempting to present a linguistic theory, I mention here several restrictions that might be placed on the class of attribute-value structures. These restrictions define subclasses of the full class of attribute-value structures; in Section 2.7 I discuss the effect of allowing only these subclasses on the logic of the language for describing of attribute-value structures developed here.

One obvious restriction on attribute-value structures is that each must contain only a finite amount of 'structure'. Since the 'structure' of an attribute-value structure is represented by the function δ, we have the following definition.

Definition 2: *An attribute-value structure* $A = \langle F,C,\delta \rangle$ *is* FINITE *iff the cardinality of* δ *is finite. The class* Fin *is the class of finite attribute-value structures.*

It might be argued that some restriction of this kind is motivated by psychological considerations: surely with finite resources only finite structures can be represented, hence a psychologically realistic theory should admit only finite structures.

Interestingly, I show in Section 2.7.1 that including infinite attribute-value structures does not affect the logic of the language for describing attribute-value structures or the correctness of the algorithms that determine the satisfiability of a description of an attribute-value structure. Thus although it is not possible to construct infinite objects using finite means, it is possible to perform computations about infinite objects using only finite means. (In fact it shows something stronger: as far as the theory developed here is concerned, it does not matter whether we consider infinite attribute-value structures as possible feature structures).

Another restriction that could be placed on attribute-value structures is the requirement that any two distinct non-constant elements must differ in the value they take on some attribute. One might want to impose this restriction if one thought that the complex elements of an attribute-value structure were completely determined by the values that their attributes have.

Definition 3: *Given an attribute-value structure* $A = \langle F,C,\delta \rangle$ *two elements* f_1, f_2 *in* $F - C$ *are* INDISCERNIBLE *iff for every* g *in* F, $\delta(f_1,g)$ *is defined iff* $\delta(f_2,g)$ *is defined, and for all* g *such that* $\delta(f_1,g)$ *is defined,* $\delta(f_1,g) = \delta(f_2,g)$. *An attribute-value structure* $A = \langle F,C,\delta \rangle$ *is* DISCERNIBLE *iff no two distinct elements* f_1, f_2 *in* $F - C$ *are indiscernible. The class* Disc *is the class of discernible attribute-value structures.*

The attribute-value structure of Example 1 of Section 2.1.3, for example, is not discernible because the complex elements *d* and *e* are indiscernible, i.e., have exactly the same attributes, and agree on the values for all of their attributes. I show in Section 2.7.2 that requiring discernibility does not affect the logic of the language for describing attribute-value structures or the correctness of the algorithms for determining satisfiability of a given description.

A third restriction that might be placed on attribute-value structures is that they be acyclic. I know of no linguistic motivation for this restriction, but it has been made for formal or technical reasons in several treatments of attribute-value structures, including those by Kasper and Rounds (1986) and Kaplan and Bresnan (1982). In contrast to the two restrictions just discussed, restricting attention to acyclic attribute-value structures does affect the satisfiability of a description of an attribute-value structure. In Section 2.7.3 I discuss acyclic attribute-value structures and the acyclically valid descriptions.

Readers familiar with the literature on attribute-value approaches to grammar may be surprised by the omission of 'partiality' and 'unification' in the discussion of attribute-value structures above. In this work I treat attribute-value structures as totally defined objects, rather than as partial descriptions or approximations to other objects, simplifying the treatment of disjunction and negation in the logic of attribute-value structures. I discuss the relationship between my work and standard unification-based treatments in Section 2.10.

To summarize, in this section I have identified three formal restrictions on the class of attribute-value structures that a particular linguistic theory might make. At the end of this chapter I return to these three subclasses of attribute-value structures and discuss the effect these restrictions have on the logic of the language for describing attribute-value structures.

2.2 A Language for Describing Attribute-Value Structures

In this section I describe in detail a family of languages called attribute-value languages for describing attribute-value structures. The languages in this family differ only in the sets of constant symbols *Const* and variable symbols *Var* they are constructed from. Formulae from these languages appear in lexical entries and syntactic rules of the attribute-value grammars presented in the next chapter.

2.2.1 The Syntax of Attribute-Value Languages

Let *Const* and *Var* be finite or denumerably infinite, disjoint sets not containing the symbols '(', ')', '~', '∨', '∧', '≈', *True* or *False*. The attribute-value language $\mathcal{A}$(Const,Var) is defined as follows:

Definition 4: *The* PRIMITIVE SYMBOLS *of* $\mathcal{A}$*(Const,Var) are the following:*

(a) Improper symbols: ( ) ~ ∨ ∧ ≈

(b) Individual variables: members of *Var*, e.g., $x\ y\ z\ x_1\ y_1\ z_1$

(c) Individual constant symbols: members of *Const*, e.g., $a\ b\ c\ a_1\ b_1\ c_1$

(d) Truth values: *True, False*

The TERMS *and the* WFFS *(well-formed formulae) of* $\mathcal{A}$*(Const,Var) are defined inductively by the following formation rules:*

(a) Each individual variable or constant symbol is a term.

(b) If $\mathbf{t}_1$ and $\mathbf{t}_2$ are terms, then so is $\mathbf{t}_1(\mathbf{t}_2)$.

(c) If $\mathbf{t}_1$ and $\mathbf{t}_2$ are terms, then $\mathbf{t}_1 \approx \mathbf{t}_2$ is a wff. These are the ATOMIC WFFS

(d) The truth values are wffs.

(e) If **A** is a wff, so is ~**A**.

(f) If **A** and **B** are wffs, so is (**A** ∨ **B**).

(g) If **A** and **B** are wffs, so is (**A** ∧ **B**).

When the sets *Const* and *Var* are clear from the context I will simply write $\mathcal{A}$ instead of $\mathcal{A}$(*Const,Var*).

A term of the form $\mathbf{t}_1(\mathbf{t}_2)$ is called a COMPOUND TERM, and $\mathbf{t}_1$ is called the FUNCTOR and $\mathbf{t}_2$ is called the ARGUMENT of the term $\mathbf{t}_1(\mathbf{t}_2)$. An INCOHERENT TERM is a term **t** that contains a subterm of the form $\mathbf{c}(\mathbf{t}_1)$ for some constant **c** and some term $\mathbf{t}_1$.

Following the standard presentation of the propositional calculus, I next introduce several abbreviations.

(a) $\mathbf{A} \supset \mathbf{B}$ stands for $\sim\mathbf{A} \vee \mathbf{B}$.

(b) $\mathbf{A} \approxeq \mathbf{B}$ stands for $(\mathbf{A} \supset \mathbf{B}) \wedge (\mathbf{B} \supset \mathbf{A})$.

(c) $\mathbf{A} \not\approx \mathbf{B}$ stands for $\sim(\mathbf{A} \approx \mathbf{B})$.

For the sake of convenience I introduce the following convention to permit the omission of brackets when writing terms and wffs:

(a) $\mathbf{t}(\mathbf{t}_1 \ldots \mathbf{t}_n)$ stands for $\mathbf{t}(\mathbf{t}_1) \ldots (\mathbf{t}_n)$.

(b) The outermost brackets of a wff may be omitted.

Finally, a comment about notation. It is sometimes necessary to distinguish between a language $\mathcal{A}$, which is the object of study, and the language (English, supplemented with mathematical terminology) in which $\mathcal{A}$ is discussed. The former is called the OBJECT LANGUAGE and the latter is called the METALANGUAGE. It is convenient to have metalanguage symbols that represent arbitrary terms or wffs, just as in mathematics a letter such as x is sometimes used to represent an arbitrary real number. Henceforth I will use **x, y, z** to represent arbitrary variables; **a, b, c,** to represent arbitrary constants; **s, t, u, v, w** to represent arbitrary terms, and **A, B, C** to represent arbitrary wffs.

For the rest of this chapter I use '$\approx$' as the object language equality predicate of $\mathcal{A}$ and '$\approxeq$' as the object language material equivalence connective of $\mathcal{A}$. This is so I can use '=' to denote identity of terms, wffs or entities. Thus $\mathbf{t}_1 \approx \mathbf{t}_2$ is a wff of $\mathcal{A}$, while $\mathbf{t}_1 = \mathbf{t}_2$ is a metalevel statement asserting the (string) identity of the terms denoted by the variables over terms $\mathbf{t}_1$ and $\mathbf{t}_2$.

Example 2: *If Const* $\supseteq \{a, c, c_1, c_2\}$ *and Var* $\supseteq \{x, y, z\}$, *then* $x, c, x(a), y(z(a))$ *and* $x(c_1\ c_2)$ *are coherent terms of* $\mathcal{A}$, *where* $x(c_1\ c_2)$ *is an abbreviation for* $x(c_1)(c_2)$, *and* $y(c(x))$ *is an incoherent term. Moreover,* $x \approx y$, $(x \approx z(a)) \wedge (x \not\approx c)$, *and True* $\vee$ *False are examples of wffs of* $\mathcal{A}$, *where* $(x \approx z(a)) \wedge (x \not\approx c)$ *is an abbreviation for* $((x \approx z(a)) \wedge \sim(x \approx c))$.

2.2.2 The Semantics of Attribute-Value Languages

Now I turn to the intended semantics of the languages $\mathcal{A}$ for describing attribute-value structures.

Recall the definition of an attribute-value structure from Section 2.1.3:

Definition 1: *An attribute value structure A is a triple* $\langle F, C, \delta\rangle$, *where F is a set, C is a subset of F, and* δ *is a partial function from* $F \times F$ *into F such that* $\delta(c,f)$ *is undefined for all* $c \in C$ *and* $f \in F$. *The set F is called the set of* ATTRIBUTE-VALUE ELEMENTS *of A, and the set C is called the set of* CONSTANT ELEMENTS *of A.*

In an interpretation of $\mathcal{A}$, variables may denote any attribute-value element in some attribute-value structure, while each constant symbol of

$\mathcal{A}$ is to denote a constant element of that structure. I further require that distinct constant symbols of $\mathcal{A}$ denote distinct constant elements.

If $\mathbf{t}_1$ denotes the attribute-value element f_1 and $\mathbf{t}_2$ denotes the attribute-value element f_2, then the term $\mathbf{t}_1(\mathbf{t}_2)$ denotes the value in f_1 of the attribute f_2; i.e., the attribute-value element $\delta(f_1,f_2)$ if $\delta(f_1,f_2)$ is defined. The additional object '$\perp$' distinct to the members of F is used to provide a denotation for undefined terms. Equality in $\mathcal{A}$ means equality of objects in F only. That is, for two terms to be equal, both must be defined and denote the same object in F.

Definition 5: *A* (ATTRIBUTE-VALUE) MODEL *is a quintuple* $\mathcal{M} = \langle F,C,\delta,\varphi,\chi\rangle$, *where* $\langle F,C,\delta\rangle$ *is an attribute value structure,* φ *is a function from Var to F, and* χ *is an injective function from Const to C.* [12]

Example 3: *Let* $\langle F,C,\delta\rangle$ *be the attribute-value structure defined in of Example 1 of Section 2.1.3, namely:*

(i) F = *{subj, obj, pred, tense, agr, pers, num, mary, john, 3rd, sg, chase, past, a, b, c, d, e}*

(ii) $C = F - \{a, b, c, d, e\}$

(iii)

$\delta(a,subj) = b$	$\delta(a,obj) = c$	$\delta(a,pred) = chase$
$\delta(a,tense) = past$	$\delta(b,pred) = mary$	$\delta(b,agr) = d$
$\delta(c,pred) = john$	$\delta(c,agr) = e$	$\delta(d,num) = sg$
$\delta(d,pers) = 3rd$	$\delta(e,num) = sg$	$\delta(e,pers) = 3rd$

and put

(iv) $Var = \{x, x_1, x_2, x_{2\cdot1}, x_{2\cdot2}\}$

(v) $Const = C$

(vi) $\varphi(x) = a,\ \varphi(x_1) = b,\ \varphi(x_2) = a,\ \varphi(x_{2\cdot1}) = a,\ \varphi(x_{2\cdot2}) = c.$

(vii) $\forall\, \mathbf{c} \in Const,\ \chi(\mathbf{c}) = \mathbf{c}.$

Then $\langle F,C,\delta,\varphi,\chi\rangle$ is a model.

Models can be depicted by adding to the diagrams used to depict attribute-value structures annotations indicating which elements are denoted by particular variables and which constant elements are denoted by which constant symbols. I will usually take each constant symbol to denote itself, although strictly speaking one might want to

12 For each language $\mathcal{A}$, a model must assign a distinct element in C to each symbol in *Const*. Note that the distinctness requirement forces the cardinality of C, and hence F, to be at least as large as the cardinality of *Const*.

distinguish between the constant symbols of the language $\mathcal{A}$, and the constant elements of the attribute-value structure, which might be linguistic or psychological entities.

Example 4: *The model defined in Example 3 can be represented as in Figure 7.*

$$
\begin{matrix} x \\ x_2 \\ x_{2\cdot 1} \end{matrix}
\begin{bmatrix}
\text{subj} = {}_{x_1}\begin{bmatrix} \text{agr} = \begin{bmatrix}\text{pers} = \text{3rd}\\ \text{num} = \text{sg}\end{bmatrix} \\ \text{pred} = \text{mary}\end{bmatrix} \\
\text{obj} = {}_{x_{2\cdot 2}}\begin{bmatrix} \text{agr} = \begin{bmatrix}\text{pers} = \text{3rd}\\ \text{num} = \text{sg}\end{bmatrix} \\ \text{pred} = \text{john}\end{bmatrix} \\
\text{pred} = \text{chase} \\
\text{tense} = \text{past}
\end{bmatrix}
$$

Figure 7 A representation of a model

The denotations of terms and satisfaction of formulae are defined as follows. Terms take their denotation in $F \cup \{\bot\}$, where $\bot$ is distinct to the elements of F.

Definition 6: *The* DENOTATION $\llbracket \mathbf{t} \rrbracket_{\mathcal{M}}$ *of a term t with respect to a model* $\mathcal{M}$ *is defined as follows*:

(i) $\llbracket \mathbf{c} \rrbracket = \chi(\mathbf{c})$ for $\mathbf{c} \in$ *Const*.

(ii) $\llbracket \mathbf{x} \rrbracket = \varphi(\mathbf{x})$ for $\mathbf{x} \in$ *Var*.

(iii) $\llbracket \mathbf{t}_1(\mathbf{t}_2) \rrbracket = \delta(\llbracket \mathbf{t}_1 \rrbracket, \llbracket \mathbf{t}_2 \rrbracket)$ provided $\llbracket \mathbf{t}_1 \rrbracket \neq \bot$, $\llbracket \mathbf{t}_2 \rrbracket \neq \bot$ and $\delta(\llbracket \mathbf{t}_1 \rrbracket, \llbracket \mathbf{t}_2 \rrbracket)$ is defined; otherwise $\llbracket \mathbf{t}_1(\mathbf{t}_2) \rrbracket = \bot$.

The SATISFACTION RELATION *between a model and a formula of* $\mathcal{A}$ *is defined as*:

For every model $\mathcal{M}$,

(i) $\mathcal{M} \models$ *True*

(ii) $\mathcal{M} \not\models$ *False*

(iii) $\mathcal{M} \models \mathbf{t}_1 \approx \mathbf{t}_2$ iff $\llbracket \mathbf{t}_1 \rrbracket = \llbracket \mathbf{t}_2 \rrbracket \neq \bot$.

(iv) $\mathcal{M} \models \mathbf{A} \wedge \mathbf{B}$ iff $\mathcal{M} \models \mathbf{A}$ and $\mathcal{M} \models \mathbf{B}$.

(v) $\mathcal{M} \models \mathbf{A} \vee \mathbf{B}$ iff $\mathcal{M} \models \mathbf{A}$ or $\mathcal{M} \models \mathbf{B}$.

(vi) $\mathcal{M} \models \sim\mathbf{A}$ iff $\mathcal{M} \not\models \mathbf{A}$.

A wff **A** is a VALID, written $\models \mathbf{A}$, iff for every model $\mathcal{M}$, $\mathcal{M} \models \mathbf{A}$. A wff **A** is SATISFIABLE iff there exists a model $\mathcal{M}$ such that $\mathcal{M} \models \mathbf{A}$. A wff **A** is called a CONTRADICTION iff there is no model $\mathcal{M}$ such that $\mathcal{M} \models \mathbf{A}$. These are the standard definitions of these terms found in model-theoretic semantics (e.g., Andrews 1986, p. 77).

Example 5: *If $\mathcal{M}$ is the model defined in Example 3 above, then the following hold*:

(i) $\mathcal{M} \models x \approx x$.

(ii) $\mathcal{M} \models x \approx x_2$.

(iii) $\mathcal{M} \not\models x_1(agr) \approx x_{2 \cdot 2}(agr)$.

(iv) $\mathcal{M} \models x(num) \not\approx x(num)$.

Example 6: *If $\mathcal{M}$ is any model,* **c** *any constant and* **x** *any variable then*

(v) $\mathcal{M} \not\models \mathbf{c}(\mathbf{x}) \approx \mathbf{c}(\mathbf{x})$.

Since constants have no attributes, $\mathbf{c}(\mathbf{x})$ *must denote* $\perp$ *irrespective of the denotation of* **x**. *But a term can only be equal to another term if it denotes an element in* $\mathcal{M}$, *hence an equality involving* $\mathbf{c}(\mathbf{x})$ *can never be satisfied. Therefore the following holds:*

(vi) $\models \mathbf{c}(\mathbf{x}) \not\approx \mathbf{c}(\mathbf{x})$.

Example 7: *We can generalize the previous result as follows. Let* $\mathbf{t}_c$ *be an incoherent term, i.e., a term that contains a subterm of the form* $\mathbf{c}(\mathbf{t}')$ *for some constant* **c** *and term* $\mathbf{t}'$, *and let* **t** *be any term. Since* $[\![\mathbf{t}_1(\mathbf{t}_2)]\!] = \perp$ *if either* $[\![\mathbf{t}_1]\!] = \perp$ *or* $[\![\mathbf{t}_2]\!] = \perp$, *and since for any model* $\mathcal{M}$ *it must be the case that* $[\![\mathbf{c}(\mathbf{t}')]\!] = \perp$, *by induction on the structure of* $\mathbf{t}_c$ *it follows that* $[\![\mathbf{t}_c]\!] = \perp$ *as well. Thus the following holds*:

(vii) $\models \mathbf{t}_c \not\approx \mathbf{t}$.

2.3 Attribute-Value Logic

In this section I develop a logic of $\mathcal{A}$ called AVL (for Attribute-Value Logic) by presenting a Hilbert-style deductive system for the valid wffs of $\mathcal{A}$. In this section I present axiom schemata and an inference rule that define the notion of proof. In the three following sections I show that the provable wffs are exactly the valid wffs identified in the last section, i.e., the logic is sound and complete with respect to its intended interpretation. I also show that the language is compact, from which a generalization of completeness follows.

The axioms can be divided into two groups: the propositional axioms that determine the properties of the propositional connectives, and the equality axioms that determine the properties of the equality predicate '≈'. In this system '≈' is a logical constant, i.e., its interpretation is fixed, so it has a fixed set of properties, which the equality axiom schemata express. The sole inference rule is the rule of Modus Ponens. The formulation of the axioms and the inference rule given here are based on those given in Andrews' (1986) treatment of first-order logic.

For all wffs **A**, **B**, **C**, variables **x**, terms $\mathbf{t}, \mathbf{t}_1, \mathbf{t}_2$, and constants $\mathbf{c}, \mathbf{c}_1, \mathbf{c}_2$ we have the following axioms.

The Propositional Axioms:

(P1) *True.*

(P2) *~False.*

(P3) $(\mathbf{A} \vee \mathbf{A}) \supset \mathbf{A}$.

(P4) $\mathbf{A} \supset (\mathbf{B} \vee \mathbf{A})$.

(P5) $(\mathbf{A} \supset \mathbf{B}) \supset ((\mathbf{C} \vee \mathbf{A}) \supset (\mathbf{B} \vee \mathbf{C}))$.

(P6) $(\mathbf{A} \wedge \mathbf{B}) \approxeq {\sim}({\sim}\mathbf{A} \vee {\sim}\mathbf{B})$.

The Equality Axioms:

(E1) $\mathbf{x} \approx \mathbf{x}$

(E2) $\mathbf{c} \approx \mathbf{c}$

(E3) $\mathbf{c}_1 \not\approx \mathbf{c}_2$ for $\mathbf{c}_1 \neq \mathbf{c}_2$.

(E4) $\mathbf{t}_c \not\approx \mathbf{t}$, where $\mathbf{t}_c$ is any incoherent term.

(E5) $\mathbf{t}_1 \approx \mathbf{t}_2 \supset \mathbf{t} \approx \mathbf{t}$, where **t** is a subterm of $\mathbf{t}_1$.

(E6) $\mathbf{t}_1 \approx \mathbf{t}_2 \supset (\mathbf{A}[\mathbf{x}/\mathbf{t}_1] \supset \mathbf{A}[\mathbf{x}/\mathbf{t}_2])$, where $\mathbf{A}[\mathbf{x}/\mathbf{t}]$ is the expression that results from substituting every occurrence of the variable **x** in **A** with the term **t**.

AVL has one inference rule, Modus Ponens:

(MP) From **A** and $\mathbf{A} \supset \mathbf{B}$ infer **B**.

I now define the notion of 'proof' in AVL. I use $\mathcal{E}$ as a syntactical variable for a set of wffs. A PROOF of a wff **A** from a set $\mathcal{E}$ of hypotheses is a finite sequence $\mathbf{A}_1, \ldots, \mathbf{A}_n$ of wffs such that $\mathbf{A}_n$ is **A** and for each k, $1 \leq k \leq n$, at least one of the following conditions is satisfied:

(i) $\mathbf{A}_k$ is an axiom.

(ii) $\mathbf{A}_k$ is a member of $\mathcal{E}$.

(iii) $\mathbf{A}_k$ follows by Modus Ponens from $\mathbf{A}_i$ and $\mathbf{A}_j$, where $i<k$ and $j<k$.

I write $\mathcal{E} \vdash \mathbf{A}$ to indicate that there is a proof of **A** from $\mathcal{E}$. A THEOREM of AVL is a wff which has a proof from the empty set of hypotheses $\mathcal{E} = \varnothing$. I write $\vdash \mathbf{A}$ to indicate that **A** is a theorem.

The propositional axiom schemata and inference rule of AVL are substitution instances of the axiom schemata and inference rule of the propositional calculus. Hence assuming these axioms amounts to assuming all substitution instances of the propositional calculus theorems as axioms of AVL. Consequently we have the following:

Rule P: *If* **A** *is a tautology of the propositional calculus where* $\mathbf{p}_1, \ldots, \mathbf{p}_n$ *are the propositional variables in* **A** *and* $\mathbf{B}_1, \ldots, \mathbf{B}_n$ *are arbitrary wffs of* $\mathcal{A}$, *then* $\mathbf{A}[\mathbf{p}_1/\mathbf{B}_1]\ldots[\mathbf{p}_n/\mathbf{B}_n]$ *is a theorem of AVL.*

Proof: If A is a tautology of the propositional calculus there is a proof $A_1, \ldots, A_n$ of A in the propositional calculus. Then by induction on i, $A_i[p_1/B_1]\ldots[p_n/B_n]$ is a theorem of AVL for $1 \leq i \leq n$. □

The Transitive Law of Implication and the Deduction Theorem hold in AVL, just as in first-order logic. I state these metatheorems without proof since their proof is exactly the same as their proof for the propositional calculus, which can be found in standard texts on mathematical logic (e.g., Andrews 1986).

Transitive Law of Implication (Trans): *If* $\mathcal{E} \vdash \mathbf{A}_1 \supset \mathbf{A}_2$, $\mathcal{E} \vdash \mathbf{A}_2 \supset \mathbf{A}_3, \ldots,$ *and* $\mathcal{E} \vdash \mathbf{A}_{n-1} \supset \mathbf{A}_n$, *then* $\mathcal{E} \vdash \mathbf{A}_1 \supset \mathbf{A}_n$ *for arbitrary wffs* $\mathbf{A}_1, \ldots, \mathbf{A}_n$ *of AVL.*

Deduction Theorem: *If* $\mathcal{E} \cup \{\mathbf{A}\} \vdash \mathbf{B}$, *then* $\mathcal{E} \vdash \mathbf{A} \supset \mathbf{B}$ *for arbitrary wffs* **A**, **B** *of AVL.*

The equality axioms characterize the properties of equality in this system. Axiom schemata (E1) through (E4) present pairs of terms that are necessarily equal or unequal. I show immediately below that axiom schemata (E6) allows the substitution of equals for equals.

Note that $\mathbf{t} \approx \mathbf{t}$ must *not* be a theorem of AVL for all terms $\mathbf{t}$ because of the possibility that for some terms $[\![\mathbf{t}]\!] = \bot$.

To conclude this section I produce some examples of theorems (strictly speaking, theorem schemata) of AVL. These theorems demonstrate that the axiomatization of equality presented here gives it all of the usual properties other than Reflexivity, viz. Symmetry, Transitivity and Substitutivity. The proofs are based on the corresponding theorems of Andrews (1986).

Symmetry of Equality: $\vdash (\mathbf{t}_1 \approx \mathbf{t}_2) \approxeq (\mathbf{t}_2 \approx \mathbf{t}_1)$.

Proof:

(.1)	$\vdash (\mathbf{t}_1 \approx \mathbf{t}_2) \supset (\mathbf{t}_1 \approx \mathbf{t}_1 \supset \mathbf{t}_2 \approx \mathbf{t}_1)$	(Axiom E6, $\mathbf{A} = \mathbf{x} \approx \mathbf{t}_1$)
(.2)	$\vdash (\mathbf{t}_1 \approx \mathbf{t}_2) \supset (\mathbf{t}_1 \approx \mathbf{t}_1)$	(Axiom E5)
(.3)	$\vdash (\mathbf{t}_1 \approx \mathbf{t}_2) \supset (\mathbf{t}_2 \approx \mathbf{t}_1)$	(Rule P) □

Transitivity of Equality: $\vdash (\mathbf{t}_1 \approx \mathbf{t}_2 \wedge \mathbf{t}_2 \approx \mathbf{t}_3) \supset (\mathbf{t}_1 \approx \mathbf{t}_3)$.

Proof:

(.1)	$\vdash (\mathbf{t}_2 \approx \mathbf{t}_1) \supset (\mathbf{t}_2 \approx \mathbf{t}_3 \supset \mathbf{t}_1 \approx \mathbf{t}_3)$	(Axiom E6)
(.2)	$\vdash (\mathbf{t}_1 \approx \mathbf{t}_2) \supset (\mathbf{t}_2 \approx \mathbf{t}_3 \supset \mathbf{t}_1 \approx \mathbf{t}_3)$	(Symmetry, Rule P) □

Substitutivity of Equality: $\vdash (\mathbf{t}_1 \approx \mathbf{t}_2) \wedge \mathbf{A} \approxeq (\mathbf{t}_1 \approx \mathbf{t}_2) \wedge \mathbf{A}[\mathbf{t}_1/\mathbf{t}_2]$.

Proof: Let $\mathbf{B} = \mathbf{A}[\mathbf{t}_1/\mathbf{x}]$, where $\mathbf{x}$ is a variable that does not appear in $\mathbf{A}$.

(.1)	$\vdash \mathbf{t}_1 \approx \mathbf{t}_2 \supset (\mathbf{B}[\mathbf{x}/\mathbf{t}_1] \supset \mathbf{B}[\mathbf{x}/\mathbf{t}_2])$	($\mathbf{B}[\mathbf{x}/\mathbf{t}_2] = \mathbf{A}[\mathbf{t}_1/\mathbf{t}_2]$, Axiom E6)
(.2)	$\vdash \mathbf{t}_1 \approx \mathbf{t}_2 \wedge \mathbf{A} \supset \mathbf{A}[\mathbf{t}_1/\mathbf{t}_2]$	(.1, Substitute for **B**, Rule P)
(.3)	$\vdash \mathbf{t}_1 \approx \mathbf{t}_2 \wedge \mathbf{A} \supset \mathbf{t}_1 \approx \mathbf{t}_2 \wedge \mathbf{A}[\mathbf{t}_1/\mathbf{t}_2]$	(.2, Rule P)
(.4)	$\vdash \mathbf{t}_2 \approx \mathbf{t}_1 \supset (\mathbf{B}[\mathbf{x}/\mathbf{t}_2] \supset \mathbf{B}[\mathbf{x}/\mathbf{t}_1])$	(Axiom E6)
(.5)	$\vdash \mathbf{t}_2 \approx \mathbf{t}_1 \wedge \mathbf{A}[\mathbf{t}_1/\mathbf{t}_2] \supset \mathbf{A}$	(.4, Substitute for **B**, Rule P)
(.6)	$\vdash \mathbf{t}_1 \approx \mathbf{t}_2 \wedge \mathbf{A}[\mathbf{t}_1/\mathbf{t}_2] \supset \mathbf{t}_1 \approx \mathbf{t}_2 \wedge \mathbf{A}$	(.5, Symmetry, Rule P) □

2.4 Soundness of AVL

In the two previous sections I defined validity $\models$ and provability $\vdash$ as distinct properties of wffs. I now commence to show that these are extensionally the same, i.e., for each wff $\mathbf{A}$, $\vdash \mathbf{A}$ iff $\models \mathbf{A}$. I begin in this section by proving the left-to-right half of the equivalence.

Theorem 7 (Soundness Theorem): *Every theorem of AVL is valid, i.e.,* $\vdash \mathbf{A}$ *implies* $\models \mathbf{A}$.

Proof: Since $\vdash \mathbf{A}$ only if $\mathbf{A}$ is derivable from the axioms of AVL by applications of Modus Ponens, it suffices to show that the axioms of

AVL are valid and that Modus Ponens preserves validity. We consider the axiom schemata and inference rule case by case. The soundness result then follows by an induction on the length of a proof.

The validity of axioms that are instances of axiom schemata (P1) through (P6) and the fact that Modus Ponens preserves validity can be proven using the standard techniques of the propositional calculus (Andrews 1986). I show here that all instances of axiom schema (P3) are valid; the other axioms can be shown valid using similar techniques.

Let $\mathcal{M}$ be any model and let $\mathbf{A}$ be any wff of AVL. If $\mathcal{M} \models \mathbf{A} \vee \mathbf{A}$, then by the definition of '$\vee$', $\mathcal{M} \models \mathbf{A}$. Thus $(\mathbf{A} \vee \mathbf{A}) \supset \mathbf{A}$ is a tautology for all wffs $\mathbf{A}$.

Now consider the equality axiom schemata (E1) and (E2). For any model $\mathcal{M} = \langle F,C,\delta,\phi,\chi \rangle$ and any variable $\mathbf{x}$, $[\![\mathbf{x}]\!] = \phi(\mathbf{x}) \in F$, and thus $\mathcal{M} \models \mathbf{x} \approx \mathbf{x}$. Similarly, for any constant symbol $\mathbf{c}$, $[\![\mathbf{c}]\!] = \chi(\mathbf{c}) \in F$, and thus $\mathcal{M} \models \mathbf{c} \approx \mathbf{c}$.

Consider the instances of axiom schema (E3). For any model $\mathcal{M} = \langle F,C,\delta,\varphi,\chi \rangle$, χ is an injective function, thus for $\mathbf{c}_1 \neq \mathbf{c}_2$, $[\![\mathbf{c}_1]\!] = \chi(\mathbf{c}_1) \neq \chi(\mathbf{c}_2) = [\![\mathbf{c}_2]\!]$, and hence $\mathcal{M} \models \mathbf{c}_1 \not\approx \mathbf{c}_2$.

Now consider axiom schema (E4). Let $\mathbf{t}_c$ be any incoherent term. Then as noted in Example 7 of Section 2.2.2, $[\![\mathbf{t}_c]\!] = \bot$, and hence for any model $\mathcal{M}$, $\mathcal{M} \models \mathbf{t}_c \not\approx \mathbf{t}$, as required.

Now consider the axioms of schema (E5). If $\mathcal{M} \models \mathbf{t}_1 \approx \mathbf{t}_2$, then $[\![\mathbf{t}_1]\!] \neq \bot$. Let $\mathbf{t}$ be any subterm of $\mathbf{t}_1$, and suppose $[\![\mathbf{t}]\!] = \bot$. Then by induction on the structure of $\mathbf{t}_1$ it must be the case that $[\![\mathbf{t}_1]\!] = \bot$, which is a contradiction. So $[\![\mathbf{t}]\!] \neq \bot$ and hence $\mathcal{M} \models \mathbf{t} \approx \mathbf{t}$, as required.

Finally consider the instances of axiom schema (E6). For any model $\mathcal{M} = \langle F,C,\delta,\varphi,\chi \rangle$ let $\mathcal{M}_f^x = \langle F,C,\delta,\varphi_f^x,\chi \rangle$, where $\varphi_f^x(\mathbf{y}) = \varphi(\mathbf{y})$ for all variables $\mathbf{y} \neq \mathbf{x}$ and $\varphi_f^x(\mathbf{x}) = f$. For any term $\mathbf{t}$, if $[\![\mathbf{t}]\!]_{\mathcal{M}} = f$ for any $f \in F$, then by induction on the structure of any wff $\mathbf{A}$, $\mathcal{M}_f^x \models \mathbf{A}$ iff it is the case that $\mathcal{M} \models \mathbf{A}[\mathbf{x}/\mathbf{t}]$. The axioms of axiom schema (E6) are wffs of the form:

$$\mathbf{t}_1 \approx \mathbf{t}_2 \supset (\mathbf{A}[\mathbf{x}/\mathbf{t}_1] \supset \mathbf{A}[\mathbf{x}/\mathbf{t}_2]).$$

If $\mathcal{M} \models \mathbf{t}_1 \approx \mathbf{t}_2$ then $[\![\mathbf{t}_1]\!]_{\mathcal{M}} = [\![\mathbf{t}_2]\!]_{\mathcal{M}} = f \in F$. Then $\mathcal{M} \models \mathbf{A}[\mathbf{x}/\mathbf{t}_1]$ iff $\mathcal{M}_f^x \models \mathbf{A}$ iff $\mathcal{M} \models \mathbf{A}[\mathbf{x}/\mathbf{t}_2]$, which implies $\mathcal{M} \models \mathbf{A}[\mathbf{x}/\mathbf{t}_1] \supset \mathbf{A}[\mathbf{x}/\mathbf{t}_2]$, and hence $\mathcal{M}$ satisfies the axiom.

To see that the inference rule Modus Ponens preserves validity, recall that $\mathbf{A} \supset \mathbf{B}$ is an abbreviation for $\sim\mathbf{A} \vee \mathbf{B}$. Now suppose that $\mathbf{A}$ and $\sim\mathbf{A} \vee \mathbf{B}$ are valid, i.e., for every $\mathcal{M}$, $\mathcal{M} \models \mathbf{A}$ and $\mathcal{M} \models \sim\mathbf{A} \vee \mathbf{B}$. Let $\mathcal{M}$ be any model; since $\mathcal{M} \models \sim\mathbf{A} \vee \mathbf{B}$ and $\mathcal{M} \not\models \sim\mathbf{A}$, $\mathcal{M} \models \mathbf{B}$. Thus $\mathbf{B}$ is valid, as required. □

Example 8: *The soundness of AVL implies that if* $\vdash$ **A** $\approx$ **B** *then* $\models$ **A** $\approx$ **B**. *But if* $\models$ **A** $\approx$ **B** *then for any model* $\mathcal{M}$, $\mathcal{M} \models$ **A** *iff* $\mathcal{M} \models$ **B**. *Thus if* $\vdash$ **A** $\approx$ **B** *then exactly the same models satisfy* **A** *and* **B**.

2.5 Decidability and Completeness of AVL

In this section I prove that all of the valid wffs of $\mathcal{A}$ are theorems of AVL. I also provide an algorithm that will determine the validity of any wff of $\mathcal{A}$.

The completeness theorem is considerably more complex than the soundness theorem. To prove it I use several intermediate results. Decidability of the satisfiability and validity problems follows from the techniques I use to prove completeness.

First, I define a set of wffs of $\mathcal{A}$ that I call reduced forms, which I prove are all satisfiable. Reduced forms are characterized in terms of their syntactic form alone, and there is an algorithm for determining whether a given wff of $\mathcal{A}$ is a reduced form or not.

Second, I prove a series of theorem schemata of the form **L** $\approx$ **R**, whose instances are theorems of AVL.

Third, I define a positive integer valued norm $\|\mathbf{A}\|$ on terms and wffs of $\mathcal{A}$. This norm has the property that for any terms $\mathbf{t}_1$, $\mathbf{t}_2$, $\|\mathbf{t}_1\| = \|\mathbf{t}_2\|$ iff $\mathbf{t}_1 = \mathbf{t}_2$. Moreover, I establish that for any instance **L′** $\approx$ **R′** of these theorem schemata, $\|\mathbf{R'}\| < \|\mathbf{L'}\|$.

Fourth, I show that these equivalences can be used from left to right as rewriting rules in a reduction algorithm that rewrites wffs to provably equivalent wffs (i.e., if **A** is reduced to **B**, then $\vdash$ **A** $\approx$ **B**). The reduction algorithm terminates only when the wff has been rewritten to *False* or a reduced form. Because each rewriting step decreases the norm of the wff, the reduction algorithm must terminate. Thus any wff **A** reduces ultimately to *False* if **A** is unsatisfiable, and reduces ultimately to some reduced form **R** if **A** is satisfiable. This result together with the Soundness Theorem just established shows that the satisfiability and validity problems in AVL are decidable.

Finally, I show completeness. If **A** is valid then ~**A**, being unsatisfiable, does not reduce to a reduced form **R**, since that would require ~**A** to be satisfiable. Thus ~**A** must reduce to *False*. But if **B** reduces to **B′** then $\vdash$ **B** $\approx$ **B′**, so there exists a proof of ~**A** $\supset$ *False*, and thus a proof of **A**. Thus the axioms and inference rule of AVL are complete.

2.5.1 Reduced Forms

In this section I define the reduced forms of $\mathcal{A}$, wffs that are patently satisfiable on inspection of their syntactic form. I show then how to construct a model for any reduced form. This model is constructed from the terms and subterms of the reduced form itself.

I use the following auxiliary definitions.

Definition 8: *A* POSITIVE LITERAL *is an atomic wff of $\mathcal{A}$ of the form* $\mathbf{t}_1 \approx \mathbf{t}_2$ *for some terms* $\mathbf{t}_1, \mathbf{t}_2$. *A* NEGATIVE LITERAL *is a wff of $\mathcal{A}$ of the form* $\mathbf{t}_1 \not\approx \mathbf{t}_2$ *for some terms* $\mathbf{t}_1, \mathbf{t}_2$. *A* LITERAL *is a wff that is either a positive literal or a negative literal.*

A wff **R** *of $\mathcal{A}$ is a* REDUCED FORM *iff it is True or a disjunction of conjunctive reduced forms.*

A wff **C** *of $\mathcal{A}$ is a* CONJUNCTIVE REDUCED FORM *iff* **C** *is a conjunction of literals such that for each positive literal* $\mathbf{t} \approx \mathbf{t}'$ *in* **C** :

(i) **t** and **t′** are coherent,

(ii) $\mathbf{t}' \notin$ *Const* (i.e., **t′** is not a constant symbol), and

(iii) if **t′** is not the same term as **t**, then **t′** does not occur elsewhere in **C** (even as a subterm of some other term in **C**).

and for each negative literal $\mathbf{t} \not\approx \mathbf{t}'$ *in* **C** :

(iv) if **t** is the same term as **t′**, then **t** is neither a variable nor a constant, and moreover **t** does not occur in any positive literal in **C** (even as a subterm).

Thus a reduced form is necessarily in disjunctive normal form, but not all disjunctive normal form wffs are reduced forms.

Example 9: *The following examples are wffs in conjunctive reduced form:*

(i) $x_1 \approx x(subj) \;\wedge\; sleep \approx x(pred) \;\wedge\; john \approx x_1(pred).$

(ii) $y \approx x(agr) \;\wedge\; y \approx x(subj)(agr) \;\wedge\; 3rd \not\approx y(pers) \;\wedge\; sg \not\approx y(num).$

The following is an example of a conjunctive form that is not reduced:

(iii) $x \approx y \;\wedge\; z \approx y.$

Reduced forms are defined so as to always be satisfiable. I show that they have this property by showing how to construct a model for any conjunctive reduced form. Intuitively, this is because no right-hand term of any positive literal appears as a subterm of any other term in **C**, so a term model for **C** can be constructed by letting the left-hand terms of positive literals denote themselves, and setting the denotation of each right-hand term to be the denotation of the term to its left. Condition (iv) of of Definition 8, is required for the following reason. If **C** contains a negative literal of the form $\mathbf{t} \not\approx \mathbf{t}$, then in any satisfying model $[\![\mathbf{t}]\!] = \bot$. Condition (iv) ensures that such non-denoting terms do not appear as subterms of terms appearing in positive literals of **C**, which must have a denotation other than $\bot$.

Lemma 9: *If* **R** *is a wff of* $\mathcal{A}$ *in reduced form, then* **R** *is satisfiable.*

Proof: If **R** = *True* then **R** is clearly satisfiable. Otherwise, $\mathbf{R} = \mathbf{C}_1 \vee \ldots \vee \mathbf{C}_n$, where each $\mathbf{C}_i$ is a conjunctive reduced form. Let $\mathbf{C} = \mathbf{E} \wedge \mathbf{I}$ be any $\mathbf{C}_i$, where **E** is a (possibly null) conjunction of positive literals and **I** is a (possibly null) conjunction of negative literals. I will show how to construct a model that satisfies **C**, and hence **R**.

Let the sets T_E and T and the function ϕ from T to T be defined as follows:

(i) T_E is the set of terms and subterms that appear in **E**,

(ii) $T = T_E \cap \mathit{Const} \cap \mathit{Var}$, and

(iii) ϕ is the function defined by $\phi(\mathbf{t}_2) = \mathbf{t}_1$ if $\mathbf{t}_1 \approx \mathbf{t}_2$ is a wff of **E**, $\phi(\mathbf{t}_2) = \mathbf{t}_2$ otherwise.

By condition (iii) of Definition 8, ϕ is well-defined. Let ϕ_{Const} and ϕ_{Var} denote the restriction of ϕ to *Const* and *Var* respectively. Define the partial function $\eta: T \times T \rightharpoonup T$ by $\eta(\mathbf{t}_1,\mathbf{t}_2) = \phi(\mathbf{t}_1(\mathbf{t}_2))$ when $\mathbf{t}_1(\mathbf{t}_2)$ in T, and $\eta(\mathbf{t}_1,\mathbf{t}_2)$ is undefined otherwise.

I claim $\mathcal{M}(\mathbf{E}) = \langle T, \mathit{Const}, \eta, \phi_{\mathrm{Const}}, \phi_{\mathrm{Var}} \rangle$ is a model for **C** and hence a model for **R**.

First, $\langle T, \mathit{Const}, \eta \rangle$ is an attribute-value structure. In particular, the requirement that all terms in **E** and hence in T be coherent ensures that $\eta(\mathbf{c},\mathbf{t})$ is undefined for all constant symbols **c** and terms **t**.

Second, for any $\mathbf{t} \in T$, $[\![\mathbf{t}]\!] = \mathbf{t}$ unless **t** appears on the right hand side of some equality in **E**. This can be shown as follows: Let T_R be the set of terms $\mathbf{t}_2$ that appear on the right hand side of some equality $\mathbf{t}_1 \approx \mathbf{t}_2$ in **E** for $\mathbf{t}_1 \neq \mathbf{t}_2$. Then for any term **t** in $T - T_R$, $\phi(\mathbf{t}) = \mathbf{t}$. Moreover, by the definition of T and the requirement on conjunctive reduced forms that no term in T_R is a subterm of any other term in **C** and hence T, it follows that $T - T_R$ is closed under subterms. Now $[\![\mathbf{x}]\!] = \mathbf{x}$ for all individual variables **x** in $T - T_R$ and $[\![\mathbf{c}]\!] = \mathbf{c}$ for all constant symbols **c**. Suppose $\mathbf{t}_1$, $\mathbf{t}_2$ and $\mathbf{t}_1(\mathbf{t}_2)$ are in $T - T_R$ and that $[\![\mathbf{t}_1]\!] = \mathbf{t}_1$ and $[\![\mathbf{t}_2]\!] = \mathbf{t}_2$. Then $[\![\mathbf{t}_1(\mathbf{t}_2)]\!] = \eta([\![\mathbf{t}_1]\!],[\![\mathbf{t}_2]\!]) = \eta(\mathbf{t}_1,\mathbf{t}_2) = \phi(\mathbf{t}_1(\mathbf{t}_2)) = \mathbf{t}_1(\mathbf{t}_2)$. Thus by induction $[\![\mathbf{t}]\!] = \mathbf{t}$ for any term **t** in $T - T_R$.

Now consider any positive literal $\mathbf{t}_1 \approx \mathbf{t}_2$ in **E**. By condition (iii) of Definition 8, $\mathbf{t}_1 \notin T_R$, thus $[\![\mathbf{t}_1]\!] = \mathbf{t}_1$. By conditions (i) and (ii) of Definition 8, $\mathbf{t}_2$ is a coherent term that is not an constant symbol. This means that $\mathbf{t}_2$ is either some variable $\mathbf{x}$ or a term $\mathbf{t}_{21}(\mathbf{t}_{22})$. If $\mathbf{t}_2 = \mathbf{x}$, then $[\![\mathbf{t}_2]\!] = \phi(\mathbf{x}) = \mathbf{t}_1$ and thus $\mathcal{M} \models \mathbf{t}_1 \approx \mathbf{t}_2$. If $\mathbf{t}_2 = \mathbf{t}_{21}(\mathbf{t}_{22})$, then $\mathbf{t}_{21}$ and $\mathbf{t}_{22}$ are in $T - T_R$ and hence $[\![\mathbf{t}_2]\!] = [\![\mathbf{t}_{21}(\mathbf{t}_{22})]\!] = \eta(\mathbf{t}_{21}, \mathbf{t}_{22}) = \phi(\mathbf{t}_{21}(\mathbf{t}_{22})) = \phi(\mathbf{t}_2) = \mathbf{t}_1$. Again $[\![\mathbf{t}_2]\!] = \mathbf{t}_1$, thus for all equations $\mathbf{t}_1 \approx \mathbf{t}_2$ in $\mathbf{E}$, $\mathcal{M} \models \mathbf{t}_1 \approx \mathbf{t}_2$.

Finally, consider any negative literal $\mathbf{t}_1 \not\approx \mathbf{t}_2$ in $\mathbf{I}$. By Definition 8, neither $\mathbf{t}_1$ nor $\mathbf{t}_2$ is or contains as a subterm any term of T_R. Let $\mathbf{t}$ be any term that does not contain a term in T_R as a subterm. Then $[\![\mathbf{t}]\!] = \mathbf{t}$ if $\mathbf{t}$ is in T and so in $T - T_R$, while $[\![\mathbf{t}]\!] = \bot$ otherwise. Consider two cases separately. First, suppose either $\mathbf{t}_1$ or $\mathbf{t}_2$ is not in T; then either $[\![\mathbf{t}_1]\!] = \bot$ or $[\![\mathbf{t}_2]\!] = \bot$, and hence $\mathcal{M} \models \mathbf{t}_1 \not\approx \mathbf{t}_2$. Now suppose $\mathbf{t}_1$ and $\mathbf{t}_2$ are in T, and hence in $T - T_R$, then $[\![\mathbf{t}_1]\!] = \mathbf{t}_1$ and $[\![\mathbf{t}_2]\!] = \mathbf{t}_2$. Since condition (iv) of Definition 8 requires $\mathbf{t}_1 \neq \mathbf{t}_2$ if $\mathbf{t}_1$ and $\mathbf{t}_2$ both are in T, it follows that $\mathcal{M} \models \mathbf{t}_1 \not\approx \mathbf{t}_2$. □

Example 10: *If Const = { agr, subj, 3rd, pers, num }, Var = { x, y }, and* $\mathbf{C}$ *is the conjunctive reduced form shown in (ii) of Example 9, repeated here as (i), then T,* ϕ*, and* η *are as given below.* $\langle T, Const, \eta, \phi_{Const}, \phi_{Var}\rangle$ *is a model for* $\mathbf{C}$*, as required.*

(i) $y \approx x(agr) \wedge y \approx x(subj)(agr) \wedge 3rd \not\approx y(pers) \wedge sg \not\approx y(num)$.

(ii) $T = \{agr, subj, 3rd, pers, num, x, y, x(agr), x(subj), x(subj)(agr)\}$

(iii)

$\phi(agr) = agr$	$\phi(subj) = subj$	$\phi(3rd) = 3rd$
$\phi(pers) = pers$	$\phi(num) = num$	$\phi(x) = x$
$\phi(x) = x$	$\phi(y) = y$	
$\phi(x(agr)) = y$	$\phi(x(subj)) = x(subj)$	$\phi(x(subj)(agr)) = y$

(iv) $\eta(x, agr) = y$ $\quad$ $\eta(x, subj) = x(subj)$ $\quad$ $\eta(x(subj), agr) = y$

2.5.2 Some Theorem Schemata of AVL

In this section I present the theorem schemata of AVL that will be used to define the rewriting procedure used in the reduction algorithm and completeness proof. The theorem schemata come in two varieties; those concerned with the boolean connectives '∧', '∨' and '~', and those concerned with equality.

The group 1 schemata comprise the associative and commutative laws of the boolean connectives ∧ and ∨. The group 2 schemata contain more complex equivalences that will be used left-to-right to form the basis of a rewriting system. Displayed below, all of these theorems are of the form $\mathbf{L} \approx \mathbf{R}$ for some wffs $\mathbf{L}$ and $\mathbf{R}$ of $\mathcal{A}$.

Note that these theorem schemata are not necessarily the most general ones possible; in particular the symmetry of equality and substitutivity of equality theorem schemata in fact hold irrespective of the norms $\|\mathbf{t}_1\|$ and $\|\mathbf{t}_2\|$ of $\mathbf{t}_1$ and $\mathbf{t}_2$. (The norm $\|\mathbf{t}\|$ is defined in the next section). The restrictions imposed on $\mathbf{t}_1$ and $\mathbf{t}_2$ in these schemata are needed in the completeness proof of AVL, however.

The boolean theorems are standard theorems of the propositional calculus and their proof is exactly the same as in the propositional calculus, which can be found in most standard texts on mathematical logic (e.g., Andrews 1986). The theoremhood of the simple equalities follows immediately from the equality axioms. I proved the symmetry of equality and substitutivity of equality theorem schemata above.

2.5.3 A Norm on Terms and Wffs

I now define the complexity norm on the terms of any attribute-value language $\mathcal{A}(Const,Var)$. In this section I make the assumption that both *Const* and *Var* are finite ordered sets, and that $\mathbf{c}_i$ denotes the *i*th constant symbol and $\mathbf{v}_i$ denotes the *i*th variable.

Let $n_c = |Const|$ and $n = n_c + |Var|$, and let T be the set of terms of $\mathcal{A}(Const,Var)$.

I assign to each term in T a norm in $\mathbb{N}^+$. Define the norm $\|\mathbf{t}\|_{\mathrm{Const,Var}}$ of a term $\mathbf{t}$ in T as follows:

(i) $\|\mathbf{c}_i\|_{\mathrm{Const,Var}} = i$ for $\mathbf{c}_i$ in *Const*.

(ii) $\|\mathbf{v}_i\|_{\mathrm{Const,Var}} = n_c + i$ for $\mathbf{v}_i$ in *Var*.

(iii) $\|\mathbf{t}_1(\mathbf{t}_2)\|_{\mathrm{Const,Var}} = n + 3^{\|\mathbf{t}_1\|} \cdot 2^{|\mathbf{t}_2|}$.

As usual, I will omit the subscripts on the norm when clear from the context.

Note that this norm is defined so that the constants have a lower complexity than any other terms, that $\|\mathbf{t}_1\| = \|\mathbf{t}_2\|$ iff $\mathbf{t}_1 = \mathbf{t}_2$ (this follows from the prime number factorization theorem of elementary number theory), and that if $\|\mathbf{t}_1\| < \|\mathbf{t}_2\|$, then for any $\mathbf{t}$ in T that contains $\mathbf{t}_2$ as a subterm, it must be the case that $\|\mathbf{t}[\mathbf{t}_2/\mathbf{t}_1]\| < \|\mathbf{t}\|$.

I extend the norm to wffs of $\mathcal{A}(Const,Var)$ as follows:

(i) $\|True\| = 2$.

(ii) $\|False\| = 3$.

(iii) $\|\mathbf{t}_1 \approx \mathbf{t}_2\| = 4 + 2 \cdot \|\mathbf{t}_1\| + \|\mathbf{t}_2\|$.

(iv) $\|\mathbf{A} \vee \mathbf{B}\| = \|\mathbf{A}\| + \|\mathbf{B}\| + 1$.

(v) $\|\mathbf{A} \wedge \mathbf{B}\| = \|\mathbf{A}\| \cdot \|\mathbf{B}\|$.

(vi) $\|{\sim}\mathbf{A}\| = 2^{|\mathbf{A}|}$.

Group 1 Theorem Schemata:

$\vdash ((\mathbf{A} \vee \mathbf{B}) \vee \mathbf{C}) \approxeq (\mathbf{A} \vee (\mathbf{B} \vee \mathbf{C})$ *Associativity*

$\vdash ((\mathbf{A} \wedge \mathbf{B}) \wedge \mathbf{C}) \approxeq (\mathbf{A} \wedge (\mathbf{B} \wedge \mathbf{C}))$

$\vdash (\mathbf{A} \vee \mathbf{B}) \approxeq (\mathbf{B} \vee \mathbf{A})$ *Commutativity*

$\vdash (\mathbf{A} \wedge \mathbf{B}) \approxeq (\mathbf{B} \wedge \mathbf{A})$

Group 2 Theorem Schemata:

$\vdash (\mathbf{A} \wedge (\mathbf{B} \vee \mathbf{C})) \approxeq ((\mathbf{A} \wedge \mathbf{B}) \vee (\mathbf{A} \wedge \mathbf{C}))$ *Distributivity*

$\vdash \sim(\mathbf{A} \vee \mathbf{B}) \approxeq \sim\mathbf{A} \wedge \sim\mathbf{B}$ *De Morgan*

$\vdash \sim(\mathbf{A} \wedge \mathbf{B}) \approxeq \sim\mathbf{A} \vee \sim\mathbf{B}$

$\vdash \sim\sim\mathbf{A} \approxeq \mathbf{A}$ *Double Negation*

One and Zero

$\vdash (\mathbf{A} \vee \mathit{True}) \approxeq \mathit{True}$ $\vdash (\mathbf{A} \wedge \mathit{True}) \approxeq \mathbf{A}$

$\vdash (\mathbf{A} \vee \mathit{False}) \approxeq \mathbf{A}$ $\vdash (\mathbf{A} \wedge \mathit{False}) \approxeq \mathit{False}$

Symmetry of Equality

$\vdash (\mathbf{t}_1 \approx \mathbf{t}_2) \approxeq (\mathbf{t}_2 \approx \mathbf{t}_1)$ where $\| \mathbf{t}_1 \| > \| \mathbf{t}_2 \|$.

Substitutivity of Equality

$\vdash (\mathbf{t}_1 \approx \mathbf{t}_2 \wedge \mathbf{A}) \approxeq (\mathbf{t}_1 \approx \mathbf{t}_2 \wedge \mathbf{A}[\mathbf{t}_2/\mathbf{t}_1])$ where $\| \mathbf{t}_1 \| < \| \mathbf{t}_2 \|$ and **A** contains an occurrence of $\mathbf{t}_2$.

Simple Equalities

$\vdash (\sim\mathit{False}) \approxeq \mathit{True}$ $\vdash (\sim\mathit{True}) \approxeq \mathit{False}$

$\vdash \mathbf{x} \approx \mathbf{x} \approxeq \mathit{True}$ $\vdash \mathbf{c} \approx \mathbf{c} \approxeq \mathit{True}$

$\vdash \mathbf{c}_1 \approx \mathbf{c}_2 \approxeq \mathit{False}$ for $\mathbf{c}_1 \neq \mathbf{c}_2$.

$\vdash \mathbf{t}_1 \approx \mathbf{t}_2 \approxeq \mathit{False}$ when either $\mathbf{t}_1$ or $\mathbf{t}_2$ is incoherent.

$\vdash (\mathbf{t}_1 \approx \mathbf{t}_2 \wedge \mathbf{t} \not\approx \mathbf{t}) \approxeq \mathit{False}$ for **t** a subterm of $\mathbf{t}_1$ or $\mathbf{t}_2$.

$\vdash (\mathbf{t}_1 \approx \mathbf{t}_2 \wedge \mathbf{t} \approx \mathbf{t}) \approxeq \mathbf{t}_1 \approx \mathbf{t}_2$ for **t** a subterm of $\mathbf{t}_1$ or $\mathbf{t}_2$.

Example 11: *If* $\|a\| = 1$, $\|b\| = 2$, $\|x\| = 3$ *and* $\|y\| = 4$, *then*

(i) $\|x(a)\| = 58$,

(ii) $\|x(a) \approx y\| = 124$, and

(iii) $\|x(a) \not\approx y\| = 2^{124}$ or approximately 10^{37}.

Finally, note that the norm just defined has the property that for all of the theorems $\mathbf{L} \approxeq \mathbf{R}$ that are instantiations of the group 1 theorem schemata of the previous subsection $\|\mathbf{R}\|_{Const,Var} = \|\mathbf{L}\|_{Const,Var}$, and for all of the theorems $\mathbf{L} \approxeq \mathbf{R}$ that are instantiations of the group 2 theorem schemata it is the case that $\|\mathbf{R}\|_{Const,Var} < \|\mathbf{L}\|_{Const,Var}$, where *Const* is any set of constant symbols containing all of the constant symbols appearing in **L** and *Var* is any set of variables containing the variables appearing in **L**. (Note that the norms of the wffs **R** are well-defined, since all of the constant symbols and variables occurring in **R** also occur in **L**). This will be of crucial importance in proving that the algorithm presented in the next section terminates.

For example, consider the De Morgan rule $\sim(\mathbf{A} \vee \mathbf{B}) \approxeq \sim \mathbf{A} \wedge \sim\mathbf{B}$. For all wffs **A** and **B**, we have:

$$
\begin{aligned}
\|\sim(\mathbf{A} \vee \mathbf{B})\| &= 2^{|\mathbf{A}|+|\mathbf{B}|+1} \\
&= 2 \cdot 2^{\|\mathbf{A}\|} \cdot 2^{|\mathbf{B}\|} \\
&> 2^{|\mathbf{A}|} \cdot 2^{|\mathbf{B}\|} \\
&= \|\sim\mathbf{A} \wedge \sim\mathbf{B}\|
\end{aligned}
$$

Similar calculations show that for the other theorem schemata of group 2, for every instantiation $\mathbf{L} \approxeq \mathbf{R}$, it is the case that $\|\mathbf{R}\| < \|\mathbf{L}\|$.

2.5.4 An Algorithm for Reducing Wffs to Reduced Forms

In this section I show that the theorem schemata of Section 2.5.2 can be used from left to right as rewriting rules in a reduction algorithm that rewrites wffs to provably equivalent wffs (that is, if **A** is reduced to **B**, then $\vdash \mathbf{A} \approxeq \mathbf{B}$). The reduction algorithm terminates only when the wff has been rewritten to *False* or a reduced form.

Informally speaking, the propositional equivalences (i.e., the Distributivity, de Morgan's rules and Double Negation equivalences) are used to reduce the wff ultimately to disjunctive normal form.[13] The

[13] It is important to note that the algorithm does not require a rewriting to disjunctive normal form before the other equivalences can be used. Indeed, it may be advantageous computationally to delay conversion to DNF by reducing

Symmetry of Equality equivalence is used to reorder equalities so that their right hand terms are more complex than their left hand terms. The One and Zero and the Simple Equality equivalences are used to simplify 'obviously' valid or invalid wffs to *True* or *False* respectively or by eliminating *True* or *False*. The main work of exploiting atomic subwffs (equalities) to license reduction is done by applications of the Substitutivity of Equality equivalence, which allows one term be substituted for an equal one (in the object language sense) of higher complexity.

Because each rewriting step decreases the norm of the wff, the reduction algorithm must terminate. Further if any wff **B** reduces to *False* then **B** is unsatisfiable, while if **B** reduces to some reduced form **R** then there is a model that satisfies **B**, thus showing that the satisfiability and validity problems for formulae of $\mathcal{A}$ are decidable.

The reduction algorithm is as follows:

Algorithm R:

Input: A wff **A**.

Output: Either the wff *False* or a reduced form **R**.

(i) Set $\mathbf{A}_0$ to **A**, the wff to be reduced, and set *i* to 0.

(ii) Set $\mathbf{S}_i$ to the set of all wffs that can be obtained by repeatedly substituting **R** for **L** in $\mathbf{A}_i$, where $\mathbf{L} \approx \mathbf{R}$ is an instance of a group 1 theorem schema (the associative and commutative equivalences).

(iii) If there is a subwff **L** of any wff **B** in $\mathbf{S}_i$ and a wff $\mathbf{R} \neq \mathbf{L}$ such that $\mathbf{L} \approx \mathbf{R}$ is an instance of a group 2 theorem schema, then set $\mathbf{A}_{i+1}$ to the result of substituting **R** for every occurrence of **L** in **B**, set *i* to *i*+1, and go to step (ii).[14] Otherwise go to step (iv).

(iv) Return $\mathbf{A}_i$ and halt.

The purpose of step (ii) in the algorithm above is to reorder the sub-wffs so that they are appropriately structured to match the left

---

according to the Distributivity equivalence only when the other equivalences cannot apply.

14 Strictly speaking, in order for the above to be an algorithm I should specify which wff **B** and which equivalence instance $\mathbf{L} \approx \mathbf{R}$ should be used in the event that more than one wff/equivalence pair meets the conditions in (iii). However, I will show the algorithm is correct irrespective of which wff/equivalence pair is used in the reduction. That is, the order in which the reductions are performed is not important for the correctness or termination of the algorithm.

hand sides of the group 2 theorem schemata. The actual reduction step is in (iii), where the wff is rewritten as a simplified wff.

Clearly steps (ii) and (iii) are effective. The sets $\mathbf{S}_i$ defined in step (ii) are always finite, since associative and commutative rules involve equivalences between wffs with equal numbers of symbols, and there is a simple algorithm for actually computing the set $\mathbf{S}_i$ for any given $\mathbf{A}_i$. Further, for any wff **B** and any theorem schema $\mathbf{L} \approx \mathbf{R}$ in group 2 there is an algorithm for determining whether a subwff of **B** is an instance of **L**, for finding the corresponding instance of **R**, and for replacing each occurrence of the former in **B** by the latter.

It is easy to see that the algorithm R terminates on any input **A**. Let *Const* be the set of constant symbols that appear in **A** and *Var* the set of variables that appear in **A**. That the algorithm terminates follows from the fact that for all $\mathbf{A}_i$ and $\mathbf{B}_i \in \mathbf{S}_i$, we have $\| \mathbf{A}_i \|_{Const,Var} = \| \mathbf{B}_i \|_{Const,Var}$ (by the associativity and commutativity of addition and multiplication respectively), and $\| \mathbf{B}_i \|_{Const,Var} > \| \mathbf{A}_{i+1} \|_{Const,Var}$, since the theorem schemata $\mathbf{L} \approx \mathbf{R}$ in group 2 have the property that for all the instances $\mathbf{L}' \approx \mathbf{R}'$, $\| \mathbf{L}' \|_{Const,Var} > \| \mathbf{R} \|_{Const,Var}$. Thus $\| \mathbf{A}_i \|_{Const,Var} > \| \mathbf{A}_{i+1} \|_{Const,Var}$, so the norm of the formula being reduced strictly decreases with each iteration. Since the norm of any wff is a positive integer, the algorithm must halt after at most $\| \mathbf{A}_0 \|_{Const,Var} = \| \mathbf{A} \|_{Const,Var}$ reduction steps. Thus the algorithm terminates irrespective of the particular sequence of equivalences used.

When the algorithm terminates, it returns either *False* or a reduced form **R**, since any wff that is not *True, False* or a reduced form always possesses a sub-wff that can be reduced by one of the group 2 theorem schemata. As is well known from the propositional calculus, De Morgan's rules and the double negation rule allow any wff other than *True* or *False* to be rewritten as one in which negation only has scope over atomic wffs (i.e., equalities). The distributivity schema allows a wff with a conjunction taking scope over a disjunction to be rewritten as one in which the disjunction has wider scope. Thus the algorithm cannot terminate producing a wff other than *True* or *False* which is not in disjunctive normal form.

Within each disjunct the symmetry of equality rule will apply to a subwff $\mathbf{t}_1 \approx \mathbf{t}_2$ if $\| \mathbf{t}_1 \| > \| \mathbf{t}_2 \|$, and the substitutivity of equality rule will apply to a subwff $(\mathbf{t}_1 \approx \mathbf{t}_2) \wedge \mathbf{A}$ whenever $\mathbf{t}_2$ is a subterm of some term in **A** and $\| \mathbf{t}_1 \| < \| \mathbf{t}_2 \|$, so the algorithm will never terminate with a wff that contains a subwff of the form $(\mathbf{t}_1 \approx \mathbf{t}_2) \wedge \mathbf{B}$, where **B** contains $\mathbf{t}_2$ as a subterm.

Nor can $\mathbf{t}_2$ be a constant symbol in any subwff $\mathbf{t}_1 \approx \mathbf{t}_2$ of the output since the symmetry of equality rule will be applicable if $\mathbf{t}_1$ is a variable or a compound term and a simple equality rule applies if $\mathbf{t}_1$ is also a constant symbol. No incoherent term can appear in the algorithm's output because of a simple equality rule.

Finally, if a subwff $\mathbf{t} \not\approx \mathbf{t}$ occurs in the output, then $\mathbf{t}$ is not a constant symbol, a variable or a subterm occurring in any positive literal occurring in the output, because of the simple equality rules.

Example 12: *Given the following complexity assignment to constants and variables,*

$$\|subj\| = 1,\ \|num\| = 2,\ \|sg\| = 3,\ \|pl\| = 4,\ \|x\| = 5,\ \|y\| = 6,$$

the following is an example of a reduction performed by algorithm R.

A_0	$x(subj) \approx y \wedge x(subj)(num) \not\approx sg \wedge y(num) \approx pl$	Input
A_1	$y \approx x(subj) \wedge x(subj)(num) \not\approx sg \wedge y(num) \approx pl$	Symmetry
A_2	$y \approx x(subj) \wedge sg \not\approx x(subj)(num) \wedge y(num) \approx pl$	Symmetry
A_3	$y \approx x(subj) \wedge sg \not\approx x(subj)(num) \wedge pl \approx y(num)$	Symmetry
A_4	$y \approx x(subj) \wedge sg \not\approx y(num) \wedge pl \approx y(num)$	Substitutivity
A_5	$y \approx x(subj) \wedge sg \not\approx pl \wedge pl \approx y(num)$	Substitutivity
A_6	$y \approx x(subj) \wedge \sim False \wedge pl \approx y(num)$	Simple Equality
A_7	$y \approx x(subj) \wedge True \wedge pl \approx y(num)$	Simple Equality
A_8	$y \approx x(subj) \wedge pl \approx y(num)$	Simple Equality

At step A_8 no more equivalences apply, so the algorithm terminates. A_8 is in reduced normal form and hence is satisfiable. Since $\vdash A_i \approxeq A_{i+1}$ for $0 \le i < 8$, $\vdash A_0 \approxeq A_8$ and hence A_0 is satisfiable as well.

Example 13: *With the same complexity assignment to constants and variables the following is an example of a reduction performed by algorithm R.*

A_0	$y \approx x(subj) \wedge sg \approx x(subj)(num) \wedge pl \approx y(num)$	Input
A_1	$y \approx x(subj) \wedge sg \approx y(num) \wedge pl \approx y(num)$	Substitutivity
A_2	$y \approx x(subj) \wedge sg \approx pl \wedge pl \approx y(num)$	Substitutivity
A_3	$y \approx x(subj) \wedge False \wedge pl \approx y(num)$	Simple Equality
A_4	$False$	One and Zero

At A_4 no more equivalences apply, so the algorithm terminates. A_4 is equal to *False* and hence not satisfiable. Since $\vdash A_i \approxeq A_{i+1}$ for $0 \le i < 4$, $\vdash A_0 \approxeq A_4$ and hence A_0 is unsatisfiable as well.

Example 14: *Given the following complexity assignment to constants and variables,*

$$\|subj\| = 1,\ \|num\| = 2,\ \|sg\| = 3,\ \|pers\| = 4,\ \|3rd\| = 5,$$
$$\|x\| = 6,\ \|y\| = 7,$$

the following is an example of a reduction performed by algorithm R.

A_0	$y{\approx}x(subj) \wedge sg \approx y(num) \wedge {\sim}(sg \approx x(subj)(num) \wedge 3rd \approx x(subj)(pers))$	Input
A_1	$y{\approx}x(subj) \wedge sg \approx y(num) \wedge {\sim}(sg \approx y(num) \wedge 3rd \approx y(pers))$	Substitutivity
A_2	$y{\approx}x(subj) \wedge sg \approx y(num) \wedge (sg \not\approx y(num) \vee 3rd \not\approx y(pers))$	de Morgan
A_3	$y{\approx}x(subj) \wedge (((sg \approx y(num) \wedge sg \not\approx y(num)) \vee (sg \approx y(num) \wedge 3rd \not\approx y(pers)))$	Distributivity
A_4	$y{\approx}x(subj) \wedge (((sg \approx y(num) \wedge sg \not\approx sg) \vee (sg \approx y(num) \wedge 3rd \not\approx y(pers)))$	Substitutivity
A_5	$y{\approx}x(subj) \wedge (((sg \approx y(num) \wedge {\sim}True) \vee (sg \approx y(num) \wedge 3rd \not\approx y(pers)))$	Simple Equality
A_6	$y{\approx}x(subj) \wedge (((sg \approx y(num) \wedge False) \vee (sg \approx y(num) \wedge 3rd \not\approx y(pers)\ )\ )$	One and Zero
A_7	$y{\approx}x(subj) \wedge (False \vee (sg \approx y(num) \wedge 3rd \not\approx y(pers)))$	One and Zero
A_8	$y{\approx}x(subj) \wedge sg \approx y(num) \wedge 3rd \not\approx y(pers)$	One and Zero

At step A_8 no more equivalences apply, so the algorithm terminates. A_8 is in reduced normal form and hence is satisfiable. Since $\vdash A_i \approxeq A_{i+1}$ for $0 \leq i < 8$, $\vdash A_0 \approxeq A_8$ and hence A_0 is satisfiable as well.

The relationship between the input and the output of algorithm R can be stated more precisely as below:

Lemma 10: *For any wff* **A** *of* $\mathcal{A}$, *if the algorithm R reduces* **A** *to* **C**, *then* $\vdash \mathbf{A} \approxeq \mathbf{C}$.

Proof: The algorithm generates a finite sequence of wffs of $\mathcal{A}$ of the form $\mathbf{A} = \mathbf{A}_0, \mathbf{B}_0, \mathbf{A}_1, \mathbf{B}_1, \ldots, \mathbf{A}_{n-1}, \mathbf{B}_{n-1}, \mathbf{A}_n = \mathbf{C}$ such that $\mathbf{A}_i \approxeq \mathbf{B}_i$ is an instance of a group 1 theorem schema and $\mathbf{B}_i \approxeq \mathbf{A}_{i+1}$ is an instance of a group 2 theorem schema for $0 \leq i < n$. Thus $\vdash \mathbf{A}_i \approxeq \mathbf{B}_i$ and $\vdash \mathbf{B}_i \approxeq \mathbf{A}_{i+1}$. But then by the Transitive Law of Implication and the Deduction theorem we have both $\vdash \mathbf{A} \supset \mathbf{C}$ and $\vdash \mathbf{C} \supset \mathbf{A}$, i.e., $\vdash \mathbf{A} \approxeq \mathbf{C}$. □

Note that by the soundness theorem it follows directly that if $\vdash \mathbf{A} \approxeq \mathbf{C}$ then $\models \mathbf{A} \approxeq \mathbf{C}$, and so exactly the same models satisfy **A** and **C**. This leads directly to a proof of the decidability of the satisfiability problem and the validity problem.

Theorem 11: *There is an algorithm for determining whether any wff* **A** *of* $\mathcal{A}$ *is satisfiable, and another algorithm for determining whether* **A** *is valid. To determine the satisfiability of* **A** *apply algorithm R to* **A**; *if the output is False then* **A** *is unsatisfiable, otherwise* **A** *is satisfiable.*

To determine the validity of **A** *apply the reduction algorithm to* ~**A**; *if the output is False then* **A** *is valid, otherwise* **A** *is invalid.*

Proof: Suppose the output of the reduction algorithm with input **A** is *False*. Then ⊢ **A** ≋ *False* is a theorem of AVL, and hence by the soundness theorem, there are no models that satisfy **A** (since there are no models that satisfy *False*). Conversely, suppose the output of the algorithm is not *False*. Then it must be some reduced form **R**, and ⊢ **A** ≋ **R**. But I showed above that every reduced form is satisfiable; thus there is a model that satisfies **R**, and hence also **A**.

Given that a wff of $\mathcal{A}$ is valid iff its negation is unsatisfiable, an algorithm for determining the validity of a wff **A** can be constructed from the satisfiability algorithm as follows: present ~**A** as input to the satisfiability algorithm. **A** is valid iff ~**A** is unsatisfiable. □

Corollary 12: *Any wff* **A** *is equivalent either to False or to a satisfiable wff of the form*

$$\text{(i)} \quad \bigvee_{j=0}^{m} \left(\mathbf{E}_j \wedge \bigwedge_{i=0}^{n_j} {\sim}\mathbf{I}_{i,j} \right)$$

where the $\mathbf{E}_j$ are conjunctions of atomic wffs and the $\mathbf{I}_{i,j}$ are atomic wffs. □

Finally, I show completeness of AVL.

Theorem 13 (Completeness Theorem): *The axioms and inference rules of AVL are complete, i.e.,* ⊨ **A** *implies* ⊢ **A**.

Proof: Let **A** be any valid wff. Then ~**A** is unsatisfiable, and hence algorithm R does not reduce ~**A** to any reduced form **R**. Thus the algorithm reduces ~**A** to *False*, and therefore by Lemma 10, ⊢ ~**A** ≋ *False*. Since ⊢ ~**A** ⊃ *False*, we can show ⊢ **A**. Thus all valid formulae are theorems of AVL. □

2.6 Compactness of $\mathcal{A}$

In this section I show that the languages $\mathcal{A}$ are compact, and use this to obtain a generalized completeness result.

Definition 14: *A set of wffs* $\mathcal{E}$ *is* FINITELY SATISFIABLE *iff every finite subset of* $\mathcal{E}$ *is satisfiable.*

Theorem 15 (Compactness Theorem): *A set* $\mathcal{E}$ *of wffs of* $\mathcal{A}$ *is satisfiable if and only if* $\mathcal{E}$ *is finitely satisfiable.*

Proof: The proof from left to right is trivial.

For the other direction, let $\mathcal{E}$ be a finitely satisfiable set of wffs of $\mathcal{A}$. I show how to extend $\mathcal{E}$ to a maximal finitely satisfiable set, and prove that every maximal finitely satisfiable set is satisfiable. Since $\mathcal{E}$ is a subset of a maximal finitely satisfiable set, it follows that $\mathcal{E}$ is satisfiable.

Let $\mathbf{A}_0, \mathbf{A}_1, \ldots$ be an enumeration of all wffs of $\mathcal{A}$, and define a sequence K_i of sets of wffs as follows:

(i) $K_0 = \mathcal{E}$

(ii) $K_{i+1} = K_i \cap \{\mathbf{A}_i\}$ if $K_i \cap \{\mathbf{A}_i\}$ is finitely satisfiable, and $K_{i+1} = K_i \cap \{\sim\mathbf{A}_i\}$ otherwise.

Let $$K_\infty = \bigcup_{i=0}^{\infty} K_i,$$

whence $\mathcal{E} \subseteq K_\infty$. Note that for any wff $\mathbf{A}$ either $\mathbf{A} \in K_\infty$ or $\sim \mathbf{A} \in K_\infty$; hence if $\mathbf{A} \notin K_\infty$, $K_\infty \cap \{ \mathbf{A} \}$ is not finitely satisfiable as $\sim\mathbf{A} \in K_\infty$. Therefore K_∞ is a maximal finitely satisfiable superset of $\mathcal{E}$ if K_∞ is finitely satisfiable.

Now K_∞ is finitely satisfiable if every K_i is, since any finite unsatisfiable subset of K_∞ is a subset of some K^{i}. I prove by induction over i that each K_i is finitely satisfiable. $K_0 = \mathcal{E}$ is finitely satisfiable by hypothesis. Suppose K_i is finitely satisfiable, and let K be any finite subset of K_{i+1}. There are three cases to consider: (i) $K \subseteq K_i$, (ii) $\mathbf{A}_i \in K - K_i$, and (iii) $\sim\mathbf{A}_i \in K - K_i$. In case (i) K is finitely satisfiable by the induction hypothesis. In case (ii) $\mathbf{A}_i \in K_{i+1} - K_i$, so $K_i \cap \{ \mathbf{A}_i \} = K_{i+1}$ is finitely satisfiable by the construction of K_{i+1}; hence the finite subset K is satisfiable. In case (iii) $\sim\mathbf{A}_i \in K_{i+1} - K_i$, so $K_i \cap \{ \mathbf{A}_i \}$ is not finitely satisfiable. I show that K is satisfiable by proving that otherwise $K_i \cap \{ \mathbf{A}_i \}$ is satisfiable after all.

Let $\mathcal{M}$ be a model such that $\mathcal{M} \models K - \{ \sim\mathbf{A}_i \}$; such a model exists since $K - \{ \sim\mathbf{A}_i \} = K \cap K_i$ is a finite subset of K_i and hence is satisfiable by the induction hypothesis. Now $\mathcal{M} \models \sim\mathbf{A}_i$, since otherwise $\mathcal{M} \models \mathbf{A}_i$ and hence $\mathcal{M} \models (K \cap K_i) \cap \{ \mathbf{A}_i \}$, which is a contradiction since $K \cap K_i$ can be any finite subset of K_i. Therefore $\mathcal{M} \models K$, and since K is any finite subset of K_{i+1}, K_{i+1} is finitely satisfiable.

It remains only to show that every maximal finitely satisfiable set is satisfiable. Let K be any maximal finitely satisfiable set of wffs of $\mathcal{A}$. I construct a model of K as follows. The elements of this model will be equivalence classes of the terms that appear in the atomic wffs in K that are positive literals.

Let T be the set of terms and subterms that appear in atomic wffs belonging to K, and let $\equiv$ be the relation on T defined by:

$$\mathbf{t} \equiv \mathbf{t}' \text{ iff } \mathbf{t} \approx \mathbf{t}' \in K.$$

Since K is a maximal finitely satisfiable set, $\equiv$ is an equivalence relation on T.

(i) Suppose $\mathbf{t} \equiv \mathbf{t}'$ and $\mathbf{t}' \equiv \mathbf{t}''$, but not $\mathbf{t} \equiv \mathbf{t}''$. Then $\mathbf{t} \approx \mathbf{t}' \in K$ and $\mathbf{t}' \approx \mathbf{t}'' \in K$, and $\mathbf{t} \not\approx \mathbf{t}'' \in K$. But then K is not finitely satisfiable, which is a contradiction.

(ii) Suppose $\mathbf{t} \equiv \mathbf{t}'$ but not $\mathbf{t}' \equiv \mathbf{t}$. Then $\mathbf{t} \approx \mathbf{t}' \in K$ and $\mathbf{t}' \not\approx \mathbf{t} \in K$. But then K is not finitely satisfiable, which is a contradiction.

(iii) Suppose there is some $\mathbf{t} \in T$ such that $\mathbf{t} \equiv \mathbf{t}$ does not hold. Then $\mathbf{t} \not\approx \mathbf{t} \in K$. But by definition of T there are terms $\mathbf{t}'$, $\mathbf{t}''$ such that $\mathbf{t}$ is a subterm of $\mathbf{t}'$ such that either $\mathbf{t}' \approx \mathbf{t}''$ or $\mathbf{t}'' \approx \mathbf{t}'$ is in K. But neither $\{\mathbf{t}' \approx \mathbf{t}'', \mathbf{t} \not\approx \mathbf{t}\}$ nor $\{\mathbf{t}'' \approx \mathbf{t}', \mathbf{t} \not\approx \mathbf{t}\}$ is satisfiable if $\mathbf{t}$ is a subterm of $\mathbf{t}'$, so K is not finitely satisfiable, which is a contradiction.

Let $[\mathbf{t}]$ be the equivalence class containing $\mathbf{t}$.

Define $\delta : T/{\equiv} \times T/{\equiv} \rightharpoonup T/{\equiv}$ by $\delta([\mathbf{t}],[\mathbf{t}']) = [\mathbf{t}(\mathbf{t}')]$ iff $\mathbf{t}(\mathbf{t}') \in T$. To see that δ is well-defined, suppose the contrary, i.e., that $[\mathbf{t}_1] = [\mathbf{t}_1']$ and $[\mathbf{t}_2] = [\mathbf{t}_2']$, but $[\mathbf{t}_1(\mathbf{t}_2)] \neq [\mathbf{t}_1'(\mathbf{t}_2')]$. Then $\mathbf{t}_1(\mathbf{t}_2) \not\approx \mathbf{t}_1'(\mathbf{t}_2')$, $\mathbf{t}_1(\mathbf{t}_2) \approx \mathbf{t}_1(\mathbf{t}_2)$, $\mathbf{t}_1'(\mathbf{t}_2') \approx \mathbf{t}_1'(\mathbf{t}_2')$, $\mathbf{t}_1 \approx \mathbf{t}_1'$ and $\mathbf{t}_2 \approx \mathbf{t}_2'$ are all wffs in K. But then K is not finitely satisfiable, which is a contradiction.

Now define $\varphi: T \to T/{\equiv}$ as $\varphi(\mathbf{t}) = [\mathbf{t}]$, and let φ_{Const} and φ_{Var} be the restriction of φ to *Const* and *Var* respectively. Note that $Const \subseteq T$ and $Var \subseteq T$, since $\mathbf{c} \approx \mathbf{c}$ and $\mathbf{x} \approx \mathbf{x}$ are valid for all constants $\mathbf{c}$ and for all variables $\mathbf{x}$.

Then I claim $\mathcal{M} = \langle T/{\equiv}, Const/{\equiv}, \delta, \varphi_{\text{Const}}, \varphi_{\text{Var}} \rangle$ is a model for K. To see this, first note that by induction on the structure of any term $\mathbf{t}$ in T, $[\![\mathbf{t}]\!]_{\mathcal{M}} = [\mathbf{t}]$. Moreover, if $\mathbf{t} \approx \mathbf{t}'$ is a positive literal in K then $[\mathbf{t}] = [\mathbf{t}']$, so $\mathcal{M} \models \mathbf{t} \approx \mathbf{t}'$. Conversely, if $\mathbf{t} \approx \mathbf{t}'$ is an atomic wff not in K then $\mathcal{M} \not\models \mathbf{t} \approx \mathbf{t}'$, since otherwise $[\mathbf{t}] = [\![\mathbf{t}]\!] = [\![\mathbf{t}']\!] = [\mathbf{t}']$, i.e., $\mathbf{t} \equiv \mathbf{t}'$ and thus $\mathbf{t} \approx \mathbf{t}'$ is in K after all.

Now consider the non-atomic wffs in K. I prove by induction on the structure of any wff $\mathbf{A}$ that $\mathbf{A} \in K$ iff $\mathcal{M} \models \mathbf{A}$. I proved the basis of the induction for the atomic wffs immediately above. If $\mathbf{A}$ is a non-atomic wff, then either:

(i) $\mathbf{A} = {\sim}\mathbf{B}$. Then $\mathbf{A} \in K$ iff $\mathbf{B} \notin K$ iff $\mathcal{M} \not\models \mathbf{B}$ (by the inductive hypothesis) iff $\mathcal{M} \models \mathbf{A}$.

(ii) $\mathbf{A} = \mathbf{B}_1 \wedge \mathbf{B}_2$. Then $\mathbf{A} \in K$ iff $\mathbf{B}_1 \in K$ and $\mathbf{B}_2 \in K$ iff $\mathcal{M} \models \mathbf{B}_1$ and $\mathcal{M} \models \mathbf{B}_2$ (by the inductive hypothesis) iff $\mathcal{M} \models \mathbf{A}$.

(iii) $\mathbf{A} = \mathbf{B}_1 \vee \mathbf{B}_2$. Similar to (ii).

Thus the model $\mathcal{M}$ satisfies every wff in K and hence K is satisfiable, as was to be proven. □

The compactness theorem and the completeness theorem together imply a generalized completeness theorem.

Theorem 16 (Generalized Completeness): *If* $\mathcal{E} \models \mathbf{A}$ *then* $\mathcal{E} \vdash \mathbf{A}$.

Proof: If $\mathcal{E} \models \mathbf{A}$ then the set $\mathcal{E} \cap \{\sim\mathbf{A}\}$ is unsatisfiable. By the compactness theorem there must exist a finite subset $\mathcal{E}' = \{\mathbf{B}_1, \ldots, \mathbf{B}_n, \sim\mathbf{A}\}$ of $\mathcal{E} \cap \{\sim\mathbf{A}\}$ that is unsatisfiable. Then $\{\mathbf{B}_1, \ldots, \mathbf{B}_n\} \models \mathbf{A}$, in which case $\models \mathbf{B}_1 \supset (\ldots(\mathbf{B}_n \supset \mathbf{A})\ldots)$, and hence by completeness $\vdash \mathbf{B}_1 \supset (\ldots(\mathbf{B}_n \supset \mathbf{A})\ldots)$. Thus $\{\mathbf{B}_1, \ldots, \mathbf{B}_n\} \vdash \mathbf{A}$ by n applications of Modus Ponens, from which it follows that $\mathcal{E} \vdash \mathbf{A}$. □

2.7 Restricting the Class of Attribute-Value Structures

At the beginning of this chapter I pointed out that a particular linguistic theory might place restrictions on attribute-value structures, and I defined several subclasses of attribute-value structures. In this section I discuss the effect that restricting attention to these subclasses has on the satisfiability and validity of wffs of $\mathcal{A}$.

Definition 17: *If K is a class of attribute-value structures then a* K-MODEL *is a model* $\mathcal{M} = \langle F, C, \delta, \varphi, \chi \rangle$ *such that* $\langle F, C, \delta \rangle$ *is an attribute-value structure in K.*

If $\mathbf{A}$ *is a wff of* $\mathcal{A}$, *then* $\mathbf{A}$ *is* K-VALID, *written* $K \models \mathbf{A}$, *iff* $\mathcal{M} \models \mathbf{A}$ *for every K-model* $\mathcal{M}$, *and* $\mathbf{A}$ *is* K-SATISFIABLE *iff there is a K-model* $\mathcal{M}$ *such that* $\mathcal{M} \models \mathbf{A}$.

2.7.1 Finite Attribute-Value Structures

One restriction that might be placed on attribute-value structures is to require that the complexity of the 'structure' be finite. Recall that an attribute-value structure $\langle F, C, \delta \rangle$ is *finite* iff the cardinality of δ is finite. The class *Fin* is the class of finite attribute-value structures. The following theorem shows that restricting attention to the finite models does not affect satisfiability or validity of wffs of $\mathcal{A}$.

Theorem 18: *For any wff* $\mathbf{A}$, $Fin \models \mathbf{A}$ *iff* $\models \mathbf{A}$.

Proof: If **A** is *Fin*-satisfiable, then **A** is satisfiable, since every finite attribute-value structure is an attribute-value structure. Furthermore, if **A** is satisfiable, then it is equivalent to a reduced wff **R**. But every reduced wff **R** has a finite model: the model $\mathcal{M}(\mathbf{R})$ constructed in proving that every reduced formula is satisfiable (Lemma 9 of Section 2.5.1) is finite. Thus if **A** is satisfiable then **A** has a finite model, and hence **A** is *Fin*-satisfiable.

Now for any wff **B**, **B** is valid/*Fin*–valid iff ~**B** is satisfiable/*Fin*–satisfiable respectively. But since ~**B** is *Fin*–satisfiable iff ~**B** is satisfiable it follows that **B** is valid iff **B** is *Fin*–valid. □

2.7.2 Discernible Attribute-Value Structures

Another restriction that can be placed on attribute-value structures is that any two distinct non-constant elements must differ on the value they take on some attribute.

Recall that in an attribute-value structure $\langle F,C,\delta\rangle$ two elements f_1, f_2 in $F - C$ are *indiscernible* iff for every g in F, $\delta(f_1,g)$ is defined iff $\delta(f_2,g)$ is defined, and for all g such that $\delta(f_1,g)$ is defined, $\delta(f_1,g) = \delta(f_2,g)$. Two elements are discernible iff they are not indiscernible. An attribute-value structure $\langle F,C,\delta\rangle$ is *discernible* iff every pair of distinct elements of $F - C$ are discernible. The class *Disc* is the class of discernible attribute-value structures. The following theorem shows that restricting attention to the discernible models does not affect satisfiability or validity of wffs of $\mathcal{A}$.

Theorem 19: *For any wff* **A**, *Disc* $\models$ **A** *iff* $\models$ **A**.

Proof: The proof from right to left is trivial. To prove the hypothesis from left to right it suffices to show that if **A** is satisfiable, then it is *Disc*–satisfiable. If **A** is satisfiable, then **A** has a model $\mathcal{M} = \langle F,C,\delta,\varphi,\chi\rangle$. I show how to construct a discernible model that satisfies **A**. Let 0 be some element not in F, and let $F' = F \cup \{0\}$. Define $\delta': F' \times F' \rightharpoonup F'$ to be the partial function that agrees with δ on $F \times F$ for those pairs on which δ is defined, $\delta'(f,0) = f$ for all f in $F - C$, and δ' is undefined elsewhere. Then if $\mathcal{M}' = \langle F',C,\delta',\varphi,\chi\rangle$, by induction on the structure of any term **t**, $[\![\mathbf{t}]\!]_{\mathcal{M}'} = [\![\mathbf{t}]\!]_{\mathcal{M}}$. Thus $\mathcal{M}'$ is a discernible model that satisfies **A**. □

Note, by the way, that if the original model is finite, then the model constructed in the proof just given is finite. Thus we have the following:

Corollary 20: *For any wff* **A**, **A** *is valid iff* **A** *is satisfied by all discernible finite models.* □

To summarize, restricting attention to the classes of finite or discernible attribute-value structures has no effect on the satisfiability or the validity of wffs from $\mathcal{A}$. Conversely, there is no set of wff of $\mathcal{A}$ that identifies precisely class of finite or the class of discernible attribute-value structures.

2.7.3 Acyclic Attribute-Value Structures

A further restriction that can be placed on attribute-value structures is that they be acyclic.

Definition 21: *For any attribute-value structure $A = \langle F,C,\delta \rangle$ define the relation D on F×F as $D(f,g)$ iff $\delta(f,h)=g$ for some $h \in F$. Then A is* ACYCLIC *iff the transitive closure of D is irreflexive. Let* Acyc *be the class of acyclic attribute-value structures.*

The cyclic attribute value structures are structures that contain an element such that the value of some sequence of attributes of that element is the element itself. Interestingly, restricting attention to acyclic attribute-value structures does affect the satisfiability of wffs of $\mathcal{A}$.

Clearly every valid wff is acyclically valid, and every acyclically satisfiable wff is satisfiable, but the set of satisfiable wffs is a proper superset of the acyclically satisfiable wffs, and hence the set of valid wffs is a proper subset of acyclically valid wffs.

Example 15: *The wff in (i) is satisfiable but not acyclically satisfiable, since any model that satisfies (i) must have $\delta(\llbracket x \rrbracket, \llbracket y \rrbracket) = \llbracket x \rrbracket$. Thus while the wff in (ii) is invalid, it is acyclically valid.*

(i) $x(y) \approx x$.

(ii) $x(y) \not\approx x$.

In the remainder of this subsection I axiomatize the acyclically valid wffs. I define an additional axiom schema, and show that this axiomatization is sound and complete.

To do this, I introduce the auxiliary notion of 'accessible element'. Intuitively, an element of an attribute-value model is accessible if and only if there is a term that denotes it, and a model is accessible if and only if all of its elements are accessible. The accessible submodel $\alpha(\mathcal{M})$ of a model $\mathcal{M}$ is the restriction of $\mathcal{M}$ to its accessible elements. Clearly, $\mathcal{M} \models \mathbf{A}$ if and only if $\alpha(\mathcal{M}) \models \mathbf{A}$. I then prove that a model satisfies every instance of the schema axiomatizing the acyclically valid wffs if and only if $\alpha(\mathcal{M})$ is acyclic. Since the accessible submodel of any acyclic model is clearly also acyclic, it follows that every acyclic model satifies a wff **B** if and only if every model that satisfies every instance of the schema also satisfies **B**. The soundness and completeness of the axiomatization follow immediately from the soundness and (generalized) completeness theorems for AVL respectively.

Definition 22: *Let* $\mathcal{M} = \langle F, C, \delta, \varphi, \chi \rangle$, *with* φ: *Var* $\to$ *F and* χ: *Const* $\to$ *C. An element* $f \in F$ *is* ACCESSIBLE *iff there is a term t of the language* $\mathcal{A}$*(Const, Var) such that* $[\![t]\!]_{\mathcal{M}} = f$. *A model is accessible if and only if every element of that model is accessible.*

Definition 23: *The model* $\alpha(\mathcal{M}) = \langle F', C', \delta', \varphi, \chi \rangle$ *is the* ACCESSIBLE SUBMODEL *of a model* $\mathcal{M} = \langle F, C, \delta, \varphi, \chi \rangle$, *where* F' *is the set of accessible elements of* $\mathcal{M}$, $C' = C \cap F'$, *and* δ' *is the restriction of* δ *to* $F' \times F' \to F'$.

The following lemma shows that a model satisfies exactly the same formulae as its accessible submodel.

Lemma 24: *For all wffs* **A** *and models* $\mathcal{M}$, $\mathcal{M} \models$ **A** *iff* $\alpha(\mathcal{M}) \models$ **A**.

Proof: By induction on the structure of any term **t**, $[\![\mathbf{t}]\!]_{\mathcal{M}} = [\![\mathbf{t}]\!]_{\alpha(\mathcal{M})}$. Hence by an induction on the structure of any wff **A**, $\mathcal{M} \models$ **A** iff $\alpha(\mathcal{M}) \models$ **A**.

□

I now proceed to axiomatize the acyclically valid wffs. I do this by providing an additional axiom schemata called (A), and show that a wff **A** is acyclically valid if and only if there is a proof of **A** from the axioms of AVL and instances of axiom schema (A). I show this by first proving that a model satisfies every instance of (A) if and only if its accessible submodel $\alpha(\mathcal{M})$ is acyclic.

Axiom schema (A) is given below. In what follows, the set *A* is the set of instances of axiom schema (A).

(A) $\mathbf{t} \neq \mathbf{t}(\mathbf{t}_1)\ldots(\mathbf{t}_n)$ for some term **t** and some non-null sequence of terms $\mathbf{t}_1, \ldots, \mathbf{t}_n$.

Theorem 25: *Let* $\mathcal{M}$ *be any model. Then* $\mathcal{M}$ *satisfies every instance of axiom schema (A) if and only if* $\alpha(\mathcal{M})$ *is acyclic.*

Proof: I begin by proving the left-to-right half of the theorem. Suppose the contrary, i.e., there exists a model $\mathcal{M}$ that satisfies every instance of axiom schema (A) such that $\alpha(\mathcal{M}) = \langle F, C, \delta, \varphi, \chi \rangle$ is a cyclic model. I show that there is an instance of **A** that $\alpha(\mathcal{M})$ and hence (by Lemma 24) $\mathcal{M}$ do not satisfy.

Because $\alpha(\mathcal{M})$ is a cyclic model there are elements $f, h_0, \ldots, h_n, g_1, \ldots, g_n$ for $n \geq 0$ such that $\delta(f, h_0) = g_1$, $\delta(g_1, h_1) = g_2$, $\ldots$, $\delta(g_n, h_n) = f$. Because

$\alpha(\mathcal{M})$ is an accessible model there are terms $\mathbf{t}, \mathbf{t}_0, \ldots, \mathbf{t}_n$, such that $[\![\mathbf{t}]\!] = f$, $[\![\mathbf{t}_0]\!] = h_0, \ldots, [\![\mathbf{t}_n]\!] = h_n$. Then by induction on the structure of $\mathbf{t}(\mathbf{t}_0)\ldots(\mathbf{t}_n)$, it follows $[\![\mathbf{t}(\mathbf{t}_0)\ldots(\mathbf{t}_n)]\!] = [\![\mathbf{t}]\!]$, and hence $\alpha(\mathcal{M})$ does not satisfy $\mathbf{t} \not\approx \mathbf{t}(\mathbf{t}_0)\ldots(\mathbf{t}_n)$, an instance of (A). Thus if $\mathcal{M}$ and hence $\alpha(\mathcal{M})$ satisfy every instance of (A), $\alpha(\mathcal{M})$ is acyclic.

Now I prove the right-to-left half of the theorem. Let $\mathcal{M}$ be any model such that $\alpha(\mathcal{M})$ is acyclic, and suppose that there is some in-- stance of (A) that $\alpha(\mathcal{M})$ does not satisfy, i.e that $\alpha(\mathcal{M}) \models \mathbf{t} \approx \mathbf{t}(\mathbf{t}_1)\ldots(\mathbf{t}_n)$ for some term $\mathbf{t}$ and some non-null sequence of terms $\mathbf{t}_1, \ldots, \mathbf{t}_n$.

If this is the case, then $\delta(\mathbf{t}, [\![\mathbf{t}_1]\!]) = [\![\mathbf{t}(\mathbf{t}_1)]\!]$, $\delta([\![\mathbf{t}(\mathbf{t}_1)]\!], [\![\mathbf{t}_2]\!]) = [\![\mathbf{t}(\mathbf{t}_1)(\mathbf{t}_2)]\!], \ldots, \delta([\![\mathbf{t}(\mathbf{t}_1)\ldots(\mathbf{t}_{n-1})]\!], [\![\mathbf{t}_n]\!]) = [\![\mathbf{t}(\mathbf{t}_1)\ldots(\mathbf{t}_n)]\!]$. Thus $D([\![\mathbf{t}]\!], [\![\mathbf{t}(\mathbf{t}_1)]\!])$, $D([\![\mathbf{t}(\mathbf{t}_1)]\!], [\![\mathbf{t}_2]\!]), \ldots, D([\![\mathbf{t}(\mathbf{t}_1)\ldots(\mathbf{t}_{n-1})]\!], [\![\mathbf{t}(\mathbf{t}_1)\ldots(\mathbf{t}_n)]\!])$. But since $\alpha(\mathcal{M}) \models \mathbf{t} \approx \mathbf{t}(\mathbf{t}_1)\ldots(\mathbf{t}_n)$, $[\![\mathbf{t}(\mathbf{t}_1)\ldots(\mathbf{t}_n)]\!] = [\![\mathbf{t}]\!]$, thus $D([\![\mathbf{t}(\mathbf{t}_1)\ldots(\mathbf{t}_{n-1})]\!], [\![\mathbf{t}]\!])$, hence the transitive closure of D is not irreflexive and $\alpha(\mathcal{M})$ is not acyclic, contrary to hypothesis. □

Since the accessible submodel of any acyclic model is clearly also acyclic, it follows immediately from Lemma 24 and Theorem 25 that every acyclic model satifies a wff **B** if and only if every model that satisfies *A* also satisfies **B**, i.e., that schema (A) describes exactly the models satisfying all of the acyclically valid wffs. Thus we have:

Corollary 26: *A wff* **B** *is acyclically valid iff* $A \models \mathbf{B}$.

Finally, by the Soundness Theorem 7 of Section 2.4 and the Generalized Completeness Theorem 16 it follows that the axiomatization of the acyclically valid wffs is sound and complete.

Corollary 27: *A wff* **B** *is acyclically valid iff* $A \vdash \mathbf{B}$.

2.8 Wffs of $\mathcal{A}$ as Descriptions of Attribute-Value Structures

The languages $\mathcal{A}$(*Const,Var*) discussed in this chapter were introduced as tools for describing attribute-value structures, where a wff of $\mathcal{A}$ describes the attribute-value models that satisfy it. In this section I investigate the structure of the space of attribute-value models with respect to a relation between models called the subsumption relation, and explain how this structure is related to the structure of the set of attribute-value models that satisfy any wff of $\mathcal{A}$. This identifies the sets of attribute-value models that wffs of $\mathcal{A}$ describe.

Informally, a model $\mathcal{M}$ subsumes another model $\mathcal{M}'$ if and only if the 'structure' of $\mathcal{M}'$ is an extension of the 'structure' of $\mathcal{M}$. Two models that have the same 'structure' are called subsumption equivalent.

Subsumption equivalence is an equivalence relation, so it partitions the set of models into equivalence classes, and the subsumption relation (modulo subsumption equivalence) is a partial order on these equivalence classes.

I then investigate the properties of the set of models that satisfy any wff **A** of $\mathcal{A}$. First I show that for any conjunction of positive literals **E** there is a model $\mathcal{M}$(**E**) that satisfies **E** and subsumes a model $\mathcal{M}$ if and only if $\mathcal{M}$ itself satisfies **E**. Thus [$\mathcal{M}$(**E**)], the equivalence class of models containing $\mathcal{M}$(**E**), is the subsumption minimal equivalence class of models satisfying **E**, and the equivalence classes of models satisfying **E** form a principal filter generated by [$\mathcal{M}$(**E**)]. Then, using the fact that any wff **A** is equivalent to *False* or a wff in reduced form, I provide a direct characterization of the set of models that satisfy any wff **A** in terms of the principal filters generated by the positive and negative literals of a reduced form equivalent to **A**.

The subsumption relation is defined in terms of a class of mappings from models to models called model homomorphisms, which I now proceed to define.

Definition 28: *Let Const and Var be fixed, and let* $\mathcal{M} = \langle F,C,\delta,\varphi,\chi\rangle$ *and* $\mathcal{M}' = \langle F',C',\delta',\varphi',\chi'\rangle$ *be two models for the same set of constant symbols and variables (i.e.,* φ: *Var* $\rightarrow$ *F,* φ': *Var* $\rightarrow$ *F',* χ: *Const* $\rightarrow$ *C, and* χ': *Const* $\rightarrow$ *C'). Then a function* $h : F \rightarrow F'$ *is a* MODEL HOMOMORPHISM *from* $\mathcal{M}$ *to* $\mathcal{M}'$ *iff:*

(i) For every $x \in Var$, $h(\varphi(x)) = \varphi'(x)$.

(ii) For every $c \in Const$, $h(\chi(c)) = \chi'(c)$.

(iii) For every $f \in C$, $h(f) \in C'$.

(iv) For every $f_1, f_2 \in F$, if $\delta(f_1,f_2)$ is defined then $\delta'(h(f_1),h(f_2))$ is defined, and $h(\delta(f_1,f_2)) = \delta'(h(f_1),h(f_2))$.

Informally speaking, conditions (i) and (ii) in the definition of model homomorphism require that *h* preserve the assignments to variables and constants. Conditions (iii) requires that *h* preserves the constant status of constant elements, while condition (iv) requires that *h* preserves the 'structure' of model that is represented by the partial function δ.

The subsumption relation is defined in terms of model homomorphisms.

Definition 29: *If there is a model homomorphism from* $\mathcal{M}$ *to* $\mathcal{M}'$*, then* $\mathcal{M}$ SUBSUMES $\mathcal{M}'$*, written as* $\mathcal{M} \sqsubseteq \mathcal{M}'$.

Example 16: *Let Const* = { *c* } *and let Var* = { *x* }. *Consider the models* $\mathcal{M}_1 = \langle F_1, C_1, \delta_1, \varphi_1, \chi_1 \rangle$ *and* $\mathcal{M}_2 = \langle F_2, C_2, \delta_2, \varphi_2, \chi_2 \rangle$ *defined in (3). The function* $h : F_1 \rightarrow F_2$ *defined in (4) is a model homomorphism from* $\mathcal{M}_1$ *to* $\mathcal{M}_2$, *so* $\mathcal{M}_1$ *subsumes* $\mathcal{M}_2$.

(3) $F_1 = \{ p, q, r \}$ $\quad F_2 = \{ u, v, w \}$

$C_1 = \{ p \}$ $\quad C_2 = \{ u \}$

$\delta_1(q,p) = r$ $\quad \delta_2(v,u) = v,$ $\quad \delta_2(w,u) = u$

$\varphi_1(x) = q$ $\quad \varphi_2(x) = v$

$\chi_1(c) = p$ $\quad \chi_2(c) = u$

(4) $h(p) = u, \quad h(q) = v, \quad h(r) = v.$

I now proceed to investigate the structure of the space of models with respect to the subsumption relation.

Lemma 30: *The subsumption relation is transitive and reflexive.*

Proof: Let $\mathcal{M} = \langle F,C,\delta,\varphi,\chi \rangle$, $\mathcal{M}' = \langle F',C',\delta',\varphi',\chi' \rangle$, $\mathcal{M}'' = \langle F'',C'',\delta'',\varphi'',\chi'' \rangle$, where $\mathcal{M} \sqsubseteq \mathcal{M}'$ and $\mathcal{M}' \sqsubseteq \mathcal{M}''$. Therefore there exist model homomorphisms $h : F \rightarrow F'$ and $h' : F' \rightarrow F''$. It is easy to verify that $h' \circ h : F \rightarrow F''$ is a model homomorphism from $\mathcal{M}$ to $\mathcal{M}''$, hence $\mathcal{M} \sqsubseteq \mathcal{M}''$.

Now consider the identity function $1_F : F \rightarrow F$. Clearly 1_F is a model homomorphism from $\mathcal{M}$ to $\mathcal{M}$, hence the subsumption relation is reflexive. □

Note that any reflexive and transitive relation R on a set S induces an equivalence relation $\equiv_R$ on S and a partial order $R/\equiv_R$ on the quotient set $S/\equiv_R$. Since the subsumption relation is a reflexive and transitive relation on the set of models, this implies that there is an equivalence relation on the set of models; this equivalence relation is called the subsumption equivalence relation.

Definition 31: *If* $\mathcal{M} \sqsubseteq \mathcal{M}'$ *and* $\mathcal{M}' \sqsubseteq \mathcal{M}$, *then* $\mathcal{M}$ *and* $\mathcal{M}'$ *are* SUBSUMPTION EQUIVALENT, *written* $\mathcal{M} \sqsupseteq\sqsubseteq \mathcal{M}'$. $[\mathcal{M}]$ *is the subsumption equivalence class containing* $\mathcal{M}$.

Then we have the following.

Corollary 32: *Subsumption equivalence is an equivalence relation on the set of models. The subsumption relation modulo the subsumption equivalence relation is a partial order on the set of models modulo the subsumption equivalence relation.* □

Now I show that for each wff **E** that is a conjunction of atomic wffs there is a model $\mathcal{M}(\mathbf{E})$ that subsumes every model that satisfies **E**.

(Recall that an atomic wff is a wff of the form $\mathbf{t} \approx \mathbf{t}'$, where $\mathbf{t}$ and $\mathbf{t}'$ are terms of $\mathcal{A}$). The model $\mathcal{M}(\mathbf{E})$ is in fact the model constructed in Section 2.5.1 in the discussion of reduced forms.

Definition 33: *Let* $\mathbf{E}$ *be a reduced wff of* $\mathcal{A}$ *that is a conjunction of positive literals. Then define the model* $\mathcal{M}(\mathbf{E}) = \langle T, Const, \eta, \phi_{Const}, \phi_{Var} \rangle$ *for* $\mathbf{E}$ *as follows:*

(i) T_E is the set of terms and subterms appearing in $\mathbf{E}$, and let $T = T_E \cap Const \cap Var$.

(ii) Let $\phi : T \rightarrow T$ be the function defined by $\phi(\mathbf{t}') = \mathbf{t}$ if $\mathbf{t} \approx \mathbf{t}'$ is a wff of $\mathbf{E}$, $\phi(\mathbf{t}') = \mathbf{t}'$ otherwise. Then ϕ_{Const} and ϕ_{Var} are the restrictions of ϕ to *Const* and *Var* respectively.

(iii) $\eta : T \times T \rightharpoonup T$ is the partial function defined by $\eta(\mathbf{t},\mathbf{t}') = \phi(\mathbf{t}(\mathbf{t}'))$ for $\mathbf{t}(\mathbf{t}')$ in T, and undefined otherwise.

I showed in Section 2.5.1 that the model $\mathcal{M}(\mathbf{E})$ satisfies $\mathbf{E}$. Now I show that any model that satisfies $\mathbf{E}$ is subsumed by $\mathcal{M}(\mathbf{E})$.

Lemma 34: $\mathcal{M}'$ *is a model that satisfies wff* $\mathbf{E}$ *of* $\mathcal{A}$ *that is a conjunction of atomic wffs if and only if* $\mathcal{M}(\mathbf{E}) \sqsubseteq \mathcal{M}'$.

Proof: First, suppose $\mathcal{M}' \models \mathbf{E}$, where $\mathcal{M}' = \langle F, C, \delta, \varphi, \chi \rangle$, and let T be defined as above. Then for every $\mathbf{t} \in T$, $[\![\mathbf{t}]\!]_{\mathcal{M}'} \neq \bot$.

Let $h : T \rightarrow F$ be defined by $h(\mathbf{t}) = [\![\mathbf{t}]\!]_{\mathcal{M}'}$. By the previous remark, h is well-defined. I claim that h is a model homomorphism from $\mathcal{M}'$ to $\mathcal{M}(\mathbf{E}) = \langle T, Const, \eta, \phi_{Const}, \phi_{Var} \rangle$, so $\mathcal{M}(\mathbf{E}) \sqsubseteq \mathcal{M}'$.

If $\mathbf{t} \in Const$ then $h(\phi_{Const}(\mathbf{t})) = [\![\phi_{Const}(\mathbf{t})]\!]_{\mathcal{M}} = [\![\mathbf{t}]\!]_{\mathcal{M}} = \chi(\mathbf{t})$ as required, since $\phi_{Const}(\mathbf{t}) = \mathbf{t}$.

For $\mathbf{t} \in Var$ there are two cases. Suppose $\phi_{Var}(\mathbf{t}) = \mathbf{t}$. Then, $h(\phi_{Var}(\mathbf{t})) = [\![\mathbf{t}]\!]_{\mathcal{M}'} = \varphi(\mathbf{t})$ as required. Now suppose $\phi_{Var}(\mathbf{t}) = \mathbf{t}'' \neq \mathbf{t}$. By the definition of ϕ, $\mathbf{E}$ must contain an equation of the form $\mathbf{t}'' \approx \mathbf{t}$, so it must be the case that $\varphi(\mathbf{t}) = [\![\mathbf{t}]\!]_{\mathcal{M}'} = [\![\mathbf{t}'']\!]_{\mathcal{M}'}$, since $\mathcal{M}' \models \mathbf{E}$ and hence $\mathcal{M}' \models \mathbf{t}'' \approx \mathbf{t}$. Then $h(\phi_{Var}(\mathbf{t})) = [\![\mathbf{t}'']\!]_{\mathcal{M}'} = \varphi(\mathbf{t})$, as required.

Consider terms $\mathbf{t}, \mathbf{t}', \mathbf{t}'' \in T$ such that $\eta(\mathbf{t},\mathbf{t}') = \phi(\mathbf{t}(\mathbf{t}')) = \mathbf{t}''$. Again, there are two cases to consider. Suppose $\mathbf{t}'' = \mathbf{t}(\mathbf{t}')$. Then it must be the case that $h(\eta(\mathbf{t},\mathbf{t}')) = [\![\mathbf{t}(\mathbf{t}')]\!]_{\mathcal{M}'} = \delta([\![\mathbf{t}]\!]_{\mathcal{M}'}, [\![\mathbf{t}']\!]_{\mathcal{M}'}) = \delta(h(\mathbf{t}), h(\mathbf{t}'))$. Now suppose that $\eta(\mathbf{t},\mathbf{t}') = \mathbf{t}'' \neq \mathbf{t}(\mathbf{t}')$. Then by the definition of ϕ, $\mathbf{E}$ must contain an equation of the form $\mathbf{t}'' \approx \mathbf{t}(\mathbf{t}')$, so it must be the case that $\delta([\![\mathbf{t}]\!]_{\mathcal{M}'}, [\![\mathbf{t}']\!]_{\mathcal{M}'}) = [\![\mathbf{t}(\mathbf{t}')]\!]_{\mathcal{M}'} = [\![\mathbf{t}'']\!]_{\mathcal{M}'}$, since $\mathcal{M} \models \mathbf{E}$. Then $h(\eta(\mathbf{t},\mathbf{t}')) = [\![\mathbf{t}'']\!]_{\mathcal{M}'} = \delta([\![\mathbf{t}]\!]_{\mathcal{M}'}, [\![\mathbf{t}']\!]_{\mathcal{M}'}) = \delta(h(\mathbf{t}), h(\mathbf{t}'))$, as required.

Thus if $\mathcal{M}' \models \mathbf{E}$ then $\mathcal{M}(\mathbf{E}) \sqsubseteq \mathcal{M}'$.

Now suppose $\mathcal{M}(\mathbf{E}) \sqsubseteq \mathcal{M}'$. Then there exists a model homomorphism $h : T \rightarrow F$. By induction on the structure of any term $\mathbf{t} \in T$ it follows that $[\![\mathbf{t}]\!]_{\mathcal{M}'} = h(\phi(\mathbf{t}))$. Let $\mathbf{t} \approx \mathbf{t}'$ be any positive literal in $\mathbf{E}$. Then by construction $\phi(\mathbf{t}) = \phi(\mathbf{t}')$, so $[\![\mathbf{t}]\!]_{\mathcal{M}'} = [\![\mathbf{t}']\!]_{\mathcal{M}'}$, and thus $\mathcal{M}' \models \mathbf{t} \approx \mathbf{t}'$ as required.

Thus if $\mathcal{M}(\mathbf{E}) \sqsubseteq \mathcal{M}'$ then $\mathcal{M}' \models \mathbf{E}$. □

An immediate corollary of this is that the set of equivalence classes of the models that satisfy a conjunction of atomic wffs **E** have a particularly simple structure.

Definition 35: *If $<$ is a partial order on a set S, then the* PRINCIPLE FILTER $\psi(\mathrm{a})$ *generated by an element $a \in S$ is the set* $\psi(\mathrm{a}) = \{ b : b \in S, \ a < b \}$.

Corollary 36: *The set of subsumption equivalence classes of models that satisfy a wff* **E** *that is a conjunction of positive literals is the principal filter generated by* $[\mathcal{M}(\mathbf{E})]$. □

This means that the set of equivalence classes of models that satisfy a wff **E** can be viewed as an infinite 'cone' ascending from its generator $[\mathcal{M}(\mathbf{E})]$, as sketched in Figure 8.

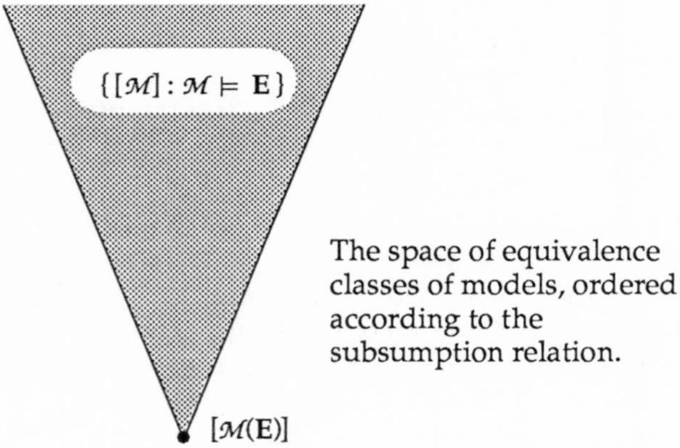

Figure 8 The equivalence classes of models satisfying E

This result can be used to characterize the set of equivalence classes of models that satisfy an arbitrary wff of $\mathcal{A}$. Corollary 12 of Section 2.5.4 showed that any wff **A** of $\mathcal{A}$ is equivalent to either *True, False,* or a disjunction of conjunctive reduced forms (recall that a conjunctive reduced form is a conjunction of atomic wffs and negations of atomic wffs).

Consider an arbitrary conjunctive reduced form $\mathbf{C} = \mathbf{E} \wedge \sim\mathbf{I}_1 \wedge \ldots \sim\mathbf{I}_n$, where **E** is a conjunction of atomic wffs, and each $\mathbf{I}_i$ is an atomic wff. Any model that satisfies **C** must satisfy **E**, so it must lie in one of the equivalence classes in the principal filter generated by $[\mathcal{M}(\mathbf{E})]$. Further, any model that satisfies **C** also must not satisfy any of the $\mathbf{I}_i$, and hence must lie outside all of the equivalence classes in the union of the principle filters generated by the $[\mathcal{M}(\mathbf{I}_i)]$. Thus the set of subsumption equivalence classes of models that satisfy **C** is given by:

(iii) $$\psi([\mathcal{M}(\mathbf{E})]) - \left(\bigcup_{i=0}^{n} \psi([\mathcal{M}(\mathbf{I}_i)]) \right)$$

This set of subsumption equivalence classes is sketched in Figure 9; the set equivalence classes of satisfying models corresponds to the shaded area in the figure.

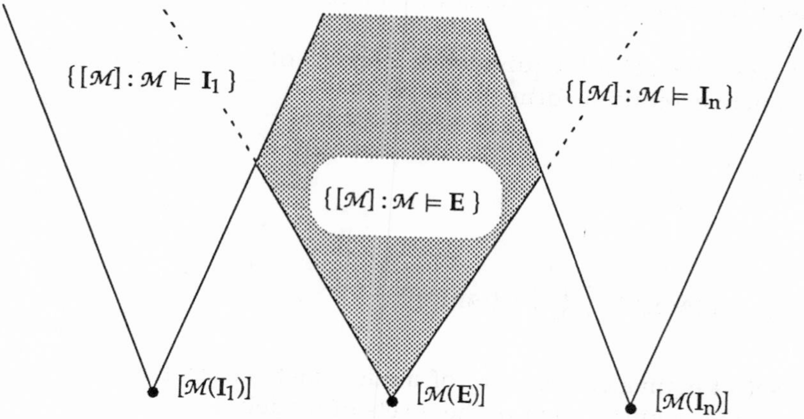

Figure 9 The equivalence classes of models satisfying a conjunctive reduced form

This, together with the fact that an arbitrary wff **A** is equivalent to either *True, False* or a disjunction of conjunctive normal forms enables us to characterize the set of models that satisfy **A** in the following way:

Theorem 37: *The set of subsumption equivalence classes of models that satisfy any wff* **A** *of* $\mathcal{A}$ *can be expressed as:*

$$\bigcup_{j=0}^{m} \left(\psi([\mathcal{M}_j]) - \left(\bigcup_{i=0}^{n_j} \psi([\mathcal{M}_{i,j}]) \right) \right)$$

where each of the $\mathcal{M}_j$ and $\mathcal{M}_{i,j}$ are finite models.

Proof: By Corollary 12 of Section 2.5.4 any wff **A** of $\mathcal{A}$ is equivalent to *True, False* or a disjunction of conjunctions of positive and negative literals. If **A** is equivalent to *True* then all models satisfy **A**, so the set of subsumption equivalence classes of models that satisfy **A** is $\psi([\mathcal{M}(\mathbf{c} \approx \mathbf{c})])$ for any constant symbol **c**, since any model satisfies $\mathbf{c} \approx \mathbf{c}$. If **A** is equivalent to *False* then no model satisfies **A**, so the set of subsumption equivalence classes of models that satisfy **A** is $\varnothing = \psi([\mathcal{M}(\mathbf{c} \approx \mathbf{c})]) - \psi([\mathcal{M}(\mathbf{c} \approx \mathbf{c})])$ for any constant symbol **c**. Finally, if **A** is equivalent to a reduced form not equal to *True* then

(i) $$\mathbf{A} \equiv \bigvee_{j=0}^{m} \left(\mathbf{E}_j \wedge \bigwedge_{i=0}^{n_j} \sim\mathbf{I}_{i,j} \right)$$

where the $\mathbf{E}_j$ are conjunctions of atomic wffs and the $\mathbf{I}_{i,j}$ are atomic wffs.

Since the set of equivalence classes of models that satisfy a conjunctive reduced form

(ii) $$\mathbf{E}_j \wedge \bigwedge_{i=0}^{n_j} \sim\mathbf{I}_{i,j}$$

is

(iii) $$\psi([\mathcal{M}(\mathbf{E}_j)]) - \left(\bigcup_{i=0}^{n_j} \psi([\mathcal{M}(\mathbf{I}_{i,j})]) \right)$$

the set of equivalence classes of models that satisfy a reduced form is given by the finite union of these sets of models, i.e.,

(iv) $$\bigcup_{j=0}^{m} \left(\psi([\mathcal{M}(\mathbf{E}_j)]) - \left(\bigcup_{i=0}^{n_j} \psi([\mathcal{M}(\mathbf{I}_{i,j})]) \right) \right)$$

But since an arbitrary wff not equivalent to either *True* or *False* is equivalent to some reduced form, the set of equivalence classes of models that satisfy an arbitrary wff is the form shown in (iv).

Finally, note that all of the models $\mathcal{M}(\mathbf{E}_j)$ and $\mathcal{M}(\mathbf{I}_{i,j})$ are finite models, so the hypothesis of the theorem follows from (iv) with $\mathcal{M}_j = \mathcal{M}(\mathbf{E}_j)$ and $\mathcal{M}_{i,j} = \mathcal{M}(\mathbf{I}_{i,j})$. □

Thus the set of equivalence classes of models that satisfy an arbitrary wff **A** of $\mathcal{A}$ can be depicted as shown in Figure 10, where the satisfying equivalence classes lie in the shaded areas.

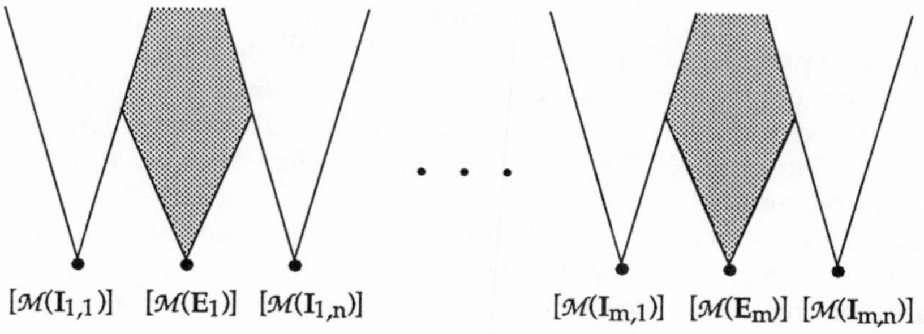

Figure 10 The sets of equivalence classes satisfying an arbitrary wff

Example 17: *Let* $\mathbf{A} = sg \approx y(num) \wedge y \approx x(subj) \wedge \sim(sg \approx x(subj)(num) \wedge 3rd \approx x(subj)(pers))$. *Then by the reduction algorithm* $\mathbf{A} \equiv sg \approx y(num) \wedge y \approx x(subj) \wedge 3rd \not\approx y(pers)$, *(see Example 14 of Section 2.5.4) so the set of equivalence classes of models that satisfy* $\mathbf{A}$ *is given by:*

$$\psi([\mathcal{M}(sg \approx y(num) \wedge y \approx x(subj))]) - \psi([\mathcal{M}(3rd \approx y(pers))]).$$

This set is sketched in Figure 11.

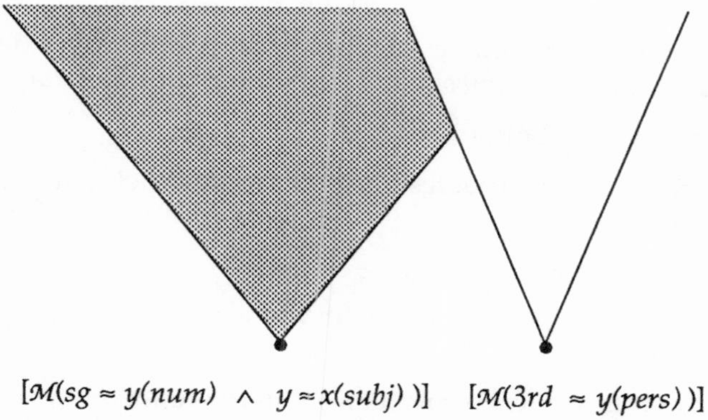

Figure 11 The equivalence classes of models satisfying $sg \approx y(num) \wedge y \approx x(subj) \wedge \sim(sg \approx x(subj)(num) \wedge 3rd \approx x(subj)(pers))$

2.9 The Quantifier-Free Theory with Equality

In this section I investigate the relationship between the language $\mathcal{A}$ and the quantifier-free first-order languages with function symbols and equality. I do this by defining a translation from the wffs of $\mathcal{A}$ to the wffs of the quantifier-free first order language with function symbols and equality, such that a wff of $\mathcal{A}$ is satisfiable if and only if its translation is satisfiable. The existence of this translation shows that the expressive power of the the quantifier-free first order language with function symbols and equality is greater than or equal to the expressive power of $\mathcal{A}$.

Moreover, since the translation involved can be performed in polynomial time, and since the satisfiability problem for wffs from the quantifier free first-order languages with equality is $\mathcal{NP}$-complete, it follows as a corollary that the satisfiability problem for wffs of $\mathcal{A}$ is $\mathcal{NP}$-easy. But since SAT can be reduced to the satisfiability problem for wffs of $\mathcal{A}$ I show that the satisfiability problem for wffs of $\mathcal{A}$ is in fact $\mathcal{NP}$-complete.

2.9.1 Quantifier-Free First-order Languages with Equality

In this section I briefly review the quantifier-free first order theory with function symbols and equality. For more detailed treatments, see Nelson and Oppen (1980) and Gallier (1986). The quantifier-free first order languages with function symbols and equality $\mathcal{L}$ are defined as follows:

Definition 39: *The primitive symbols of a quantifier-free first order language with function symbols and equality $\mathcal{L}$ are the following*:

(a) Improper symbols: ( ) $\neg \vee \wedge \doteq$

(b) n-ary function variables: $f^n, g^n, h^n, \ldots$ for each natural number $n \geq 0$.

(c) Truth values: *True, False.*

The terms and the wffs of $\mathcal{L}$ are defined inductively by the following formation rules:

(a) If $\mathbf{t}_1, \ldots, \mathbf{t}_n$ are terms and $\mathbf{f}^n$ is an n-ary function variable, then $\mathbf{f}^n(\mathbf{t}_1, \ldots, \mathbf{t}_n)$ is a term.

(b) If $\mathbf{t}_1$ and $\mathbf{t}_2$ are terms, then $\mathbf{t}_1 \doteq \mathbf{t}_2$ is a wff.

(c) If $\mathbf{A}$ is a wff, so is $\neg\mathbf{A}$.

(d) If $\mathbf{A}$ and $\mathbf{B}$ are wffs, so is $\mathbf{A} \wedge \mathbf{B}$ and $\mathbf{A} \vee \mathbf{B}$.

The 0-ary function variables are also called *individual variables.* When the arity of a function variable is clear from the context I omit the superscript that indicates arity. Now I present the intended semantics of $\mathcal{L}$.

Definition 40: *A* DOMAIN OF INDIVIDUALS *is a set $\mathcal{D}$. An assignment into $\mathcal{D}$ is a function ϕ defined on the function variables of $\mathcal{L}$ such that $\phi(f^n)$ is a function from $\mathcal{D}^n$ to $\mathcal{D}$.*

Given a domain of individuals $\mathcal{D}$ and an assignment ϕ into $\mathcal{D}$, we define the VALUE $\mathcal{V}(\mathbf{f}^n(\mathbf{t}_1, \ldots, \mathbf{t}_n))$ *of a term* $\mathbf{f}^n(\mathbf{t}_1, \ldots, \mathbf{t}_n)$ *of $\mathcal{L}$ as* $(\phi(\mathbf{f}^n))\ (\mathcal{V}(\mathbf{t}_1), \ldots, \mathcal{V}(\mathbf{t}_n))$.

Finally, the SATISFACTION RELATION $\models$ *between pairs consisting of a domain $\mathcal{D}$ and an assignment ϕ into $\mathcal{D}$, and wffs of $\mathcal{L}$ is defined as follows:*

(a) If $\mathbf{A}$ is $\mathbf{t}_1 \doteq \mathbf{t}_2$, then $\langle \mathcal{D}, \phi \rangle \models \mathbf{A}$ iff $\mathcal{V}(\mathbf{t}_1) = \mathcal{V}(\mathbf{t}_2)$.

(b) If $\mathbf{A}$ is $\neg\mathbf{B}$, then $\langle \mathcal{D}, \phi \rangle \models \mathbf{A}$ iff $\langle \mathcal{D}, \phi \rangle \not\models \mathbf{B}$.

(c) If $\mathbf{A}$ is $\mathbf{B} \wedge \mathbf{C}$, then $\langle \mathcal{D}, \phi \rangle \models \mathbf{A}$ iff $\langle \mathcal{D}, \phi \rangle \models \mathbf{B}$ and $\langle \mathcal{D}, \phi \rangle \models \mathbf{C}$.

(d) If $\mathbf{A}$ is $\mathbf{B} \vee \mathbf{C}$, then $\langle \mathcal{D}, \phi \rangle \models \mathbf{A}$ iff $\langle \mathcal{D}, \phi \rangle \models \mathbf{B}$ or $\langle \mathcal{D}, \phi \rangle \models \mathbf{C}$.

(e) $\langle \mathcal{D}, \phi \rangle \models$ *True*, $\langle \mathcal{D}, \phi \rangle \not\models$ *False*.

Example 19: *If x and y are 0-ary function symbols and f is a unary function symbol, then (5) is an example of a wff of $\mathcal{L}$.*

(5) $f(x) \doteq y \wedge f(y) \doteq x \wedge \neg\, x \doteq y.$

If $\mathcal{D} = \{0, 1\}$, $\phi(x) = 0$, $\phi(y) = 1$, and $(\phi(f))(0) = 1$, $(\phi(f))(1) = 0$, then:

(6) $\langle \mathcal{D}, \phi \rangle \models f(x) \doteq y \wedge f(y) \doteq x \wedge \neg\, x \doteq y.$

2.9.2 A Translation from $\mathcal{A}$ into $\mathcal{L}$

I now provide a translation from the wffs of $\mathcal{A}$ into the wffs of $\mathcal{L}$ which has the property that a wff $\mathbf{A}$ of $\mathcal{A}$ is satisfiable if and only if its translation $\tau(\mathbf{A})$ in $\mathcal{L}$ is satisfiable.

Informally, the language $\mathcal{L}$ differs from the language $\mathcal{A}$ in two important ways:

(i) Terms of $\mathcal{L}$ always have a value in $\mathcal{D}$, while terms of $\mathcal{A}$ need not always have as their denotation an element of the attribute-value model.

(ii) The language $\mathcal{L}$ makes a syntactic distinction between 0-ary and unary function symbols, while the language $\mathcal{A}$ makes no such distinction. For example, both occurrences of the symbol f in the wff $f(a) \approx f$ of $\mathcal{A}$ are the same variable of $\mathcal{A}$, while in the wff $f(a) \doteq f$ of $\mathcal{L}$ the first occurrence of the symbol f is a unary function symbol, while the second occurrence is an individual variable.

The first of these differences is accounted for by introducing an auxiliary individual variable '0', whose value is the value of the translations of non-denoting terms of $\mathcal{A}$. The second difference is accounted for by the introduction of an auxiliary binary function variable *apply*, where the value of *apply*($\mathbf{t}_1$,$\mathbf{t}_2$) is the value of 'applying' $\mathbf{t}_1$ to $\mathbf{t}_2$. (This will become clear in the exposition of the translation procedure).

Definition 41: *Let the variables and constant symbols of $\mathcal{A}$ plus the additional function variable '0' be the 0-ary function variables of $\mathcal{L}$, and let* APPLY *be a binary function symbol of $\mathcal{L}$. For any wff* **A** *of $\mathcal{A}$, let* Term(**A**) *be the set of terms that appear in* **A**, Const(**A**) *the set of constant symbols that appear in* **A**, *and* Var(**A**) *the set of variables that appear in* **A**. *Then define the function τ_t from terms of $\mathcal{A}$ to terms of $\mathcal{L}$ and the functions τ_{c1}, τ_{c2}, τ_v, τ_d and τ_w from wffs of $\mathcal{A}$ to wffs of $\mathcal{L}$ as follows:*

(a) If **t** is a variable or a constant symbol then $\tau_t(\mathbf{t}) = \mathbf{t}$. If $\mathbf{t} = \mathbf{t}_1(\mathbf{t}_2)$ is a complex term then $\tau_t(\mathbf{t}) = apply(\tau_t(\mathbf{t}_1), \tau_t(\mathbf{t}_2))$.

(b) $\tau_{c1}(\mathbf{A}) = \bigwedge_{c_i,\, c_j \in Const(\mathbf{A}),\, c_i \neq c_j} \neg\, c_i \doteq c_j.y$

(c) $\tau_{c2}(\mathbf{A}) = \bigwedge_{c \in Const(\mathbf{A}),\, t \in Term(\mathbf{A})} apply(\mathbf{c}, \tau_t(\mathbf{t})) \doteq 0.$

(d) $\tau_v(\mathbf{A}) = \bigwedge_{u \in Const(\mathbf{A}) \cap Var(\mathbf{A})} \neg\, \mathbf{u} \doteq 0.$

(e) $\tau_d(\mathbf{A}) = \bigwedge_{t \in Term(\mathbf{A})} apply(\tau_t(\mathbf{t}),0) \doteq 0 \wedge apply(0,\tau_t(\mathbf{t})) \doteq 0.$

(f) If **A** is $\mathbf{t}_1 \approx \mathbf{t}_2$ then $\tau_w(\mathbf{A})$ is $\tau_t(\mathbf{t}_1) \doteq \tau_t(\mathbf{t}_2) \wedge \neg\tau_t(\mathbf{t}_1) \doteq 0$,
if **A** is ~**B** then $\tau_w(\mathbf{A})$ is $\neg\tau_w(\mathbf{B})$,
if **A** is $\mathbf{B} \vee \mathbf{C}$ then $\tau_w(\mathbf{A})$ is $\tau_w(\mathbf{B}) \vee \tau_w(\mathbf{C})$,
if **A** is $\mathbf{B} \wedge \mathbf{C}$ then $\tau_w(\mathbf{A})$ is $\tau_w(\mathbf{B}) \wedge \tau_w(\mathbf{C})$,
if **A** is *True* then $\tau_w(\mathbf{A})$ is *True*, and
if **A** is *False* then $\tau_w(\mathbf{A})$ is *False*.

Then define the translation $\tau(\mathbf{A})$ *of any wff* **A** *of $\mathcal{A}$ as:*

(g) $\tau(\mathbf{A}) = \tau_{c1}(\mathbf{A}) \wedge \tau_{c2}(\mathbf{A}) \wedge \tau_v(\mathbf{A}) \wedge \tau_w(\mathbf{A})$.

Informally, $\tau_t(\mathbf{t})$ is the translation of a term **t**. $\tau_{c1}(\mathbf{A})$ ensures that the value of the translation of every constant appearing in **A** is has a distinct value, $\tau_{c2}(\mathbf{A})$ ensures that the value of any attribute of any constant symbol appearing in **A** is undefined, $\tau_v(\mathbf{A})$ ensures that the value of (the translation of) any constant symbol or variable appearing in **A** is not equal to 0 (i.e., it requires that every constant symbol and variable appearing in **A** has a denotation not equal to $\perp$), and $\tau_d(\mathbf{A})$ ensures that if the value of a term of $\mathcal{L}$ that is the translation of a subterm of a term **t** appearing in **A** is 0, then the value of the translation of **t** is also 0 (i.e., that a term has a denotation not equal to $\perp$ only if all of its subterms do). Finally, $\tau_w(\mathbf{A})$ translates an equality of $\mathcal{A}$ into an equality of $\mathcal{L}$, with the added condition that the terms appearing in the equality must not equal 0, and translates the boolean structure of wffs in the obvious way.

Example 20: *Let* **A** *be the wff* $x(a) \approx y \wedge y(b) \approx a$*, where* x *and* y *are variables of* $\mathcal{A}$*, and* a *and* b *are constant symbols of* $\mathcal{A}$*. Then the following hold:*

$$\tau_{c1}(\mathbf{A}) = \neg\, a \doteq b\,.$$

$$\tau_{c2}(\mathbf{A}) = apply(a,a) \doteq 0 \wedge apply(a,b) \doteq 0 \wedge apply(a,x(a)) \doteq 0 \wedge apply(a,y(b)) \doteq 0 \wedge apply(b,a) \doteq 0 \wedge apply(b,b) \doteq 0 \wedge apply(b,x(a)) \doteq 0 \wedge apply(b,y(b)) \doteq 0.$$

$$\tau_v(\mathbf{A}) = \neg\, a \doteq 0 \wedge \neg\, b \doteq 0 \wedge \neg\, x \doteq 0 \wedge \neg\, y \doteq 0.$$

$$\tau_d(\mathbf{A}) = apply(a,0) \doteq 0 \wedge apply(b,0) \doteq 0 \wedge apply(x,0) \doteq 0 \wedge apply(y,0) \doteq 0 \wedge apply(x(a),0) \doteq 0 \wedge apply(y(b),0) \doteq 0 \wedge apply(0,a) \doteq 0 \wedge apply(0,b) \doteq 0 \wedge apply(0,x) \doteq 0 \wedge apply(0,y) \doteq 0 \wedge apply(0,x(a)) \doteq 0 \wedge apply(0,y(b)) \doteq 0.$$

$$\tau_w(\mathbf{A}) = apply(x,a) \doteq y \wedge \neg apply(x,a) \doteq 0 \wedge apply(y,b) \doteq a \wedge \neg apply(y,b) \doteq 0.$$

Thus $\tau(\mathbf{A}) = \tau(\mathbf{A}) = \tau_{c1}(\mathbf{A}) \wedge \tau_{c2}(\mathbf{A}) \wedge \tau_v(\mathbf{A}) \wedge \tau_w(\mathbf{A})$ *is as given below.*

$$\tau(\mathbf{A}) = \neg\, a \doteq b \wedge apply(a,a) \doteq 0 \wedge apply(a,b) \doteq 0 \wedge apply(a,x(a)) \doteq 0 \wedge apply(a,y(b)) \doteq 0 \wedge apply(b,a) \doteq 0 \wedge apply(b,b) \doteq 0 \wedge apply(b,x(a)) \doteq 0 \wedge apply(b,y(b)) \doteq 0 \wedge \neg\, a \doteq 0 \wedge \neg\, b \doteq 0 \wedge \neg\, x \doteq 0 \wedge \neg\, y \doteq 0 \wedge apply(a,0) \doteq 0 \wedge apply(b,0) \doteq 0 \wedge apply(x,0) \doteq 0 \wedge apply(y,0) \doteq 0 \wedge apply(x(a),0) \doteq 0 \wedge apply(y(b),0) \doteq 0 \wedge apply(0,a) \doteq 0 \wedge apply(0,b) \doteq 0 \wedge apply(0,x) \doteq 0 \wedge apply(0,y) \doteq 0 \wedge apply(0,x(a)) \doteq 0 \wedge apply(0,y(b)) \doteq 0 \wedge apply(x,a) \doteq y \wedge \neg apply(x,a) \doteq 0 \wedge apply(y,b) \doteq a \wedge \neg apply(y,b) \doteq 0.$$

I now prove that a wff and its translation are equisatisfiable.

Theorem 42: *For any wff* **A** *of* $\mathcal{A}$, **A** *is satisfiable iff its translation* $\tau(\mathbf{A})$ *in the quantifier-free first-order language with equality is satisfiable.*

Proof: Suppose **A** is satisfiable. Then there exists a model $\mathcal{M} = \langle F, C, \delta, \varphi, \chi \rangle$ such that $\mathcal{M} \models \mathbf{A}$. Define $\mathcal{D}$ and ϕ as follows:

(i) $\mathcal{D} = F \cap \{ \perp \}$,

(ii) $\phi(\mathbf{c}) = \chi(\mathbf{c})$ for $\mathbf{c} \in$ *Const*,
$\phi(\mathbf{x}) = \varphi(\mathbf{x})$ for $\mathbf{x} \in$ *Var*,
$\phi(0) = \perp$,
$(\phi(apply))(e,e') = \delta(e,e')$ when $\delta(e,e')$ is defined,
$(\phi(apply))(e,e') = 0$ otherwise.

Then I claim $\langle \mathcal{D},\phi \rangle$ satisfies $\tau(\mathbf{A})$. To see this, first note that for any term $\mathbf{t}$ in *Term*(**A**), $[\![\mathbf{t}]\!]_{\mathcal{M}} = \mathcal{V}(\tau_t(\mathbf{t}))$. (This follows by an induction on the structure of $\mathbf{t}$). It follows directly that $\langle \mathcal{D},\phi \rangle$ satisfies $\tau_{c1}(\mathbf{A})$, $\tau_{c2}(\mathbf{A})$, $\tau_v(\mathbf{A})$ and $\tau_d(\mathbf{A})$. Finally, since $\mathcal{M} \models \mathbf{t}_1 \approx \mathbf{t}_2$ implies that $[\![\mathbf{t}_1]\!]_{\mathcal{M}} \neq \perp$, it follows by an induction on the structure of $\tau_w(\mathbf{A})$ that $\langle \mathcal{D},\phi \rangle$ satisfies $\tau_w(\mathbf{A})$. Thus $\langle \mathcal{D},\phi \rangle$ satisfies $\tau(\mathbf{A})$, as required.

Now suppose $\tau(\mathbf{A})$ is satisfiable. Then there exist $\mathcal{D}$ and ϕ such that $\langle \mathcal{D},\phi \rangle$ satisfies $\tau(\mathbf{A})$. Define the model $\mathcal{M} = \langle F,C,\delta,\varphi,\chi \rangle$ as follows:

(i) $F = \{ \phi(\tau_t(\mathbf{t})) : \mathbf{t} \in Term(\mathbf{A}) \} - \{ \phi(0) \}$,

(ii) $C = \{ \phi(\tau_t(\mathbf{c})) : \mathbf{c} \in Const(\mathbf{A}) \}$,

(iii) $\delta(e,e') = (\phi(apply))(e,e')$, for e, e' and $(\phi(apply))(e,e')$ in F, and δ is undefined elsewhere,

(iv) $\varphi(\mathbf{x}) = \phi(\mathbf{x})$ for $\mathbf{x} \in Var(\mathbf{A})$, and

(v) $\chi(\mathbf{c}) = \phi(\mathbf{c})$ for $\mathbf{c} \in Const(\mathbf{A})$.

I claim $\mathcal{M}$ satisfies **A**. To see this, first note that $\mathcal{M}$ is a well-formed attribute-value model. Since $\langle \mathcal{D},\phi \rangle$ satisfies $\tau_{c2}(\mathbf{A})$ it must be the case that for every $c \in C$ and every $f \in F$, $\delta(c,f)$ is undefined. Further, since $\langle \mathcal{D},\phi \rangle$ satisfies $\tau_v(\mathbf{A})$ it must be the case that $\varphi(\mathbf{x})$ and $\chi(\mathbf{c})$ are both defined for all variables in *Var*(**A**) and *Const*(**A**) respectively,[15] and since $\langle \mathcal{D},\phi \rangle$ satisfies $\tau_{c1}(\mathbf{A})$ it follows that χ is an injective function into C. Thus $\mathcal{M}$ is a well-formed attribute-value model.

Now, by induction on the structure of any term $\mathbf{t}$ in *Var*(**A**) it follows that if $\phi(\tau_t(\mathbf{t})) \neq \phi(0)$ then $\phi(\tau_t(\mathbf{t})) = [\![\mathbf{t}]\!]_{\mathcal{M}}$, and if $\phi(\tau_t(\mathbf{t})) = \phi(0)$ then $[\![\mathbf{t}]\!]_{\mathcal{M}} = \perp$. Thus it follows that for any two terms $\mathbf{t}_1$, $\mathbf{t}_2$ in *Var*(**A**), $\mathcal{M} \models \mathbf{t}_1 \approx \mathbf{t}_2$ iff $\langle \mathcal{D},\phi \rangle \models \tau_t(\mathbf{t}_1 \approx \mathbf{t}_2)$, so by an induction on the structure of **A** it follows that if $\langle \mathcal{D},\phi \rangle$ satisfies $\tau(\mathbf{A})$ then $\mathcal{M}$ satisfies **A**. □

2.9.3 The Computational Complexity of Satisfiability in $\mathcal{A}$

We can use this result to show that the satisfiability problem for wffs of $\mathcal{A}$ is $\mathcal{NP}$-complete. I do this in two steps: first I show that the

[15] Strictly speaking this is not sufficient, since φ and χ should also provide denotations for the variables and constants of the language $\mathcal{A}$ that do not appear in **A**. This requirement can be satisfied by including extra elements in the sets F and C that function as the denotation of the variables and constants not appearing in **A**.

satisfiability problem is $\mathcal{NP}$-easy, and then I show that an $\mathcal{NP}$-complete problem can be reduced to the satisfiability problem for wffs of $\mathcal{A}$, showing this problem to be $\mathcal{NP}$-complete.[16]

The first step requires the following result from Oppen (1980).

Theorem 43 (Oppen): *The satisfiability problem for formulae from the quantifier free languages with equality and function symbols is $\mathcal{NP}$-complete.* □

This leads directly to the following theorem.

Theorem 44: *The satisfiability problem for wffs of $\mathcal{A}$ is $\mathcal{NP}$-complete.*

Proof: First, note that the translation $\tau(\mathbf{A})$ can be computed in polynomial time in the length of **A**, so any instance of the satisfiability problem for wffs of $\mathcal{A}$ can be reduced in polynomial time to an instance of the satisfiability problem for wffs of the quantifier-free first-order language with function symbols and equality. Thus the satisfiability problem for wffs of $\mathcal{A}$ is $\mathcal{NP}$-easy.

To see that the satisfiability problem is $\mathcal{NP}$-complete, note that an $\mathcal{NP}$-complete problem, the satisfiability problem for propositional calculus (SAT),[17] can be reduced to the satisfiability problem for wffs of $\mathcal{A}$. If **P** is a wff of the propositional calculus and V is the set of (propositional) variables in **P**, let **P′** be the wff of $\mathcal{A}(\{c\}, V)$ with exactly the same propositional structure as **P**, except that each propositional variable **x** in **P** has been replaced with the atomic wff $\mathbf{x} \approx c$. Clearly this translation can be computed in polynomial time.

Suppose **P** is satisfiable with variable assignment $\mathcal{V}: V \rightarrow \{T, F\}$. Clearly the model $\langle\{T, F\}, \{T\}, \emptyset, \mathcal{V}, \{\langle c, T\rangle\}\rangle$ satisfies **P′**. Conversely, suppose some model $\mathcal{M}$ satisfies **P′**. Clearly the variable assignment $\mathcal{V}(\mathbf{x}) = T$ iff $[\![\mathbf{x}]\!]_{\mathcal{M}} = [\![\mathbf{c}]\!]_{\mathcal{M}}$ satisfies **P**. Thus the reduction is correct, and thus the satisfiability problem for wffs of $\mathcal{A}$ is $\mathcal{NP}$-complete. □

2.10 Attribute-Value Structures and Partiality

Readers familiar with the literature on attribute-value approaches to linguistics may have been surprised by omission of 'partiality' and 'unification' in my presentation of the important properties of attribute-value structures. These two notions have played leading roles in the development of attribute-value approaches to language (see,

---

16 This result can also be proven directly using the method that Oppen (1980) uses to prove the $\mathcal{NP}$-completeness of the satisfiability problem for the quantifier free languages with equality.

17 See Garey and Johnson (1979) for further details about this and many other $\mathcal{NP}$-complete problems.

e.g., Shieber 1986). In this section I discuss the 'unification approach' to attribute-value structures, and then explain how the approach I have taken here differs from this 'unification approach'. There is no universally accepted formulation of the 'unification approach'; I use the term here to refer to a set of 'leading ideas' rather than any specific treatment. In order to facilitate comparison of the 'unification approach' with the material presented above I formulate the 'unification approach' using the formal devices developed in this chapter. For other presentations of the 'unification approach' see Pereira and Shieber (1984), Shieber (1986), Kasper and Rounds (1986), Moshier and Rounds (1987), and Pereira (1987).

2.10.1 Satisfaction and the 'Unification Approach'

In the next chapter I show that solving the recognition problem for an attribute-value grammar may involve determining whether there exists a linguistic structure that simultaneously satisfies a finite set of constraints. These constraints are wffs of the language $\mathcal{A}$, and linguistic structures are attribute-value models, as defined above. Thus this problem is to determine if there is a model that simultaneously satisfies all of a given finite set of wffs. In parsing attribute-value grammars in general, we are not only interested in determining whether a particular finite set of wffs are satisfiable, but also in characterizing the sets of models that satisfy them. This problem can be stated more precisely as follows:

(7) Given a set of wffs $\{ \mathbf{A}_1, \mathbf{A}_2, \ldots, \mathbf{A}_n \}$, find a characterization of

$$M = \bigcap_{i=1}^{n} M(\mathbf{A}_i), \text{ where } M(\mathbf{A}) \text{ is the set of models that satisfy } \mathbf{A}.$$

The problem can be represented graphically as in Figure 12:

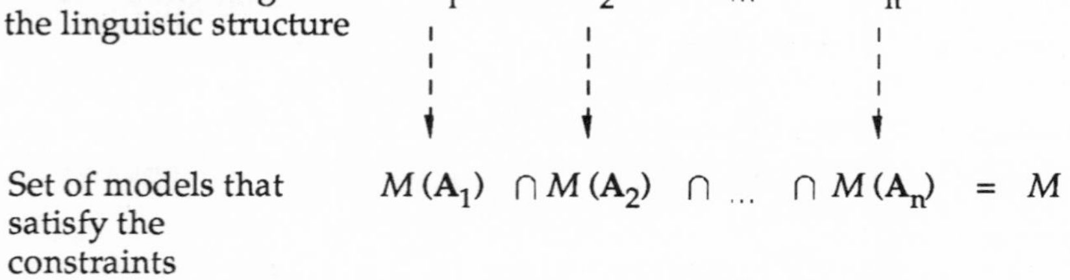

Figure 12 An abstract formulation of the parsing problem for an attribute-value grammar

If the sets $M(\mathbf{A}_i)$ were finite sets one might be able to computationally characterize the set M by enumerating and then intersecting the $M(\mathbf{A}_i)$. Since the $M(\mathbf{A}_i)$ are in general infinite sets of models, they cannot be exhaustively enumerated with only finite resources, so this strategy cannot be guarantied to terminate.

Instead the strategy adopted under the 'unification approach' is to find 'finite characterizations' of the sets $M(\mathbf{A}_i)$, call them $C(\mathbf{A}_i)$, and an abstract operation '∇' on these characterizations such that $C(\mathbf{A}_i) \nabla C(\mathbf{A}_j)$ 'characterizes' the set $M(\mathbf{A}_i) \cap M(\mathbf{A}_j)$. That is, the operation '∇' in the space of characterizations 'corresponds' to (i.e., is the dual of) the intersection operation in the space of sets of models. Given that the characterizations $C(\mathbf{A}_i)$ are finite and computable from the $\mathbf{A}_i$, and given that the operation '∇' on the $C(\mathbf{A}_i)$ is also computable, one way of characterizing the set of models that satisfy all of the $\mathbf{A}_i$ is to compute the $C(\mathbf{A}_i)$, and then apply the operation '∇' to them to yield a characterization C of the set of satisfying models M. This processes is sketched in Figure 13.

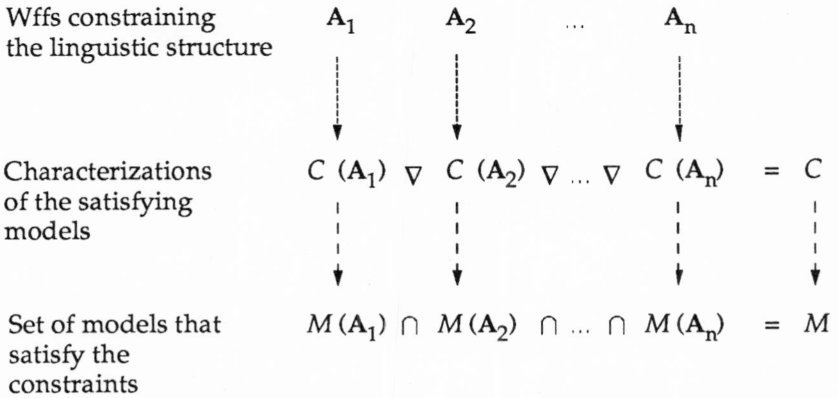

Figure 13 Using characterizations to solve the abstract problem

Now the potentially infinite sets $M(\mathbf{A}_i)$ and M need not be enumerated; the computation is performed on the finite objects $C(\mathbf{A}_i)$. The computation produces as output the characterization C, which can be regarded as a characterization or a description of the satisfying models S rather than the set S itself.

2.10.2 Partial Descriptions and Unification

In the 'unification approach', attribute-value structures play a double role: namely, they are regarded not only as linguistic structures but also as approximations to or partial descriptions of linguistic structures. If the value of some attribute of a complex element is not specified by a particular attribute-value structure, then in the 'unification approach' the value of that attribute is regarded as 'unknown'. Thus the sequence of attribute-value models represented in Figure 14 are interpreted as providing successively more information about some linguistic structure.

$$ {}_{x}\begin{bmatrix} \text{pred} = \text{sleep} \\ \text{subj} = {}_{y}\begin{bmatrix} \text{pred} = \text{john} \end{bmatrix} \end{bmatrix} $$

$$ {}_{x}\begin{bmatrix} \text{tense} = \text{past} \\ \text{pred} = \text{sleep} \\ \text{subj} = {}_{y}\begin{bmatrix} \text{pred} = \text{john} \end{bmatrix} \end{bmatrix} $$

$$ {}_{x}\begin{bmatrix} \text{pred} = \text{sleep} \\ \text{tense} = \text{past} \\ \text{subj} = {}_{y}\begin{bmatrix} \text{pred} = \text{john} \\ \text{agr} = \begin{bmatrix} \text{pers} = \text{3rd} \\ \text{num} = \text{sg} \end{bmatrix} \end{bmatrix} \end{bmatrix} $$

Figure 14 A sequence successively more instantiated of models

According to the 'unification approach' the subsumption relation between models (defined in the last section) orders models in terms of their 'information content'; a more general attribute-value structure (i.e., one that carries less information) subsumes a more specific attribute-value structure (i.e., one that carries more information). Thus a model $\mathcal{M}$ is interpreted as being a partial description of all the models that lie in the equivalence classes $\psi([\mathcal{M}])$. In terms of the 'characterizations' mentioned above a model $\mathcal{M}$ 'characterizes' the set of models that lie in $\psi([\mathcal{M}])$.

The unification operation is an operation on two or more partial descriptions that yields another partial description containing all of the information present in the two original descriptions. In terms of the 'unification approach', where attribute-value models are regarded as partial descriptions of other models, the unification $\mathcal{M}_1 \sqcup \mathcal{M}_2$ of models $\mathcal{M}_1$ and $\mathcal{M}_2$ is a model such that $\psi([\mathcal{M}_1 \sqcup \mathcal{M}_2]) = \psi([\mathcal{M}_1]) \cap \psi([\mathcal{M}_2])$, if such a model exists.[18]

Figure 15 presents an example of the unification of two attribute-value models.

$$ {}_x\begin{bmatrix} \text{pred} = \text{sleep} \\ \text{subj} = {}_y\begin{bmatrix} \text{pred} = \text{john} \end{bmatrix} \end{bmatrix} \quad \textit{and} \quad {}_x\begin{bmatrix} \text{tense} = \text{past} \\ \text{pred} = \text{sleep} \\ \text{subj} = {}_y\begin{bmatrix} \text{agr} = \begin{bmatrix} \text{pers} = \text{3rd} \\ \text{num} = \text{sg} \end{bmatrix} \end{bmatrix} \end{bmatrix} $$

unify to produce

$$ {}_x\begin{bmatrix} \text{pred} = \text{sleep} \\ \text{tense} = \text{past} \\ \text{subj} = {}_y\begin{bmatrix} \text{pred} = \text{john} \\ \text{agr} = \begin{bmatrix} \text{pers} = \text{3rd} \\ \text{num} = \text{sg} \end{bmatrix} \end{bmatrix} \end{bmatrix} $$

Figure 15 An example of unification

Sometimes two attribute-value models (interpreted as partial descriptions) contain incompatible or conflicting information, i.e., it is not possible that these two descriptions describe the same object. In that case there are no unifiers for the attribute-value models and the unification of these two structures is said to *fail*. An example of two incompatible attribute-value models is presented in Figure 16, where the outline font identifies the incompatible values.

Thus unification is an operation on attribute-value models which, when the models are interpreted as partial descriptions, produces as output a model which contains all of the information present in its inputs, and fails if the inputs contain incompatible information.

[18] Unification can thus be defined as the 'meet' operation in the semilattice of equivalence classes of models defined by the subsumption order of section 2.8.

$$ {}_{x}\begin{bmatrix} \text{tense} = \textbf{past} \\ \text{pred} = \text{sleep} \\ \text{subj} = {}_{y}\begin{bmatrix} \text{agr} = \begin{bmatrix} \text{pers} = \text{3rd} \\ \text{num} = \text{sg} \end{bmatrix} \end{bmatrix} \end{bmatrix} \qquad {}_{x}\begin{bmatrix} \text{tense} = \textbf{present} \\ \text{pred} = \text{sleep} \\ \text{subj} = {}_{y}\begin{bmatrix} \text{agr} = \begin{bmatrix} \text{pers} = \text{3rd} \\ \text{num} = \text{sg} \end{bmatrix} \end{bmatrix} \end{bmatrix} $$

Figure 16 Two incompatible attribute-value models

2.10.3 Unification and Satisfaction of Atomic Wffs

Now consider the problem introduced in Section 2.9.1. of determining the satisfiability of a set wffs $\{\mathbf{A}_1, \ldots, \mathbf{A}_n\}$. To begin, suppose each $\mathbf{A}_i$ to be a conjunction of atomic wffs (I discuss disjunction and negation later in this section). Then by Corollary 36 of Section 2.8 the set of equivalence classes of models that satisfy each $\mathbf{A}_i$ is exactly the principal filter $\psi[\mathcal{M}(\mathbf{A}_i)]$, so clearly these sets are each characterized by the models $\mathcal{M}(\mathbf{A}_i)$. Thus under the standard view each of the models $\mathcal{M}(\mathbf{A}_i)$ is interpreted as a partial description or characterization $C(\mathbf{A}_i)$ of the set of satisfying models $M(\mathbf{A}_i)$.

This means that one can determine whether a finite set of conjunctions of atomic wffs $\{\mathbf{E}_1, \mathbf{E}_2, \ldots, \mathbf{E}_n\}$ can be simultaneously satisfied by:

(i) Computing the models $\mathcal{M}(\mathbf{E}_1), \mathcal{M}(\mathbf{E}_2), \ldots, \mathcal{M}(\mathbf{E}_n)$, and if they exist, then

(ii) Unifying the minimal models $\bigsqcup_{i=0}^{n} \mathcal{M}(\mathbf{E}_i) = \mathcal{M}$.

If the result of the unification operation in (ii) exists, then $\psi([\mathcal{M}])$ is the set of equivalence classes of models that satisfy $\{\mathbf{E}_1, \mathbf{E}_2, \ldots, \mathbf{E}_n\}$, otherwise the set of constraints is not satisfiable. This process can be represented pictorially as in Figure 17.

Thus under the 'unification approach' the attribute-value structure models play two roles: they are both the objects that function as the linguistic structure whose existence is being determined, and, as minimal models, also as approximations to or descriptions of the linguistic structures that actually satisfy these constraints.

2.10.4 Unification and Satisfaction of Arbitrary Wffs

The fact that attribute-value structures are used both as linguistic structures and descriptions of linguistic structures causes problems for the 'unification approach' if the constraints on linguistic structures are

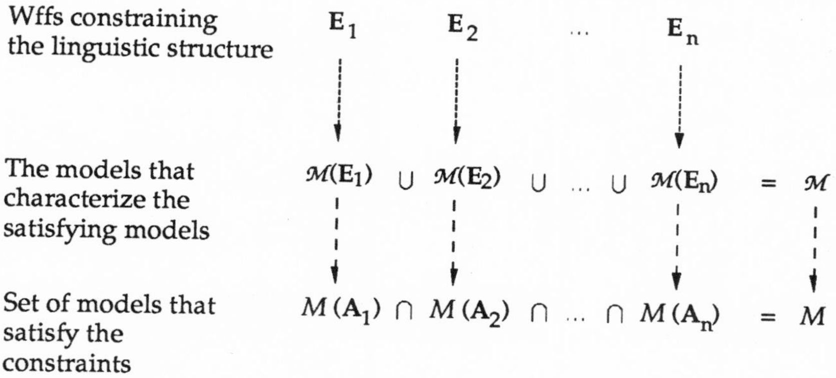

Figure 17 The 'unification approach' of determining satisfiability

not restricted to be conjunctions of atomic wffs, since in general it is not the case that the set of equivalence classes of satisfying models form a principal filter, and therefore the set of models that satisfy a constraint cannot be described in terms of a single model.

A variety of ingenious solutions to this problem have been proposed in the literature for the case involving arbitrary conjunctions and disjunctions of atomic wffs (Karttunen 1984, Kasper and Rounds 1986, Kasper 1987), and for the case involving negation and disjunction (Moshier and Rounds, 1987). Many of these extensions are problematical, either because they rely on mechanisms whose correctness has not been demonstrated (e.g., Karttunen 1984), or because of the complexity of their formulation and the associated algorithms (e.g., the use of intuitionistic logic in Moshier and Rounds 1987).

Interestingly, the results of Section 2.8 can be used to show how one can find finite characterizations of the set of models that satisfy constraints that are arbitrary wffs involving disjunction and negation. Theorem 37 of Section 2.8 showed that the set of equivalence classes of models that satisfy any wff **A** can be described as:

(i) $$\bigcup_{j=0}^{m} \left(\psi([\mathcal{M}_j]) - \left(\bigcup_{i=0}^{n_j} \psi([\mathcal{M}_{i,j}]) \right) \right)$$

This means that the set of models that satisfy any wff **A** can be finitely characterized in terms of a finite number of finite models $\mathcal{M}_j$ and $\mathcal{M}_{i,j}$.

Now suppose we are given two wffs **A** and **A′**, and characterize the satisfying models of **A** as (ii) and the satisfying models of **A′** as (iii).

(ii) $$\bigcup_{j=0}^{m} \left(\psi([\mathcal{M}_j]) - \left(\bigcup_{i=0}^{n_j} \psi([\mathcal{M}_{i,j}]) \right) \right)$$

(iii) $$\bigcup_{j'=0}^{m'} \left(\psi([\mathcal{M}'_{j'}]) - \left(\bigcup_{i=0}^{n_{j'}} \psi([\mathcal{M}'_{i,j'}]) \right) \right)$$

Then clearly the set of equivalence classes of models that simultaneously satisfy both **A** and **A′** is given by (iv).

(iv) $$\bigcup_{j=0}^{m} \bigcup_{j'=0}^{m'} \left(\psi([\mathcal{M}_j]) \cap \psi([\mathcal{M}'_{j'}]) - \left(\bigcup_{i=0}^{n_j} \psi([\mathcal{M}_{i,j}]) \right) - \left(\bigcup_{i=0}^{n_{j'}} \psi([\mathcal{M}'_{i,j'}]) \right) \right)$$

$$= \bigcup_{j=0}^{m} \bigcup_{j'=0}^{m'} \left(\psi([\mathcal{M}_j \sqcup \mathcal{M}'_{j'}]) - \left(\bigcup_{i=0}^{n_j} \psi([\mathcal{M}_{i,j}]) \right) - \left(\bigcup_{i=0}^{n^{j'}} \psi([\mathcal{M}'_{i,j'}]) \right) \right)$$

Thus if the set of equivalence classes of models that satisfy a constraint is characterized in terms of a finite number of models as in (i) above, (iv) shows that the operation on these characterizations that corresponds to intersection of the sets of satisfying models is one that can be constructed directly from the unification operation on models. This means that using the results developed in this chapter it is possible to extend the 'unfication approach' in a sound and complete fashion to deal with negation and disjunction.

2.10.5 A Comparison with the 'Unification Approach'

The approach I have taken in this book differs primarily from the 'unification approach' in that I do not regard attribute-value structures as partial descriptions of or approximations to linguistic structures. I view attribute-value structures as actual linguistic structures, rather than partial approximations to them. An attribute-value structure is therefore a complete rather than a partial object. In contrast to the 'unification approach' I make a strong distinction between the linguistic structures, of which attribute-value structures are a part, and the descriptions of those linguistic structures, which I take to be formulae from a specialized language for describing those structures.

On the 'unification view' attribute-value structures play a double role: they are both linguistic structures, and the descriptions of those structures. Under the view I am proposing, attribute-value structures are only linguistic structures (and as such complete objects), rather than descriptions of those structures. For example, I interpret an undefined value of some attribute of a complex element as simply indicating that that element does not have a value for that attribute, rather than that value being 'unknown'.

According to the view proposed here, determining the satisfiability of a set of formulae $\{\mathbf{A}_1, \mathbf{A}_2, \ldots, \mathbf{A}_n\}$ is accomplished by determining the satisfiability of the conjoined formula $\mathbf{A}_1 \wedge \mathbf{A}_2 \wedge \ldots \wedge \mathbf{A}_n$, perhaps using the algorithm described in the last chapter. This algorithm reduces the formula $\mathbf{A}_1 \wedge \mathbf{A}_2 \wedge \ldots \wedge \mathbf{A}_n$ to a logically equivalent reduced form $\mathbf{A}$, which can be interpreted as a description of the models that satisfy the original constraints as shown in Section 2.8. Expressions from the description language itself serve as the partial descriptions that characterize the linguistic structure being determined in the computational process. This process is sketched in Figure 18.

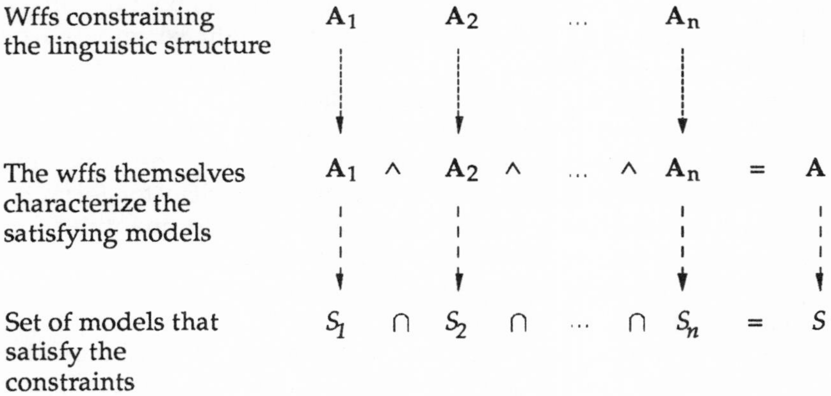

Figure 18 Determining satisfiability using AVL

The two approaches seem quite different, but in fact there are strong similarities between them. If we restrict attention to conjunctions of positive literals, then the reduced forms presented earlier correspond directly to the minimal models of the 'unification approach' just described. In fact the term model constructed in the proof of satisfiability is the minimal model for that formula. Further, the equivalences used in reduction algorithm correspond directly to the primitive computational steps of the standard unification algorithm for attribute-value structures (Kasper 1987).

Indeed, it is possible to interpret the attribute-value structures manipulated in the unification algorithm as terms from the language $\mathcal{A}$, with the result that the unification algorithm itself can be viewed as an algorithm for reducing any conjunction of positive literals to reduced form. Thus so long as we restrict attention to conjunction of positive literals the two approaches are effectively equivalent. Moreover, the results contained in this chapter show how one can extend the 'unification approach' to account for negation and disjunction.

2.11 Conclusion

In this chapter I investigated the properties of attribute-value structures, and proposed a language $\mathcal{A}$ for describing them. By axiomatizing its valid formulae I developed a logic of this language, and used this to develop algorithms for determining the satisfiability and the validity of formulae.

The definition of attribute-value structures was deliberately broad, and I investigated a series of restrictions that might be imposed on these structures, and determined how imposing these restrictions affects the satisfiability of formulae from the language $\mathcal{A}$.

I then investigated the expressive power of the language $\mathcal{A}$. First, I characterized the sets of structures that formulae of $\mathcal{A}$ describe, and then I provided a reduction of the satisfiability problem for formulae of $\mathcal{A}$ to the satisfiability problem of formulae of the quantifier-free first-order languages with function symbols and equality. As a corollary, I showed that determining the satisfiability of wffs of $\mathcal{A}$ is an $\mathcal{NP}$-complete problem.

Finally, I compared my approach to the study of attribute-value structures to the 'unification approach' standardly adopted, and showed how some of the results of this work might be applied there.

Chapter 3

The Use of Attribute-Value Structures

This chapter explains how attribute-value structures are used in attribute-value based theories of grammar and shows how the logic of language for describing attribute-value structures presented in the last chapter might be used in natural language processing.

First I define the linguistic structures of an attribute-value based theory of grammar that characterize a fluent speaker's linguistic knowledge of that utterance. These objects are called annotated constituent structures. Each annotated constituent structure consists of a constituent structure tree and an attribute-value structure, together with a function which associates each constituent structure node with an attribute-value element, and a function that identifies or names the constituent elements in the attribute-value structure.[19]

I then define the 'generates' relation for attribute-value based theories of grammar. A grammar of a particular language characterizes a fluent speaker's linguistic knowledge of that language, and the 'generates' relation identifies the annotated constituent structures that correspond to well-formed utterances of a particular language characterized by an attribute-value grammar. In an attribute-value grammar

[19] This definition closely follows the definition used in LFG (Kaplan and Bresnan 1982). Many attribute-value theories define linguistic structures in a different fashion (e.g. Pollard and Sag 1987).

of the kind discussed here, this relation is defined in terms of node-licensing: an annotated constituent structure is generated by a grammar if and only if all of its nodes are licensed by that grammar.

The recognition problem for arbitrary attribute-value grammars is then investigated and shown to be undecidable, because the empty tape halting problem for Turing machines, an undecidable problem, can be reduced to the universal recognition problem for attribute-value grammars.

I then investigate a restriction on annotated constituent structures known as the Off-line Parsability Constraint. This constraint restricts the 'size' of the tree component of annotated constituent structures. I show that if annotated constituent structures are constrained in this fashion then the universal recognition problem for attribute-value grammars is decidable.

It is important to note that attribute-value based grammar formalism presented here is not intended to constitute a theory of grammar. It is not an attempt to characterize the nature of knowledge of language, nor the class of humanly possible languages. Rather, it is an attempt to provide a foundation of formal devices that could be used in the specification of a substantive theory of the grammars of human languages.

Whether humans processing language actually follow algorithms similiar to those given in this chapter is an open question, but this work shows that several of the important problems in the processing of attribute-value grammars are soluble, and thus provides a preliminary account as to how knowledge of language might be used in processing.

3.1 Linguistic Structures in Attribute-Value Based Theories

A linguistic structure of an attribute-value based theory can be described informally as a constituent structure skeleton, together with attribute-value element annotations for each of the nodes in the constituent structure tree. Every node of an annotated constituent structure is annotated with a category label and an element from an attribute-value structure, and every terminal node is annotated with a lexical form as well. In this section I show how annotated constituent structures can be precisely defined. In LFG terms the constituent structure corresponds to the *c*-structure of LFG, and the attribute-value structure represents the *f*-structure. A sample annotated constituent structure that might be generated by an attribute-value grammar is depicted in Figure 1.

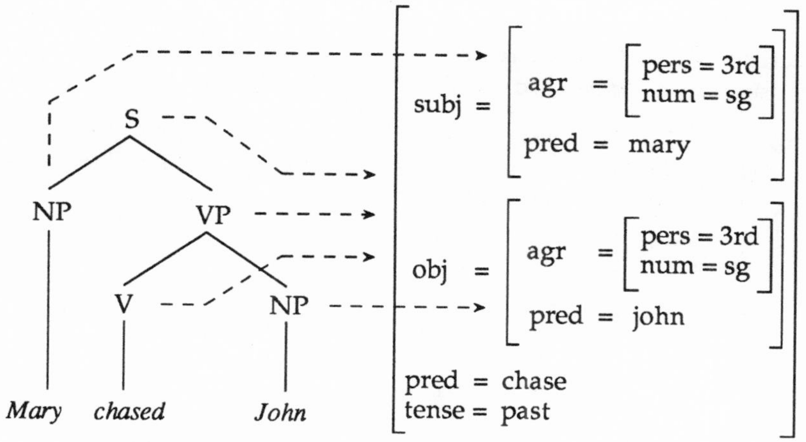

Figure 1 An annotated constituent structure

One unusual aspect of the constituent structure used in this treatment of attribute-value based theories of grammar is that the lexical items are not represented as independent nodes of the constituent structure tree. Instead, lexical forms appear as annotations of terminal nodes of the constituent structure tree. This simplifies the formal presentation, and nothing substantial follows from this aspect of the formulation.

3.1.1 Tree Domains

I use tree domains (due to Gorn (1965), see Gallier 1986 for discussion) to define the tree structure skeletons of annotated constituent structures.

Definition 1: *A* TREE DOMAIN t *is a nonempty subset of the strings in* $\mathbb{N}^*_+$, *the set of strings of positive integers, that satisfies the conditions*:

(i) For each $u \in t$, every prefix of u is also in t.

(ii) For each $u \in t$, and for every $i \in \mathbb{N}_+$, if $u \cdot i \in t$ then for every j such that $1 \leq j \leq i$, $u \cdot j$ is also in t.[20]

A tree domain t can be interpreted as a tree skeleton in which each string of integers in t corresponds to a node in the tree. The empty string ε corresponds to the *root node* of the tree, and the string $x \cdot i$, for x a string of integers and i a single integer, corresponds to the i-th daughter node (in left-to-right sequence) of the node x.

---

20 I use the '·' as a concatenation operator. For example, 1·2 refers to the two element string of integers whose first element is 1 and second element is 2.

Tree domains can be used to describe infinite as well as finite tree structures. In this book I restrict attention to finite tree domains (i.e., tree domains of finite cardinality).

Example 1: *The tree domain* $t = \{\varepsilon, 1, 1{\cdot}1, 2, 2{\cdot}1, 2{\cdot}2\}$ *corresponds to the tree skeleton depicted in Figure 2, where each node is labelled with the string in* t *corresponding to it.*

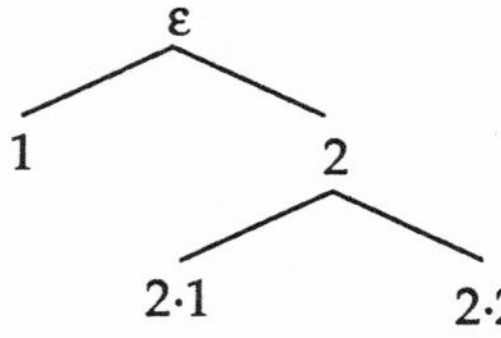

Figure 2 A tree domain and the tree it induces

I now define some functions on tree domains used later.

Definition 2: *The* SUBTREE t/u *of a tree domain* t *at a node* $u \in t$ *is the set* $\{ w : u{\cdot}w \in t \}$.

Definition 3: *The* OUTDEGREE $d_t(u)$ *of a node* u *in a tree domain* t *is the cardinality of the set* $\{ i : u{\cdot}i \in t, i \in \mathbb{N}_+ \}$.

The outdegree of a node is number of daughters of that node. I will omit the subscript 't' when it is clear from the context.

Definition 4: *The* ROOT NODE *of a tree domain* t *is the node* ε.

Informally speaking, the root node is the 'top' node of the tree.

Definition 5: *A node* $u \in t$ *is a* TERMINAL NODE *of a tree domain* t *iff* $d(u) = 0$. Term(t) *designates the set of terminal nodes of a tree domain.*

That is, a terminal node is a node that has no daughters. In the tree domain of Figure 2 the terminal nodes are 1, 2·1 and 2·2.

3.1.2 Constituent Structures

Informally, a constituent structure is a tree in which each node is labeled with a category label, and each terminal node is also labeled with a lexical item. These constituent structure trees differ from 'standard' constituent structure trees in that the lexical forms are not represented by independent nodes in the tree, but rather as annotations on terminal nodes. As remarked earlier, this aspect of the formalization is of purely notational import, and is made because it slightly simplifies the formal presentation. A sample constituent structure tree is depicted in Figure 3.

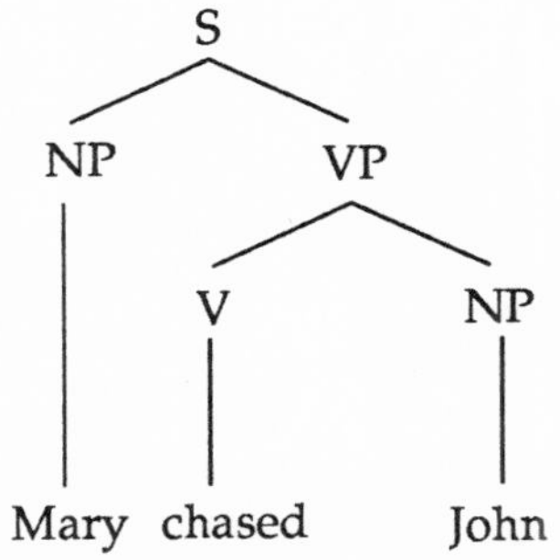

Figure 3 A Sample Constituent Structure Tree

Formally a constituent structure tree is simply a tree domain where each node is associated with a category from a finite set *Cat* of category labels, and each terminal is associated with a lexical form drawn from a finite set *Lex* of lexical forms.

Definition 6: *A* CONSTITUENT STRUCTURE TREE $p_{Cat,Lex}$ *(with respect to a finite set of categories Cat and a finite set of lexical forms Lex) is a triple* $p_{Cat,Lex} = \langle t,c,l \rangle$*, where t is a tree domain,* $c\colon t \to Cat$ *and* $l\colon term(t) \to Lex$.

The function *c* associates each node with its category, and the function *l* associates each terminal node with a lexical item. The subscripts *Cat* and *Lex* will be omitted when clear from the context.

The notions of subtree, immediate daughters and terminal nodes of a tree domain extend in the obvious way to constituent structures. In particular, the subconstituent structure of a constituent structure tree is defined as follows:

Definition 7: *The* SUBCONSTITUENT STRUCTURE p/u *of a constituent structure* $p = \langle t,c,l \rangle$ *at a node* $u \in t$ *is the constituent structure* $\langle t/u, c', l' \rangle$*, where* $c' : t/u \to Cat$ *satisfies* $\forall n \in t/u,\ c'(n) = c(u{\cdot}n)$ *and* $l' : t/u \to Lex$ *satisfies* $\forall n \in t/u,\ l'(n) = l(u{\cdot}n)$.

Example 2: *If t is the tree domain depicted in Figure 2,* $Cat = \{\text{S, NP, VP, V}\}$*,* $Lex = \{\textit{john, mary, chased}\}$ *and c and l are defined as below then* $\langle t,c,l \rangle$ *is a constituent structure tree. In fact* $\langle t,c,l \rangle$ *is the constituent structure tree depicted in Figure 3.*

(i) $c = \{ \langle \varepsilon,\text{S} \rangle, \langle 1,\text{NP} \rangle, \langle 2,\text{VP} \rangle, \langle 2{\cdot}1,\text{V} \rangle, \langle 2{\cdot}2,\text{NP} \rangle \}$ is a category labeling of *t*,

(ii) $l = \{ \langle 1,\textit{mary} \rangle, \langle 2{\cdot}1,\textit{chased} \rangle, \langle 2{\cdot}2,\textit{john} \rangle \}$ is a lexical labeling of *t*.

Finally, I define the terminal string or yield of a constituent structure. The yield function is defined recursively in terms of the subconstituent function.

Definition 8: *The* YIELD y(p) *of a constituent structure tree* $p = \langle t,c,l \rangle$ *is:*

(i) if $t = \{ \varepsilon \}$ then $y(p) = l(\varepsilon)$,

(ii) if $t \neq \{ \varepsilon \}$, then $y(p) = y(p/1) \cdot \ldots \cdot y(p/n)$, where $n = d_t(\varepsilon)$.

Example 3: *The yield of the constituent structure of Figure 3 is "mary chased john."*

3.1.3 Annotated Constituent Structures

Intuitively annotated constituent structures consist of a constituent structure tree each of whose nodes are annotated with an element from an attribute-value structure. Formally an annotated constituent structure consists of a constituent structure tree, an attribute-value structure, a function from the nodes of the constituent structure tree to elements of the attribute-value structure, and a function from a set of constant symbols to constant elements of the attribute-value structures.

The motivation for the last component of an annotated constituent structure, i.e., the function from constant symbols to constant elements, is not immediately obvious. Recall that an attribute-value structure is a triple $\langle F,C,\delta \rangle$, where F is a set of attribute-value elements, $C \subseteq F$ is a set of constant elements, and $\delta : F \times F \to F$ encodes the structural relationships that hold between the elements of F.[21] In the intended linguistic applications the elements of C will be entities denoted by symbols such as *sg* (denoting the singular number feature), *nom* (denoting the nominative case feature) and *obj* (denoting the attribute that identifies the object of a clause or phrase).

The actual nature or identity of the elements is unimportant for the treatment of annotated constituent structures proposed here; the important property of elements of C is that they can be designated by the constant symbols from the set *Const*. I assume there is an injective function $\chi : Const \to C$ that identifies the element each symbol designates. Informally, χ associates the constant symbols appearing in a grammar or elsewhere with the object that it designates.

The sets C, *Const* and the function χ are fixed by a theory of grammar or by a particular grammar; they do not vary from annotated constituent structure to annotated constituent structure within a given

21 Recall also that $\delta(c,f)$ is required to be undefined for all $c \in C$ and $f \in F$.

language. However, it is convenient to directly refer to C and χ when describing an annotated constituent structure, so they are included explicitly in the definition of an annotated constituent structure.

Definition 9: *An* ANNOTATED CONSTITUENT STRUCTURE TREE *(with respect to Cat, Lex, and Const) is a tuple* $\langle t,c,l,F,C,\delta,\varphi,\chi\rangle$, *where* $\langle t,c,l\rangle$ *is a constituent structure,* $\langle F,C,\delta\rangle$ *is an attribute-value structure,* $\varphi: t \rightarrow F$, *and* χ: *Const* $\rightarrow C$ *is an injective function.*

An annotated constituent structure tree is therefore a constituent structure tree and an attribute-value structure, together with a function φ that associates each node in the constituent structure tree with an element in the attribute-value structure and a function χ that associates constant symbols with constant elements in C.

Annotated constituent structures are related to the attribute-value models introduced in the last chapter. Recall that an attribute-value model is a quintuple $\langle F,C,\delta,\varphi,\chi\rangle$, where $\langle F,C,\delta\rangle$ is an attribute-value structure, $\varphi : Var \rightarrow F$ and $\chi : Const \rightarrow C$. In both attribute-value models and annotated constituent structures the function χ identifies or names some of the constant elements of the attribute-value structure. In an annotated constituent structure the function φ assigns attribute-value elements to nodes in the constituent structure tree, while in an attribute-value model the function φ assigns attribute-value elements to members of the set *Var* of variables. Thus an annotated constituent structure can be regarded as a pair of a constituent structure tree $\langle t,c,l\rangle$ and an attribute-value model, with the nodes in the constituent structure tree being the variables of the model, i.e., $Var = t$.

Example 4: *If* $\langle t,c,l\rangle$ *is the constituent structure depicted in Figure 3 and* $\langle F,C,\delta,\varphi,\chi\rangle$ *is the attribute-value model defined defined below, then* $\langle t,c,l,F,\delta,\varphi\rangle$ *is an annotated constituent structure. In fact* $\langle t,c,l,F,C,\delta,\varphi,\chi\rangle$ *is the annotated constituent structure depicted in Figure 1.*

(1a) $F = \{$ *subj, obj, pred, tense, agr, mary, john, 3rd, sg, chase, past, a, b, c, d, e* $\}$

(1b) $C = Const = F - \{ a, b, c, d, e \}$

(1c)

$\delta(a,subj) = b]$	$\delta(a,obj) = c$	$\delta(a,pred) = chase$
$\delta(a,tense) = past$	$\delta(b,pred) = mary$	$\delta(b,agr) = d$
$\delta(c,pred) = john$	$\delta(c,agr) = e$	$\delta(d,num) = sg$
$\delta(d,pers) = 3rd$	$\delta(e,num) = sg$	$\delta(e,num) = 3rd$

(1d)

$\varphi(\varepsilon) = a$	$\varphi(1) = b$	$\varphi(2) = a$
$\varphi(2{\cdot}1) = a$	$\varphi(2{\cdot}2) = c$	

(1e) $\chi(x) = x$ for all x in *Const*.

3.2 The 'Generates' Relation in Attribute-Value Based Theories

In this section I sketch the structure of a grammar from an attribute-value based theory and define the 'generates' relation that identifies linguistic structures that are well-formed with respect to a given grammar.

An attribute-value based grammar can be viewed as a set of *licensing conditions.* A grammar generates an annotated constituent structure if and only if every node in that annotated constituent structure is licensed by the grammar.

A grammar is a triple consisting of two finite sets called the *lexical entries* and the *syntactic rules,* and a member of *Cat* called the *start symbol.* The lexical entries license terminal nodes, while the syntactic rules license non-terminal nodes. The start symbol specifies the syntactic category of the root node of the annotated constituent structure.

Both the lexical entries and the syntactic rules express local well-formedness constraints on the linguistic structure. In order for a grammar to generate a linguistic structure, the constituent structure and its attribute-value elements associated with the consituent structure nodes must simultaneously satisfy the lexical and syntactic constraints imposed by the grammar.

A lexical entry imposes constraints that are strictly local to the terminal node being licensed. These constraints only refer to the lexical form, syntactic category and attribute-value element associated with a terminal node. The constraints imposed on a terminal node by a lexical entry are not concerned with the properties of other nodes in the annotated constituent structure or the relationship of any other nodes to the node being licensed.

The constraints imposed by a syntactic rule are local to the non-terminal node being licensed and its daughters. They only refer to the syntactic categories and attribute-value elements associated with these nodes, and are not concerned with the properties of other nodes of the annotated constituent structure or the relationship of any other nodes to the nodes being licensed.

A lexical entry consists of a lexical form, a category, and a wff from $\mathcal{A}(Const, \{x\})$, i.e., a wff in which the only variable is the variable x. A syntactic rule consists of a phrase structure rule $C \rightarrow C_1 \ldots C_n$ together with a wff from $\mathcal{A}(Const, \{x, x_1, \ldots, x_n\})$, i.e., a wff in which the only variables are the variables $x, x_1, \ldots, x_n$. Formally, they can be defined as follows:

Definition 10: *A* LEXICON *is a finite subset of Lex×Cat×𝒜(Const, {x}). A set of* SYNTACTIC RULES *is a finite subset of*

$$\bigcup_{i\geq 1} Cat\times Cat^{i}\times\mathcal{A}(Const, \{x, x_1, \ldots, x_i\}).$$

A GRAMMAR *is a triple ⟨lexicon,rules,start⟩, where* lexicon *is a lexicon,* rules *is a set of syntactic rules and* start *is a member of Cat.*

For my purposes I treat the lexicon and the syntactic rules as finite sets with no additional structure. A particular linguistic theory would probably impose additional constraints on possible lexical and syntactic rule components, perhaps following the proposals of Grimshaw (1982), Flickenger, Pollard and Wasow (1985) or Gazdar, Klein, Pullum and Sag (1986). These constraints could be viewed as constituting claims about the nature of possible knowledge of particular human languages.

The 'generates' relation for an attribute-value based theory of grammar is defined as follows:

Definition 11: *A grammar g* GENERATES *an annotated constituent structure a iff*

(i) the syntactic category label of the root node of *a* is *start,*

(ii) for every terminal node *n* in *a* there is a lexical entry *e* in *g* such that *e* licenses *n,* and

(iii) for every nonterminal node *n* in *a* there is a syntactic rule *r* in *g* such that *r* licenses *n.*

The licensing relation is defined as:

Definition 12: *A lexical entry* $\langle l(n), c(n), \mathbf{A}\rangle$ LICENSES *a terminal node n of an annotated constituent structure* $\langle t,c,l,F,C,\delta,\varphi,\chi\rangle$ *iff* $\langle F,C,\delta,\varphi,\chi\rangle \models \mathbf{A}[x/n]$.

A syntactic rule $\langle c(n), c(n\cdot 1)\cdot \ldots \cdot c(n\cdot m), \mathbf{A}\rangle$ LICENSES *a non-terminal node n of* $\langle t,c,l,F,C,\delta,\varphi,\chi\rangle$ *iff* $d(t,n) = m$ *and* $\langle F,C,\delta,\varphi,\chi\rangle \models \mathbf{A}[x/n, x_1/n\cdot 1, \ldots, x_n/n\cdot m]$.

Intuitively, the variable x in the formula associated with a lexical item or a syntactic rule 'represents' the feature structure of the node being licensed, while in a syntactic rule the variables $x_1, \ldots, x_n$ 'represent' the feature structures of the n immediate daughters of the node being licensed. These variables correspond roughly to the 'meta-variables' '↑' and '↓' of LFG.

It is useful to be able to describe the relation between a grammar and a string that corresponds to the yield of an annotated constituent structure generated by that grammar. I call this relation the 'string-generates' relation, and when clear from the context, I will simply use the term 'generates'.

Definition 13: *A grammar g* STRING-GENERATES *a string s iff g generates an annotated constituent structure* $a = \langle t,c,l,F,C,\delta,\varphi,\chi\rangle$ *and the terminal string of* $\langle t,c,l\rangle$ *is s.*

Example 5: *Consider the lexical entries is shown in (2), and the syntactic rules shown in (3).*

(2a)	*John*	NP	x(pred) = john ∧ x(agr)(num) = sg ∧ x(agr)(pers) = 3rd.
(2b)	*Mary*	NP	x(pred) = mary ∧ x(agr)(num) = sg ∧ x(agr)(pers) = 3rd.
(2c)	*chased*	V	x(pred) = chase ∧ x(tense) = past ∧ x(subj)(agr)(num) = sg ∧ x(subj)(agr)(pers) = 3rd.[22]
(3a)	S → NP VP		$x = x_2 \wedge x(\text{subj}) = x_1$.
(3b)	VP → V NP		$x = x_1 \wedge x(\text{obj}) = x_2$.

The lexical entry in (2a) licenses any terminal node n in an annotated constituent structure $\langle t,c,l,F,C,\delta,\varphi,\chi\rangle$ such that $l(n)$ = 'John', $c(n)$ = N, and where the model $\langle F,C,\delta,\varphi,\chi\rangle$ satisfies the formula in (2a) with n substituted for x.

Similiarly, the syntactic rule in (3b) licenses any nonterminal node n with two daughters in an annotated constituent structure $\langle t,c,l,F,C,\delta,\varphi,\chi\rangle$ such that $c(n)$ = VP, $c(n{\cdot}1)$ = V, and $c(n{\cdot}2)$ = NP, and where the model $\langle F,C,\delta,\varphi,\chi\rangle$ satsifies the formula in (3b) with n substituted for x, $n{\cdot}1$ substituted for x_1 and $n{\cdot}2$ substituted for x_2.

It is thus straight-forward to verify that the grammar g = $\langle lexicon,rules,S\rangle$ given in (2) and (3) generates the annotated constituent structure shown in Figure 1.

---

[22] Nothing in this lexical entry requires the verb *chased* to be transitive. I discuss the problem of accounting for subcategorization phenomena in chapter 4.

3.3 Decomposing the Parsing Problem

The definition just given can be used to determine if a given annotated constituent structure is generated by a particular grammar. In modelling natural language processing we are usually interested solving a more difficult problem: that of determining whether a given string is string generated by a given grammar, and if so, characterizing the set of annotated constituent structures generated by a given grammar that have a given string as its yield.

The problem of determining if a given grammar generates a given string is called the *universal recognition problem.* The problem of determining just which linguistic structures are both generated by a given grammar and have a given string as their yield is called the *universal parsing problem.*

I show below that these problems can be decomposed into two subproblems:

(i) The enumeration of the constituent structures $\langle t,c,l \rangle$ whose root nodes have syntactic category *start* and whose yields are the string to be parsed, and

(ii) The characterization of the annotated constituent structures $\langle t,c,l,F,C,\delta,\varphi,\chi \rangle$ generated by the grammar, given a constituent structure $\langle t,c,l \rangle$.

In the remainder of this section I show that this second subproblem can be solved using the techniques developed in the last chapter for determining the satisfiability of wffs of the language $\mathcal{A}$. In the next section I discuss the first of these subproblems in depth.

Specifically, given a constituent structure $u = \langle t,c,l \rangle$ and a grammar g I show how to construct a wff **A** of $\mathcal{A}$ such that a model $\mathcal{M} = \langle F,C,\delta,\varphi,\chi \rangle$ satisfies **A** iff g generates $\langle t,c,l,F,C,\delta,\varphi,\chi \rangle$. Since the techniques developed in the last chapter can be used to characterize the set of models that satisfy an arbitrary wff **A** of $\mathcal{A}$, these techniques can be used to characterize the set of attribute-value structures with a given constituent structure u generated by a grammar g.

The wff **A** just referred to is called the associated formula of the constituent structure. It is the conjunction of all of the constraints that the grammar imposes on the attribute-value structure component of an annotated constituent structure with that particular constituent structure tree.

Definition 14: *The* ASSOCIATED FORMULA $af_{g,u}(n)$ *of a terminal node* $n \in t$ *with respect to a grammar* $g = \langle lexicon,rules,start \rangle$ *and constituent structure* $u = \langle t,c,l \rangle$ *is:*

$$af_{g,u}(n) = \bigvee_{l(n),c(n),\mathbf{A}\rangle \in lexicon} \mathbf{A}[x/n].$$

The associated formula $af_{g,u}(n)$ of a nonterminal node $n \in t$ with respect to a grammar $g = \langle lexicon, rules\rangle$ and constituent structure $u = \langle t,c,l\rangle$ is:

$$af_{g,u}(n) = \bigvee_{\langle c(n),c(n\cdot 1)\ldots c(n\cdot m),\ \mathbf{A}\rangle \in rules,\ d(n) = m} \mathbf{A}[x/n, x_1/n\cdot 1, \ldots, x_m/n\cdot m\ ]$$

where the empty disjunction is taken to be False.

Informally, the associated formula of a node is the disjunction of all of the attribute-value formulae associated with the lexical entries or syntactic rules that could possibly license it. Since a node is licensed if and only if it satisfies at least one lexical entry or syntactic rules, it is licensed if and only if it satisfies its associated formula.

The following lemma shows that a grammar licenses a node of an annotated constituent structure $\langle t,c,l,F,C,\delta,\varphi,\chi\rangle$ if and only if the model $\langle F,C,\delta,\varphi,\chi\rangle$ satisfies the associated formula of that node.

Lemma 15: *A grammar $g = \langle lexicon, rules, start\rangle$ licenses a node $n \in t$ of an annotated constituent structure $a = \langle t,c,l,F,C,\delta,\varphi,\chi\rangle$ iff $\langle F,C,\delta,\varphi,\chi\rangle \models af_{g,\langle t,c,l\rangle}(n)$.*

Proof: Immediate from the definitions of 'license' and 'associated formula'. □

Example 6: *If g is the grammar given in (2) and (3) of Example 5 above and p is the annotated constituent structure tree of Figure 3, then the associated formula of node 2·2 is*

$$2{\cdot}2(\text{pred}) = \text{john} \wedge 2{\cdot}2(\text{agr})(\text{num}) = \text{sg} \wedge 2{\cdot}2(\text{agr})(\text{pers}) = \text{3rd}.$$

The associated formula of an entire constituent structure tree is simply the conjunction of the associated formulae of all of the nodes in the tree.

Definition 16: *The associated formula of a constituent structure $u = \langle t,c,l\rangle$ with respect to a grammar $g = \langle lexicon, rules, start\rangle$ is False if* c(ε) ≠ start, *otherwise it is the conjunction of the associated formulae of its nodes, i.e.,*

$$af_{g,u} = \bigwedge_{n \in t} af_{g,u}(t).$$

The following lemma shows that a grammar generates an annotated constituent structure $\langle t,c,l,F,C,\delta,\varphi,\chi\rangle$ if and only if the model $\langle F,C,\delta,\varphi,\chi\rangle$ satisfies the associated formula of the constituent structure tree $\langle t,c,l\rangle$.

Lemma 17: *A grammar* $g = \langle lexicon, rules, start\rangle$ *generates an annotated constituent structure* $a = \langle t,c,l,F,C,\delta,\varphi,\chi\rangle$ *iff the model* $\mathcal{M} = \langle F,C,\delta,\varphi,\chi\rangle$ *is such that* $\mathcal{M} \models af_{g,u}$, *where* $u = \langle t,c,l\rangle$.

Proof: Immediate from the definition of associated formula and the generates relation. □

Thus given a constituent structure $u = \langle t,c,l\rangle$, we are able to determine if a given grammar generates any annotated constituent structures of the form $\langle t,c,l,F,C,\delta,\varphi,\chi\rangle$ by determining if there is a model $\mathcal{M} = \langle F,C,\delta,\varphi,\chi\rangle$ that satisfies the associated formula $af_{g,u}$. This latter problem can be solved using the techniques presented in the last chapter. It is therefore possible to characterize the annotated constituent structures $\langle t,c,l,F,C,\delta,\varphi,\chi\rangle$ generated by a grammar with respect to a given constituent structure $\langle t,c,l\rangle$.

Example 7: *If g is the grammar in (2) and (3) of Example 5 and p is the constituent structure tree shown in (3), then* $af_{g,p}$ *is the wff displayed in (4)*:

(4) $\varepsilon(\text{subj}) = 1 \wedge 1 = 2 \wedge 1(\text{pred}) = \text{mary} \wedge 1(\text{agr})(\text{num}) = \text{sg} \wedge$
$1(\text{agr})(\text{pers}) = \text{3rd} \wedge 2 = 2{\cdot}1 \wedge 2(\text{obj}) = 2{\cdot}2 \wedge$
$2{\cdot}2(\text{agr})(\text{num}) = \text{sg} \wedge 2{\cdot}2(\text{agr})(\text{pers}) = \text{3rd} \wedge 1(\text{pred}) = \text{john} \wedge$
$2.1(\text{pred}) = \text{chase} \wedge 2{\cdot}1(\text{tense}) = \text{past} \wedge$
$2{\cdot}1(\text{subj})(\text{agr})(\text{num}) = \text{sg} \wedge 2{\cdot}1(\text{subj})(\text{agr})(\text{pers}) = \text{3rd}$

Note that $\langle F,C,\delta,\varphi,\chi\rangle$ as defined in (1) above satisfies (4), as required by Lemma 17.

3.4 Arbitrary Constituent Structures and Undecidability

In this section I show that the universal recognition problem for attribute-value grammars as defined in the last section is undecidable. This undecidability result depends crucially on the existence of constituent structures whose size (in terms of number of nodes) is arbitrarily larger than their yield, and serves as the computational part of the motivation for the Off-line Parsability restriction on constituent structures discussed in the next section.

Specifically, I show how to compute an attribute-value grammar $g(M)$ for any Turing machine M so that the string "halt" is generated by $g(M)$ if and only if the Turing machine M halts on an empty input tape. Since determining whether an arbitrary Turing machine halts on an empty input tape is undecidable it follows that determining whether $g(M)$ generates "halt" for arbitrary M is also undecidable. Thus there is no algorithm for determining whether an arbitrary attribute-value grammar generates an arbitrary string.

3.4.1 Turing Machines

A Turing machine is a formal model of an effective procedure. The presentation here is based on that of Hopcroft and Ullman (1979, p. 148), which should be consulted for further details.

Definition 18: *A Turing machine M is a tuple* $M = (Q, \Sigma, \Gamma, \delta, q_0, B, F)$ *where*

> Q is a finite set of *states,*
> Γ is a finite set of allowable *tape symbols* disjoint to Q,
> $B \in \Gamma$ is the *blank symbol,*
> Σ, a subset of Γ not including B, is the set of *input symbols*
> δ is the *next move function,* a mapping from $Q \times \Gamma$ to
> $Q \times \Gamma \times \{L, R\}$ (δ may be undefined for some arguments),
> q_0 in Q is the *start state,*
> $F \subseteq Q$ is the set of *final states.*

An INSTANTANEOUS DESCRIPTION (ID) *of the Turing machine M is denoted by* $\alpha_1 q \alpha_2$, *where* $q \in Q$ *is the current state of M and* $\alpha_1\alpha_2 \in \Gamma^*$ *is the contents of the tape. The tape head is assumed to be scanning the leftmost symbol of* α_2, *or if* $\alpha_2 = \varepsilon$, *the head is scanning a blank.*

A MOVE *of a Turing machine M is defined as follows: Let* $X_1 X_2 \ldots X_{i-1}\, q\, X_i \ldots X_n$ *be an ID. Suppose* $\delta(q,X_i) = (p, Y, L)$. *If* $i - 1 = n$ *then* X_i *is taken to be B. If* $i = 1$ *then there is no next ID, while if* $i > 1$ *the next ID is* $X_1 X_2 \ldots X_{i-2}\, p\, X_{i-1}\, Y\, X_{i+1} \ldots X_n$. *If* $\delta(q,X_i) = (p, Y, R)$ *then the next ID is* $X_1 X_2 \ldots X_{i-1}\, Y\, p\, X_{i+1} \ldots X_n$.

A Turing machine M ACCEPTS *an input* $w \in \Sigma^*$ *just in case there is some sequence of moves of M beginning with ID* $q_0\, w$ *and ending with an ID* $\alpha_1\, p\, \alpha_2$ *for some* $p \in F$ *and* $\alpha_1, \alpha_2 \in \Gamma^*$.

Example 8: *Let* $Q = \{q_0, q_1, q_2\}$, $\Sigma = \{0, 1\}$, $\Gamma = \{0, 1, a, B\}$, *and* $F = \{q_2\}$, *and let* δ *be defined as:*

$$\delta(q_0,0) = (q_0, 1, R) \qquad \delta(q_0,1) = (q_0, 1, R)$$

$$\delta(q_0,B) = (q_1, a, R) \qquad \delta(q_1,B) = (q_2, a, R)$$

Then the machine $M = (Q, \Sigma, \Gamma, \delta, q_0, B, F)$ *executes the following sequence of moves on input* $w = \varepsilon$.

q_0
$a\ q_1$
$a\ a\ q_2$

Thus the machine M halts on input $w = \varepsilon$.

One of the fundamental properties of Turing machines is that there is no general way of determining if a given machine will accept a given string. This is the content of the following theorem, which I present here without proof. For a sketch of the proof of this theorem, see Minsky (1967, p. 150).

Theorem 19: *There is no algorithm for deciding if a Turing machine M accepts a blank input tape (i.e.,* $w = \varepsilon$*).* □

3.4.2 Encoding a Turing Machine in Attribute-Value Grammar

In this section I show how to encode a Turing machine *M* in an attribute-value grammar *g(M)* such that *g(M)* generates the string "halt" if and only if the machine *M* halts with a blank input tape.

I do this in two steps. First I explain how a sequence of Turing machine IDs can be represented as an annotated constituent structure. Then I provide an algorithm for producing a grammar *g(M)* from a description of a Turing machine *M* such that the constituent structures *g(M)* generates are the representations of the IDs of *M* running with a blank input tape.

The key to representing Turing machine IDs as attribute-value structures is finding a way to encode arbitrary lists as attribute-value structures. There are many ways of encoding list structures in attribute-value structures; the one proposed here is based on the linked list encoding of list structures.[23] This encoding is also used in the hierarchical encoding of grammatical relations discussed in the next chapter.

The empty list or the null list is represented by a special constant element denoted by the symbol *nil*. A non-empty list is represented by a complex attribute-value element, the value of whose *first* attribute is (the representation of) the first element of that list, and the value of

---

[23] This encoding of lists is known in computer science as a *singly linked list*. This results in a *stack* data structure with the familiar set of properties (e.g. items can be accessed only from one end). Clearly, other data structures, such as doubly linked lists, circular lists, or difference lists could equally well be used to represent list structures, and result in structures with different abstract properties. See (Knuth 1973) for further details.

whose *rest* attribute is (the representation of) the list consisting of all but the first element.

Example 9: *The list [a,b,c] would be represented as the attribute-value structure shown in Figure 4, depicted here using both matrix and directed graph notation.*

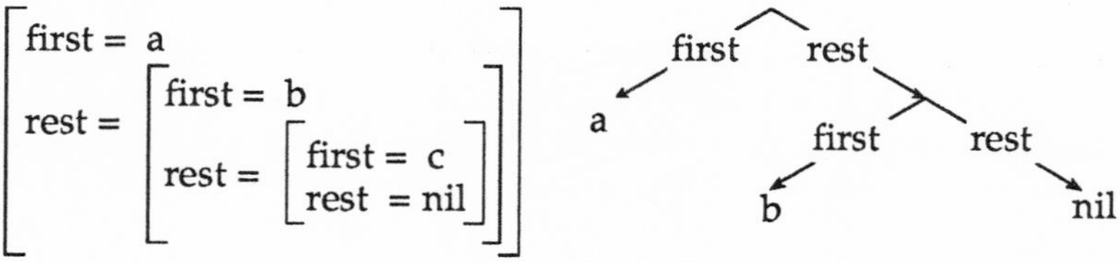

Figure 4 Encoding the list [*a*,*b*,*c*] in an attribute-value structure

A Turing machine ID $\alpha_1\ p\ \alpha_2$ is encoded as a constituent structure node in an annotated constituent structure with node label p and annotated with an attribute-value element whose *right* attribute's value is the list encoding of α_2 and whose *left* attribute's value is the list encoding of $\alpha_1{}^R$, where $\alpha_1{}^R$ is the list whose elements are the elements α_1 in reverse order.

A sequence of n Turing machine IDs ending with a final state ID is encoded as a unary branching annotated constituent structure of $n+1$ nodes, where the ith ID corresponds to the node 1^i (i.e., the ith node from the top of the tree). The ε constituent structure node (i.e., the top node of the tree) is labelled S, and the node 1^n is a terminal node with the lexical form *halts*.

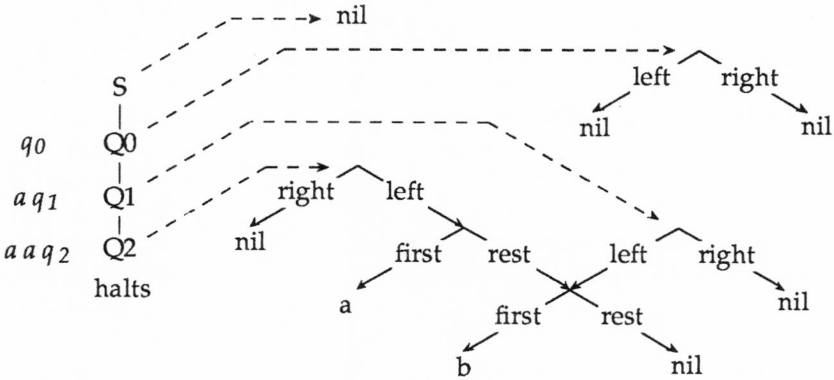

Figure 5 Encoding Turing Machine IDs

Example 10: *The sequence of Turing machine IDs of the last example would be encoded as the annotated constituent structure of Figure 5.*

The ID that each constituent structure node encodes is shown to the left of that node.

Now I specify the grammar $g(M)$ that generates annotated constituent structures that encode the sequence of moves of the Turing machine M beginning with ID q_0. There is one syntactic rule for each tuple $\langle q,X,p,Y,D \rangle$ where $\delta(q,X) = (p,Y,D)$, and one syntactic rule that 'initializes' the daughter of the top node of the constituent structure. The attribute-value formulae in these rules have the form of a disjunction; one disjunct deals with the situation in which the right-hand half of the tape is empty, and the other disjunct with the situation in which the right-hand half of the tape is not empty. There is one lexical entry for each final state (i.e., each element of F).

Definition 20: *Given a Turing machine* $M = (Q, \Sigma, \Gamma, \delta, q_0, B, F)$, *the start state of M is S, and the syntactic rules of g(M) consist of:*

(5a) $S \rightarrow q_0$ $\quad x_1(left) = nil \wedge x_1(right) = nil.$

(5b) For every q, X, p, Y such that $\delta(q,X) = (p,Y,L)$ there is a rule
$q \rightarrow p$ $\quad (x(left)(rest) = x_1(left) \wedge x(right)(rest) = x_1(right)(rest) \wedge x(right)(first) = X \wedge x_1(right)(first) = Y) \vee (x(left)(rest) = x_1(left) \wedge x(right) = nil \wedge X = B \wedge x_1(right)(rest) = nil \wedge x_1(right)(first) = Y).$

(5c) For every q, X, p, Y such that $\delta(q,X) = (p,Y,R)$ there is a rule
$q \rightarrow p$ $\quad (x(left)(rest) = x_1(left)(rest) \wedge x(right)(rest) = x_1(right) \wedge x(right)(first) = X \wedge x_1(left)(first) = Y) \vee (x(left)(rest) = x_1(left)(rest) \wedge x(right) = nil \wedge X = B \wedge x_1(right) = nil \wedge x_1(left)(first) = Y).$

The lexicon of $g(M)$ is defined as follows:

(6) For every $q \in F$ there is a lexical entry
halts q $\quad$ *True*

Example 11: *The grammar g(M) that corresponds to the Turing machine M defined in the earlier example is given below, with start state S, syntactic rules (7) and the single lexical entry (8).*

(7a) $S \rightarrow Q_0$ $\quad x_1(left) = nil \wedge x_1(right) = nil.$

(7b) $Q_0 \rightarrow Q_0$ $\quad (x(left)(rest) = x_1(left)(rest) \wedge x(right)(rest) = x_1(right) \wedge x(right)(first) = 0 \wedge x_1(left)(first) = 1) \vee (x(left)(rest) = x_1(left)(rest) \wedge$

$x(right) = nil \wedge 0 = B \wedge$
$x_1(right) = nil \wedge x_1(left)(first) = 1).$

(7c) $Q_0 \rightarrow Q_0$ $(x(left)(rest) = x_1(left)(rest) \wedge$
$x(right)(rest) = x_1(right) \wedge$
$x(right)(first) = 1 \wedge x_1(left)(first) = 1) \vee$
$(x(left)(rest) = x_1(left)(rest) \wedge$
$x(right) = nil \wedge 1 = B \wedge$
$x_1(right) = nil \wedge x_1(left)(first) = 1).$

(7d) $Q_0 \rightarrow Q_1$ $(x(left)(rest) = x_1(left)(rest) \wedge$
$x(right)(rest) = x_1(right) \wedge$
$x(right)(first) = B \wedge x_1(left)(first) = a) \vee$
$(x(left)(rest) = x_1(left)(rest) \wedge$
$x(right) = nil \wedge B = B \wedge$
$x_1(right) = nil \wedge x_1(left)(first) = a).$

(7e) $Q_1 \rightarrow Q_2$ $(x(left)(rest) = x_1(left)(rest) \wedge$
$x(right)(rest) = x_1(right) \wedge$
$x(right)(first) = B \wedge x_1(left)(first) = a) \vee$
$(x(left)(rest) = x_1(left)(rest) \wedge$
$x(right) = nil \wedge B = B \wedge$
$x_1(right) = nil \wedge x_1(left)(first) = a).$

(8) *halts* Q_2 *True.*

It is straightforward to check that the grammar in (7) and (8) generates the annotated constituent structure shown in Figure 5.

The following lemma shows that the annotated constituent structures generated by a grammar *g(M)* encode the sequence of IDs of the computation of Turing machine *M* starting with an empty input tape.

Lemma 21: *The annotated constituent structures with yield "halts" generated by g(M) encode the sequence of IDs of accepting computations of M with an empty input tape.*

Proof Sketch: First, note that the constituent structure tree is strictly unary branching because each of the syntactic rules in *g(M)* are strictly unary branching. The remainder of the proof is an induction on the nodes from root to terminal in the constituent structure tree, showing that the annotated constituents structures generated by *g(M)* encode the sequence of IDs of accepting computations of *M* with an empty input tape.

The basis step of the induction is established by showing that node '1' in the annotated constituent structure tree encodes the first ID in the computation performed by Turing machine computation *M* with an empty input tape, namely the ID q_0. This follows by direct inspection of the syntactic rule given in (5a).

Now consider the node 1^i in the annotated constituent structure, and assume that it encodes the *i*th ID in a Turing machine computation. By inspection of the grammar rules in (5b) and (5c) it follows that the node 1^{i+1} encodes the *i+1*th ID in that Turing machine computation.

By induction over $i > 0$, it follows that the 1^i node in the constituent structure encodes the ID for the *i*th ID in the Turing machine computation of *M* on an empty input tape.

Finally, for any node to be a terminal node (with a lexical form *halts*) it must be the case that that node encodes an accepting ID for *M*. Thus *g(M)* generates the string "halts" iff *M* halts on an empty input tape. □

The undecidability of the universal recognition problem for attribute-value grammars follows immediately from this.

Theorem 22: *The universal recognition problem for attribute-value grammars is undecidable.*

Proof: If there were an effective procedure for determing whether an arbitrary attribute-value grammar generates an arbitrary string, we could use it to obtain an effective procedure for determining whether an arbitrary Turing machine *M* halts on an empty input tape by determining if *g(M)* generates the string "halts." But no such effective procedure exists, therefore there is no effective procedure for determing whether an arbitrary attribute-value grammar generates an arbitrary string. □

I have just shown that the universal recognition problem for attribute-value grammars is undecidable; that is, there is no algorithm that can take any attribute-value grammar and any input string and determine if that string is string generated by that grammar. This result suffices for my purposes here; however it is easy to extend the technique for encoding a Turing machine into an attribute-value grammar presented in this section to show that for any recursively enumerable set *S*, there is an attribute-value grammar that string generates exactly *S*. This means that there are attribute-value gram-mars that generate string sets that are recursively enumerable but not recursive; i.e., attribute-value grammars for which there exists no algorithm that can determine whether a particular string is not generated by that grammar.

3.4.3 Implications of the Undecidability Result

In the last subsection I showed that the universal recognition problem for attribute-value grammars is undecidable, and mentioned that the same techniques can be used to show that there are attribute-value grammars for which the recognition problem is undecidable.

Since determining the well-formedness or grammaticality of particular utterances is probably not itself an important component of human language processing, it might seem that results showing the undecidability of the universal recognition problem and the recognition problem for specific grammars are not of direct psychological relevance.

However, it could be argued that any actual language processing will involve at least the degree of complexity of processing involved in solving these recognition problems. If it is plausible that whatever the output is from the computations humans perform when processing an utterance, it encodes in a relatively direct form information that indicates the well-formedness of that utterance, then there must be an algorithm for solving the recognition problem for any particular human language. This algorithm could be constructed by duplicating the algorithm humans use to process that language, and then inspecting its output to determine if the input given to it was well-formed.

For example, if we suppose that the output of the human language processor is a list of the well-formed linguistic structures that correspond to the input utterance, then we could construct an algorithm for solving the recognition problem for that language by merely duplicating the human parser and then determining if the set of well-formed linguistic structures is nonempty, thus 'solving' the recognition problem for the relevant language.

The undecidability of the uniform recognition problem shows that there is no single algorithm that can determine this fundamental computational problem for the entire set of attribute-value grammars (allowing arbitrary constituent structures). This means that one probably cannot hope to explain human language processing in terms of some general algorithm or strategy for 'processing' attribute-value grammars as just defined, assuming that this 'processing algorithm' 'solves' the uniform recognition problem or some other problem to which the uniform recognition problem can be reduced.

In the remainder of this section I discuss three possible ways in which such an undecidability result might be reconciled with the obvious fact that humans do succeed to process utterances from a language that they know.

First, although the uniform recognition problem for the class of all possible attribute-value grammars is undecidable, it might be the case that the uniform recognition problem for the class of grammars that a particular theory identifies as possible human grammars *is* decidable.

That is, it is possible that human languages have additional structure over and above the structure they inherit from being describable in terms of attribute-value grammars that ensures that the string sets they generate are decidable. Ideally, one would be able to show that independently motivated substantive linguistic claims about the nature of human language restrict the class of possible human languages in such a way that these languages are easy to process. I know of only one such restriction, the Off-line Parsability Constraint, which is discussed in the remainder of this chapter.

Second, it is possible that the uniform recognition problem for human languages is in fact undecidable.[24] We have no firm evidence that humans are capable of recognizing all of the well-formed utterances of a language that they know, so we have no evidence that it is possible to solve the recognition problem for a given language, much less the uniform recognition probem. Of course, the problem then is to explain just what computational processes are involved in human language processing.

Third, it is also possible that human language processing involves a computation significantly 'simpler' than the recognition problems, so the recognition problems could not be reduced to the human processing algorithm. For example, it is possible that human processing makes use of approximative or probabalistic techniques, which although not always correct, yield on the average sufficient useful information for human communication in the majority of situations they are used.

If either of the last two possibilities are in fact the case, then formal undecidability results of the kind just presented might have only mimimal importance for the study of human language processing.

3.5 The Off-Line Parsability Constraint

In the last section I showed that the universal recognition problem for attribute-value grammars was undecidable. In this section I discuss one restriction on the constituent structure components of annotated constituent structures that has the effect of making the universal recognition problem decidable. This restriction, called the Off-line Parsability Constraint (Kaplan and Bresnan 1982 p. 266, Pereira and Warren 1983), ensures that the number of constituent structures that

---

[24] There is an extensive literature discussing the decidability of the recognition problems for natural languages: see Mathews (1979), Levelt (1974), Putnam (1961) and the references cited therein.

have a given string as their yield is bounded by a computable function of the length of that string. In contrast to the local constraints on annotated constituent structures imposed by the lexical entries and syntactic rules, the Off-line Parsability Constraint is a global constraint on constituent structures.

It is possible to enumerate the finite number of off-line parsable constituent structures that have a given string as their yield and determine if at least one of their associated formulae are satisfiable, so the universal recognition problem for attribute-value theories of grammars that incorporate the Off-line Parsability Constraint is decidable.

The version of the Off-line Parsability Constraint used in this book is given below.

Definition 23: *A constituent structure satisfies the* OFF-LINE PARSABILITY CONSTRAINT *iff*

(i) it does not include a non-branching dominance chain in which the same category appears twice, and

(ii) the empty string ε does not appear as the lexical form annotation of any (terminal) node.

The first condition in the Off-line Parsability Constraint rules out the unbounded unary branching structures that were used in the encoding of Turing machine computations in the last section, and in effect places a bound on the 'height' of a constituent structure tree. The second condition requires that the number of terminal items in a constituent structure be equal to the number of lexical items in the string to be parsed, bounding the 'breadth' of a constituent structure tree.

Example 12: *The constituent structure sketched in Figure 6 violates the Off-line Parsability Constraint, since the upper node labelled 'A' exhaustively dominates another node with the same category label.*

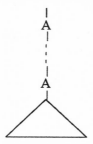

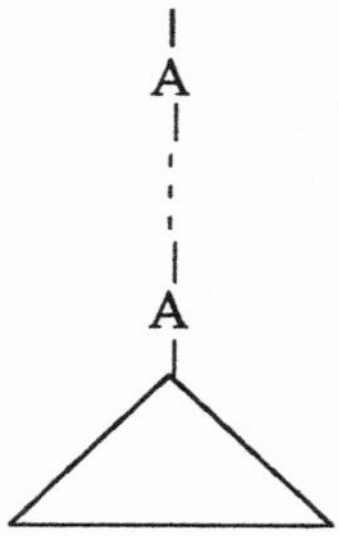

Figure 6 An Off-line Parsability Constraint violation

The effect of the Off-line Parsability Constraint is to ensure that the 'size' of any constituent structure that has a particular string as its yield is bounded by a computable function of the length of that string, which in turn bounds the number of constituent structures that dominate that string and makes the recognition problem for attribute-value grammars decidable. Bounding the size of constituent structures of course renders the reduction of the Turing machine halting problem to the uniform recognition problem for attribute-value grammars given above incorrect, since this reduction depended crucially on there being constituent structures of arbitrary size dominating a single terminal element.

The Off-line Parsability Constraint is motivated on both linguistic and computational grounds.

From the linguistic perspective Kaplan and Bresnan (1982) claim that the constituent structures ruled out by the Off-line Parsability Constraint are those that include "vacuously repetitive structures," which they claim "are without intuitive or empirical motivation." More specifically, one of the working hypotheses adopted in much recent work in attribute-value grammars (e.g., Karttunen 1986) is that the hierarchical aspects of linguistic structure should be represented in the attribute-value component of annotated constituent structures, and the constituent structure component should be correspondingly simplified so that it represents only the surface constituency of the utterance. The Off-line Parsability Constraint prohibits the constituent structure from encoding complex hierarchical structure not directly related to constituency, and so might be regarded as a formal manifestation of this hypothesis.

Computationally the off-line parsability restriction ensures the decidability of an attribute-value formalism (assuming the treatment of attribute-value structures given below), whereas without this restriction on constituent structure there are attribute-value based grammars for which the recognition problem is undecidable.

3.5.1 Enumerating OLP Constituent Structures

In this section I sketch an algorithm for enumerating the constituent structure trees that both have a given string as their yield and satisfy the off-line parsability restriction. Together with the results from the previous chapter this shows that the universal recognition problem for attribute-value grammars is in fact decidable. The enumeration algorithm is only sketched here because there are a large number of context-free grammar parsing algorithms easily adaptable for enumerating these constituent structures.[25]

The algorithm for enumerating off-line parsable constituent structures is based on two key observations:

(i) The size of any strictly unary branching chain of nodes must be less than the number of different syntactic category labels $|Cat|$.

(ii) A constituent structure tree that yields a string of length l when viewed from root to terminals consists of a (possibly null) strictly unary branching chain of nodes that immediately dominate an node with n daughters: these n daughters are constituent structure trees the sum of the lengths of whose yield must be equal to l.

Given a string of length l as input, the algorithm itself works by computing the series of sets $S_0, S_1, \ldots, S_l$, where each set S_i contains all of the constituent structure trees whose yield is of length i. The algorithm makes use of an auxiliary set U of all unary branching constituent structure tree fragments (i.e., constituent structures minus lexical annotations) that meet the Off-line Parsability Constraint, so the process of computing the off-line parsable constituent structures whose yield is of length l involves selecting in all possible ways a unary branching tree fragment from U and $n \leq l$ constituent structure trees from $\{ S_0, S_1, \ldots, S_{l-1} \}$ such that their total yield is l. This process of constructing the constituent structures in S_i is sketched in Figure 7. After computing S_l the algorithm returns all of the constituent structures that have the given input string as their yield.

The algorithm is sketched below:

Algorithm C: *The input to the algorithm is a finite set Cat of syntactic categories, a finite set Lex of lexical forms not containing* ε *and a string* $s \in Lex^*$. *The algorithm returns the set of all off-line parsable constituent structures whose yield is the string s.*

(i) Compute the set U of all unary branching constituent structure tree fragments such that within any tree fragment each node is associated with a different syntactic category (i.e., $U = \{ \langle t,c \rangle : t$ is a tree domain such that $\forall\, n \in t,\ d(n) \in \{0, 1\}$, and $c : t \rightarrow Cat$ is an injective function $\}$).

[25] A practical implementation of a parser for an attribute-value grammar would probably use one of these context free parsing algorithms for efficiency reasons. See Aho and Ullman (1972) for a discussion of a variety of different context free parsing algorithms.

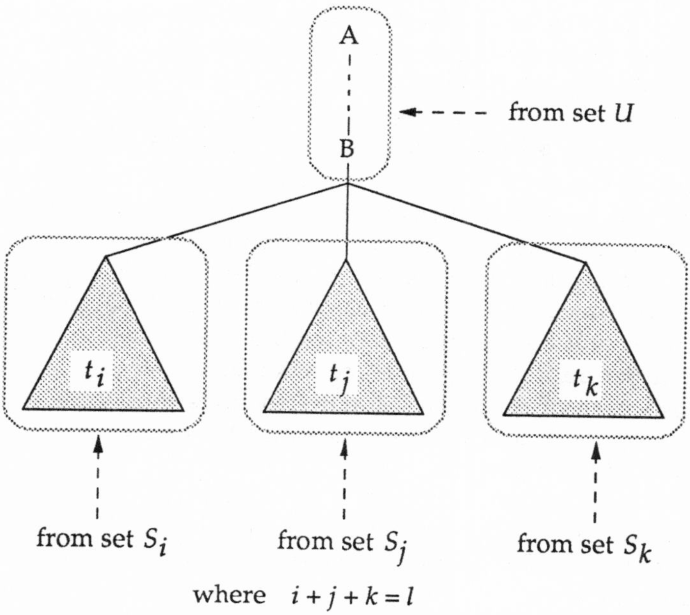

Figure 7 Construction of a Constituent Structure with yield of length l

(ii) Let S_1 be the set of all constituent structures with a yield of length 1 that meet the Off-line Parsability Constraint, (i.e., $S_1 = \{ \langle t,c,l \rangle : \langle t,c \rangle \in U, l : term(t) \rightarrow Lex \}$).

(iii) For $i = 2, \ldots, length(s)$ compute the sets S_i, each of which contains all constituent structure trees with a yield of length i constructable by extending the bottom node of a unary branching structure from U with constituent structure trees u, u', u'', ... from $\{ S_1 \cup \ldots \cup S_{i-1} \}$ (i.e., $S_i = \{ \langle t,c,l \rangle : t$ is a tree domain with a yield of length i such that $\exists \langle t',c' \rangle \in U, t' \subseteq t, \forall n \in t', c'(n) = c(n), (d_{t'}(n) = 1 \Rightarrow d_t(n) = 1), (d_{t'}(n) = 0 \Rightarrow d_t(n) = m \wedge \forall 0 < j < m, \langle t,c,l \rangle / n{\cdot}m \in \{ S_1 \cup \ldots \cup S_{i-1} \} \}$).

(iv) Return the set of constituent structures that belong to $S_{length(s)}$ whose yield is the string s. This is the set of all off-line parsable constituent structures whose yield is the string s.

The algorithm can be shown to be correct by demonstrating that each set S_i contains exactly the set of constituent structures that meet the Off-line Parsability Constraint and whose yields are of length i. This follows by an induction on i.

To establish the base of the induction, note that the set S_1 contains exactly the the set of constituent structures that meet the Off-line

Parsability Constraint and whose yields are of length 1. This follows immediately from the definition of the Off-line Parsability Constraint and the definition of the set U above.

The inductive step can be established by noting that any constituent structure u whose yield is of length n can be decomposed as sketched in Figure 7 into a unary branching constituent structure fragment and a finite sequence V of $m > 1$ constituent structure trees meeting the Off-line Parsability Constraint the sum of whose total yields is exactly n. Since the length of the yield of any constituent structure that meets the off-line parsability restriction must be greater than zero, it follows that the length of the yield of each of the m constituent structure trees in V must be less than n. But then by inductive hypothesis each of these constituent structures must be a member of some S_j for $j < n$. It follows that u is a member of the set S_n computed in step (iii) of the algorithm.

Thus the algorithm is correct if it terminates. Termination of the algorithm follows if each of the sets S_i are bounded. The size of the sets S_i can be bounded using elementary combinatorial analysis, which I now proceed to do.

Lemma 24: *The number of off-line parsable constituent structures with c different constituent structure categories and l different lexical forms that yield a string of length n is bounded above by a computable function.*

Proof: First, note that the off-line parsability restriction requires that no terminal node has an ε lexical annotation. Therefore there are n terminal nodes in any constituent structure tree that has as its yield a string of length n. Further, the number of nodes in any nonbranching dominance chain must be less than or equal to c, the number of constituent structure categories in the grammar. Thus the number of different nonbranching dominance chains $d(c)$ must be less than c^c, which is a computable function.

Second, the number $t_{c,n,l}$ of off-line parsable constituent structures with c categories and l different lexical forms whose yield is a string of length n is equal to $l^n g_{d(c),n}$, where $g_{c',n}$ is the number of trees with n leaves where each node is labelled with exactly one of c' categories and no node has exactly one daughter. This follows because:

(i) there are l^n different ways of labelling each of the n terminal nodes, and

(ii) each of the $d(c)$ different unary branching dominance chains in an off-line parsable constituent structure can be represented by one of $d(c)$ categories; hence a tree with n leaves and $d(c)$

categories without unary branching uniquely encodes an off-line parsable constituent structure with c categories.

Finally, it remains to bound $g_{c,n}$, the number of trees with n leaves where each node is labelled with exactly one of c categories and no node has exactly one daughter. Because there are at most $2n$ nodes in such a tree (i.e., the number of nodes in a binary tree with a yield of length n), there is a injective mapping of the set of these trees into the set of directed (but not necessarily connected) graphs of $2n$ nodes with c labels. Since the number of directed graphs with m nodes and c labels is less than $c^m\, 2^{m^2}$, $g_{c,n}$ must be less than $c^{2n}\, 2^{4\,n^2}$, which is a computable function.

□

Thus the number of constituent structures is bounded by a computable function, so Algorithm C for enumerating constituent structures is both correct and effective.

3.5.2 An Algorithm for Solving the Universal Parsing Problem

In this section I use the results of the previous subsection to present an algorithm for solving the universal parsing problem for attribute value grammars, where the constituent structures are constrained to satisfy the Off-line Parsability Constraint. The algorithm is a straightforward combination of Algorithm C of section 3.5.1 that enumerates constituent structures, and Algorithm R of section 2.5.4 that reduces an arbitrary wff of the language $\mathcal{A}$ for describing attribute-value structures to either *False* or a reduced form.[26]

Algorithm P:

Input: A string s and a grammar g.

Output: A list of pairs $\langle u, \mathbf{R} \rangle$, where u is a constituent structure and $\mathbf{R}$ is a reduced form of $\mathcal{A}$.

(i) Compute the set U of constituent structure trees whose yield is s using Algorithm C of section 3.5.1.

(ii) Return the set $\{ \langle u, \mathbf{R} \rangle : u \in U, \mathbf{R} \neq \mathit{False}$ is the result of applying Algorithm R of section 2.5.4 to $af_g(u)$ $\}$.

Then the string s is generated by grammar g if and only if Algorithm P returns on those inputs a non-empty set of pairs as output. Clearly, this procedure is effective. The correctness of this algorithm follows

26 A practical computational implementation of a parser for an attribute-value based theory of grammar would probably not use this algorithm, but would instead coroutine the enumeration of constituent structures and the determination of the satisfiability of the associated formulae of those constituent structures.

immediately from the decomposition of the parsing problem given in section 4.3.

In general one cannot characterize the set of annotated constituent structures generated by a given grammar that have a given string as their yield by a simple enumeration, since there may be infinitely many such structures. These annotated constituent structures can be finitely characterized, however, since for any given constituent structure *u* and grammar *g*, the set of attribute value models that can function as the attribute-value component of an annotated constituent structure generated by *g* is precisely the set of models that satisfy $af_g(u)$, and this set can in turn be characterized by a reduced form (or *False*) equivalent to $af_g(u)$. Thus the set of annotated constituent structures generated by *g* that have a string *s* as their yield is completely characterized by the sets of pairs of constituent structures and reduced forms produced by Algorithm P.

3.6 Conclusion

In this chapter I have defined attribute-value grammars and the 'generates' relation for this set of grammars. I then showed that if the set of constituent structure trees is unrestricted, then the universal recognition problem for attribute-value grammars is undecidable.

I then defined a restriction on the class of constituent structures call the Off-line Parsability Constraint, and showed that if constituent structures are restricted in this way, then the universal recognition problem is decidable. In particular I showed that one can characterize the set of annotated constituent structures that string-generate a particular string by (i) enumerating the set of constituent structures that have their yield, and (ii) for each such constituent structure, use algorithm R from Chapter 2 to produce a reduced form that characterizes the set of attribute-value models that satisfy the associated form of that constituent structure.

This result shows that there is an algorithm for characterizing the set of annotated constituent structures whose yield is a given string. Although it is extremely unlikely that humans actually use the algorithm proposed here, this work provides a starting point in the search to determine the actual procedure by which humans process linguistic information, and shows us one way in which knowledge of language can actually be put to use.

Chapter 4

The Encoding of Grammatical Relations

Until now I have been concerned with the development of the formal basis of attribute-value based theories of grammar. In this chapter I turn toward the linguistic application of these devices, and investigate how they can be employed by a theory of grammar to express substantive hypotheses about the nature of particular linguistic phenomena. I investigate two different ways of representing grammatical relations, and focus on the interaction between the Off-line Parsability Constraint (introduced in section 3.5), the representation of grammatical relations, and particular analyses of linguistic phenomena.

Specifically, I show that the following constellation of formal and substantive properties of an attribute-value based theory of grammar of the kind outlined in Chapter 3 is untenable:

(i) A 'direct encoding' of the grammatical relations,

(ii) An analysis of the Double Infinitive Construction in Dutch based on the analysis of Bresnan *et al.* (1982), and

(iii) The Off-line Parsability Constraint.

Interestingly, this constellation of properties characterizes LFG as it currently appears in the literature, so this result provides additional motivation for extensions or revisions to LFG currently being developed, specifically the use of functional uncertainty or regular path equations (see section 5.3).

In the last two chapters I showed in detail how formal devices for manipulating attribute-value structures can be used in a theory of grammar. In this chapter I investigate the interaction between the attribute-value based grammar formalism and the types of analyses of particular linguistic phenomena it can express. I focus in particular on the ways in which grammatical relations can be represented in attribute-value based theories, and how the nature of that representation influences the analyses of particular linguistic phenomena that these theories can express.

The devices for manipulating attribute-value structures that constitute the formal basis of attribute-value theories of grammar do not fully specify the way in which grammatical relations can represented in these theories. There are at least two different ways of representing grammatical relations that are consistent in an attribute-value based linguistic theory, and I show that they can lead to quite different theories of grammar.

I call the two different representations of grammatical relations the 'direct' and the 'hierarchical' encodings. In the direct encoding grammatical relations are identified by name, while in the hierarchical encoding they are identified by position in some structure. These two representations constitute two different substantive hypotheses about the nature of grammatical relations. I then discuss how these two representations of grammatical relations lead to analyses of the Dutch Double Infinitive Construction that interact differently with the formal devices out of which attribute-value based theories are constructed. I identify a particular constellation of properties that results in a theory being unable to describe certain Double Infinitive constructions in Dutch.

4.1 Encoding Grammatical Relations in AV Grammars

It should be clear from the earlier chapters that the formal basis of attribute-value framework partially restricts the types of analyses and the theory of grammar. It rules out analyses that crucially involve devices not made available in the attribute-value formalism, such as syntactic transformations, 'Move-α', etc. But there are many gross details of linguistic theories in the attribute-value frameworkthat it does not determine. As mentioned above, there are at least two ways of representing grammatical relations in a fashion compatible with the attribute-value formalism, which are called the *direct* and the *hierarchical* encodings of grammatical relations. Both of these encodings are used in current attribute-value linguistic theories. LFG

(Bresnan 1982) employs a direct encoding of grammatical relations, while HPSG (Pollard and Sag 1987) and CUG (Karttunen 1986) employ a hierarchical encoding.[27]

In what follows I will be primarily concerned with the representation of the 'nuclear' or 'governed' grammatical relations, such as subject, object and indirect object, rather than oblique arguments and adjuncts. However, a theory of obliques and adjuncts based on direct encoding have been developed in LFG (e.g., Kaplan and Bresnan 1982), and a theory of obliques and adjuncts based on hierarchical encoding has been developed in HPSG (e.g., Pollard and Sag, 1987).

4.2 The 'Direct Encoding' of Grammatical Relations

Grammatical relations can be represented by assigning each grammatical relation a unique name, and using these names as attributes of the attribute-value element associated with the clause as a whole. In a theory of grammar that uses such a direct encoding, an attribute-value structure identifies an argument phrase as bearing grammatical relation r in a clause when the attribute-value element associated with that argument is the value of attribute r of the attribute-value element associated with the clause as whole.

In LFG, the grammatical relations are given names like 'SUBJ', 'OBJ', and 'OBJ2' etc. I use these names below.

Example 1: *The lexical entries in (1) and syntactic rules in (2) constitute a fragment that uses a direct encoding of grammatical relations. (All fragments in this chapter will have S as their start category).*

(1a)	*sleeps*	V	$x(\text{subj})(\text{num}) = \text{sg} \wedge$ $x(\text{subj})(\text{pers}) = \text{3rd} \wedge$ $x(\text{pred}) = \text{sleep}.$
(1b)	*kisses*	V	$x(\text{subj})(\text{num}) = \text{sg} \wedge$ $x(\text{subj})(\text{pers}) = \text{3rd} \wedge$ $x(\text{pred}) = \text{kiss}.$
(1c)	*Mary*	NP	$x(\text{pred}) = \text{mary} \wedge$ $x(\text{pers}) = \text{3rd} \wedge$ $x(\text{num}) = \text{sg}.$

(2a)	$S \rightarrow NP\ VP$	$x = x_2 \wedge x(\text{subj}) = x_1.$
(2b)	$VP \rightarrow V$	$x = x_1.$
(2c)	$VP \rightarrow V\ NP$	$x = x_1 \wedge x(\text{obj}) = x_2.$

[27] I use the term "encodings" here because these are ways of representing grammatical relations, rather than being the relations themselves.

The grammar in (1) and (2) generates annotated constituent structures such as the one depicted in Figure 1.

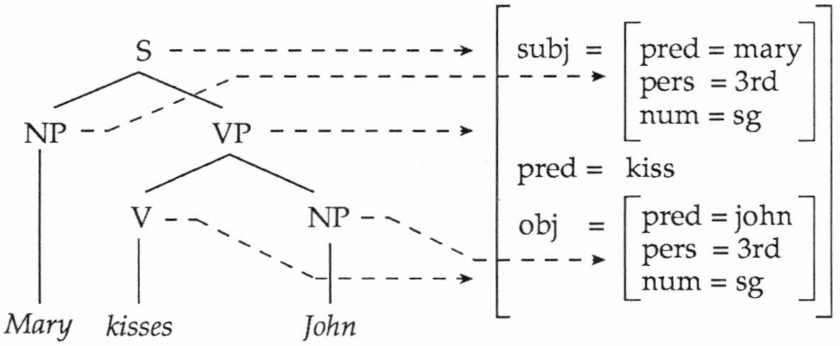

Figure 1 An annotated constituent structure with a direct encoding of grammatical relations

4.2.1 Direct Encoding and Subcategorization

One difficulty with direct encoding is that in its simplest form it gives no account of subcategorization phenomena.

Example 2: *Nothing in the grammar presented in Example 1 requires the verb 'kisses' to appear with a direct object, or prohibits the verb 'sleeps' from occurring with a direct object. Thus the annotated constituent structure depicted in Figure 2 is generated by the grammar in (1) and (2), even though its yield* *Mary sleeps John *is ungrammatical.*

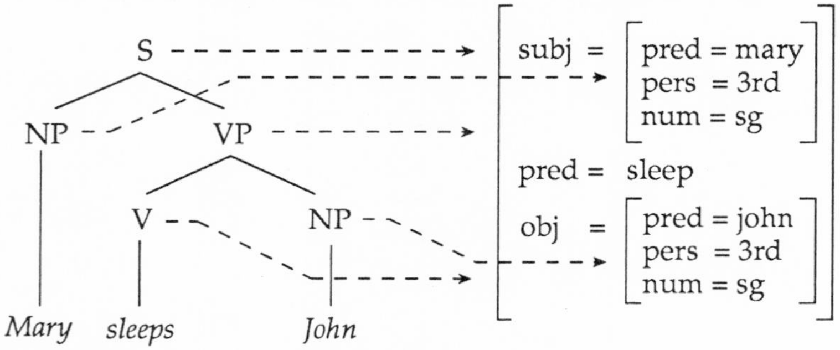

Figure 2 The failure of a simple version of direct encoding to account for subcategorization

There are at least two ways of accounting for subcategorization phenomena in an attribute-value based theory that uses direct encoding. These are discussed in the next two sections.

4.2.2 Subcategorization via Diacritic Features

First, one can annotate both the lexical entries and the grammar rules with 'diacritic features' (encoded as the value of a designated attribute in the attribute-value structure) to indicate which syntactic rules can introduce particular lexical items, thus only allowing a transitive verb to appear in the V slot of the rule that expands a VP to a V followed by an NP. This is essentially the technique used to account for subcategorization in GPSG (Gazdar *et al.*, 1986).

Example 3: *Sample lexical entries and syntactic rules for a grammar that accounts for subcategorization phenomena by using diacritic feature annotations are shown in (3) and (4). The constant symbol* diacritic *denotes the attribute whose value represents the* diacritic *feature. The attribute-value equations that make use of this attribute are identified in boldface.*

(3a) *sleeps* V x(subj)(num) = sg $\wedge$
x(subj)(pers) = 3rd $\wedge$
x(pred) = sleep $\wedge$
x(diacritic) = intrans.

(3b) *kisses* V x(subj)(num) = sg $\wedge$
x(subj)(pers) = 3rd $\wedge$
x(pred) = kisses $\wedge$
x(diacritic) = trans.

(4a) S $\rightarrow$ NP VP $x = x_2 \wedge x(\text{subj}) = x_1$.

(4b) VP $\rightarrow$ V $x = x_1 \wedge$ **x(diacritic) = intrans.**

(4c) VP $\rightarrow$ V NP $x = x_1 \wedge x(\text{obj}) = x_2 \wedge$
x(diacritic) = trans.

An annotated constituent structure generated by this grammar is depicted in Figure 3.

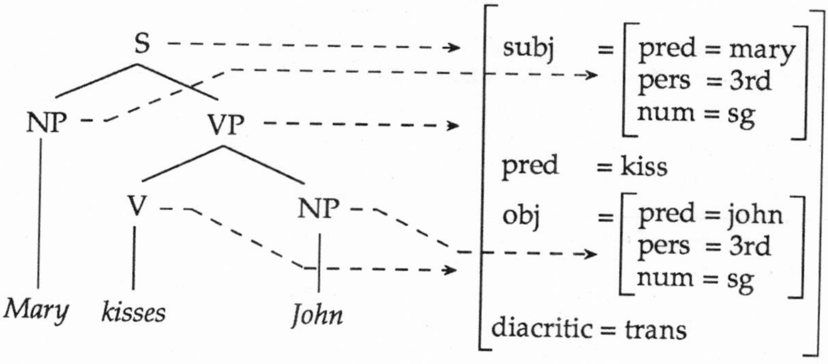

Figure 3 The use of diacritic features to account for subcategorization

The ungrammatical sentence generated by the grammar of Example 1 is not generated by this grammar, since the underlined equation associated with the lexical entry (3a) for *sleeps* requires the value of the attribute *diacritic* to be *intrans,* while the underlined equation associated with the syntactic rule (4c) used to expand VP to V NP requires the value of that attribute to be *trans.* Figure 4 depicts this ill-formedness by using braces to indicate where the constraints associated with the lexical entry and the syntactic rule require distinct values for the attribute *diacritic.*

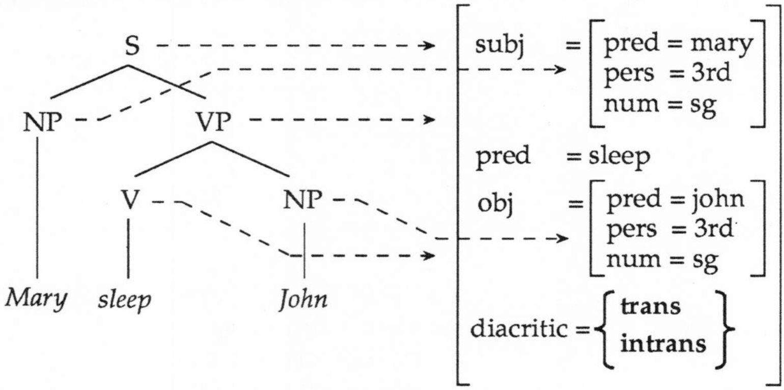

Figure 4 Incorrect subcategorization and the resulting ill-formed annotated constituent structure

4.2.3 Subcategorization via Existential Constraints

A second technique to account for subcategorization phenomena for use with grammars that use a direct encoding of grammatical relations is based on the intuition that a syntactic functor that subcategorizes for an argument bearing a particular grammatical relation requires that argument to be present in order to become 'complete'.[28] Moreover, when an argument filling a subcategorizable grammatical relation[29] is associated with a syntactic entity that does not require such an argument, that predicate becomes 'oversaturated' or 'incoherent', and ungrammaticality results. This method is used to account for subcategorization phenomena in LFG.[30]

[28] The terms 'complete' and 'coherent' in this context originate from Kaplan and Bresnan (1982, p. 203ff.).

[29] The subcategorizable grammatical relations are called 'governable grammatical functions' in Kaplan and Bresnan (1982, p. 211).

[30] Subcategorization phenomena in LFG is captured by requiring *f*-structures to meet Completeness and Consistency conditions (Kaplan and Bresnan 1982, pp. 209–213).

That is, each argument-taking predicate is associated with a set of 'existential constraints' that require that each of the attributes that represent a grammatical relation be either present or absent in the feature structure associated with the clause as a whole. As I show in the following example, these existential constraints do not appear to be straight-forwardly implementable using the devices developed for describing attribute-value structures in the last two chapters.

Example 4: *In lexical entries of (5) I have informally written the existential constraints that represent the subcategorized grammatical relations for lexical items using an 'existential quantifier' notation. These entries are intended to be used with the syntactic rules in (2) of Example 1.*

(5a)	*sleeps*	V	$x(\text{subj})(\text{num}) = \text{sg} \wedge$ $x(\text{subj})(\text{pers}) = \text{3rd} \wedge$ $x(\text{pred}) = \text{sleep} \wedge$ $\exists x(\text{subj}) \wedge \sim\exists x(\text{obj})$.
(5b)	*kisses*	V	$x(\text{subj})(\text{num}) = \text{sg} \wedge$ $x(\text{subj})(\text{pers}) = \text{3rd} \wedge$ $x(\text{pred}) = \text{kiss} \wedge$ $\exists x(\text{subj}) \wedge \exists x(\text{obj})$.

It might seem as if these existential constraints could be represented as expressions of the language $\mathcal{A}$ as follows. Since the equation $\mathbf{t} = \mathbf{t}$ of the language $\mathcal{A}$ requires that any satisfying model assign an element as the denotation of $\mathbf{t}$, it might seem that the atomic wff $\mathbf{t} = \mathbf{t}$ expresses the existential quantification $\exists\mathbf{t}$. Rewriting lexical entries of (5) according to this scheme yields the entries shown in (6).

(6a)	*sleeps*	V	$x(\text{subj})(\text{num}) = \text{sg} \wedge$ $x(\text{subj})(\text{pers}) = \text{3rd} \wedge$ $x(\text{pred}) = \text{sleep} \wedge$ $x(\text{subj}) = x(\text{subj}) \wedge x(\text{obj}) \neq x(\text{obj})$.
(6b)	*kisses*	V	$x(\text{subj})(\text{num}) = \text{sg} \wedge$ $x(\text{subj})(\text{pers}) = \text{3rd} \wedge$ $x(\text{pred}) = \text{kiss} \wedge$ $x(\text{subj}) = x(\text{subj}) \wedge x(\text{obj}) = x(\text{obj})$.

These conditions are syntactic rather than semantic constraints. For example, with a 'raising' verb such as *believe* these conditions will require the presence of a matrix object in the *f*–structure, even though semantic form of the matrix object argument does not occur in the semantic predicate-argument structure associated with *believe* (Bresnan 1982, p. 162).

Interestingly, while the lexical entry (6a) correctly prohibits the intransitive verb *sleep* from appearing with a direct object NP, the lexical entry (6b) allows the generation of annotated constituent structures such as the one depicted in Figure 5, where a transitive verb appears without a direct object NP.

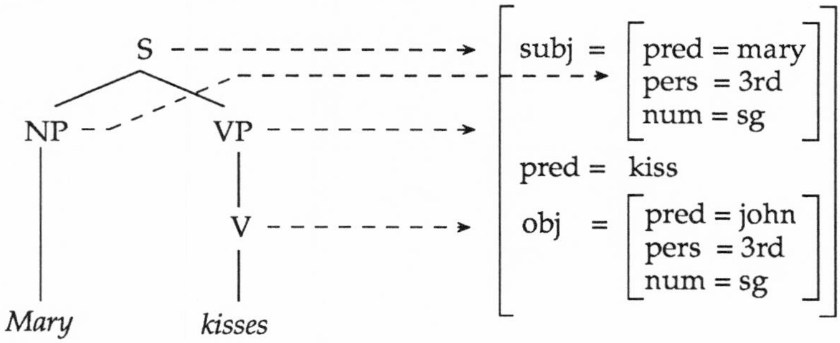

Figure 5 An an annotated constituent structure with an ungrammatical yield generated by (6)

Nothing in the grammar prohibits the attribute-value element associated with the VP constituent depicted in Figure 5 from having an *obj* attribute, even though there is no object NP argument present in the constituent structure. This suggests the existential constraints of (5) must be interpreted in some other fashion than as in (6).

Informally, the existential constraint is intended to be interpreted in a stronger sense: an existential constraint involving a term **t** is satisfied if and only if it is *independently required* that **t** denotes. Under this stronger interpretation, the annotated constituent structure depicted in Figure 5 would not be generated by the grammar of (5), since nothing in the grammar *forces* there to be an attribute-value element that is the value of the object attribute of the element associated with the constituent structure node labelled *kisses*.

Unfortunately, even though negative existential constraints can be expressed in language $\mathcal{A}$, there seems to be no straight-forward way of expressing the (positive) existential constraints. I know of no principled way of extending the language $\mathcal{A}$ for describing attribute-value structures to include such positive existential constraints.[31]

[31] For example, a potential problem for any treatment of systems containing these 'existential constraints' is the apparent non-compositionality of the boolean operators in such systems. Thus the wff $\exists\, x(subj) \wedge x(pred) = sleep \wedge x(subj)(pred) = mary$ is satisfiable under the interpretation of the existential discussed above, but

4.3 The 'Hierarchical Encoding' of Grammatical Relations

Grammatical relations can also be represented by associating positions in some configuration or structure with particular grammatical relations. In attribute-value based theories that employ this method of encoding (CUG and HPSG) this is done by associating grammatical relations with positions in a list structure associated with each predicate. This list of arguments is the value of the *subcat* attribute of the attribute-value element associated with a syntactic constituent, and its members represent the unsaturated arguments of that constituent.

As discussed in section 3.4.2, lists can be represented as attribute-value elements with two attributes *first* and *rest*. The constant element *nil* represents the null list, and the list which consists of the element *e* prepended to the list *l* is represented as an attribute-value structure whose *first* attribute has as its value *e* and whose *rest* attribute has as its value the representation of *l*. For example, the list [NP, PP] is depicted as shown in Figure 6.

$$\begin{bmatrix} \text{first} = \text{NP} \\ \text{rest} = \begin{bmatrix} \text{first} = \text{PP} \\ \text{rest} = \text{nil} \end{bmatrix} \end{bmatrix}$$

Figure 6 A attribute-value structure that represents the list [NP, PP]

Example 5. *A sample grammar and set of lexical entries using a hierarchical encoding is given in (7) and (8). The argument associated with the last position in the* subcat *list of a verb can be interpreted as the subject, and the second-to-last position as the object.*

(7a)	*sleeps*	V	x(pred) = sleep ∧ x(subcat)(first)(num) = sg ∧ x(subcat)(first)(pers) = 3rd ∧ x(subcat)(rest) = nil.
(7b)	*kisses*	V	x(pred) = kiss ∧ x(subcat)(first)(num) = sg ∧ x(subcat)(first)(pers) = 3rd ∧ x(subcat)(rest)(rest) = nil.
(7c)	*Mary*	NP	x(pred) = Mary ∧ x(num) = sg ∧ x(pers) = 3rd.

only the second of the two subwffs ∃ *x(subj)* ∧ *x(pred)* = *sleep* and *x(subj)(pred)* = *mary* is satisfiable under this interpretation.

(8a) S → NP VP x_2(subcat)(first) = x_1 ∧
x_2(subcat)(rest) = nil.

(8b) VP → V NP x_1(subcat)(rest) = x(subcat)
x_1(subcat)(first) = x_2.

(8c) VP → V $x_1 = x$.

An annotated constituent structure generated by this grammar is depicted in Figure 7.

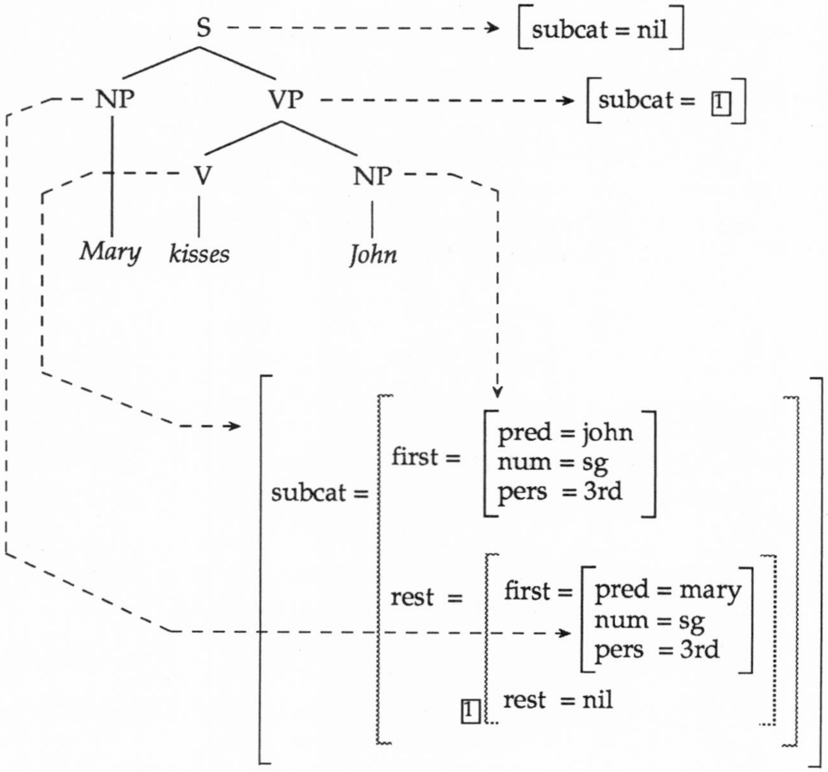

Figure 7 An annotated constituent structure generated by a grammar that uses a hierarchical encoding of grammatical relations

The list represented by the value of the *subcat* attribute of a syntactic constituent encodes the unsaturated arguments of that category in much the same way as the complex categories of a categorial grammar encode the valency of consituents. In general, in grammars with hierarchical encoding a syntactic rule that introduces an argument phrase (e.g., the rule (8b)), 'pops' the top element from the *subcat* list of the head daughter, equates it with the argument introduced in the rule, and equates the remaining undischarged arguments of the head with the *subcat* list of the mother constituent.

With hierarchical encoding and simple syntactic rules, such as the ones in (8), the order in which the arguments of a predicate combine with that predicate is determined by the order in which these arguments appear in the predicate's *subcat* list. If the syntactic rules are relatively impoverished, a rich system of lexical rules manipulating the *subcat* list is needed to generate a variety of lexical entries with arguments in the appropriate order. Alternatively, the syntatic rule system can be enriched so it can perform more complicated operations on the *subcat* list not restricted to combining arguments with the predicate in the order that they appear on the *subcat* list.

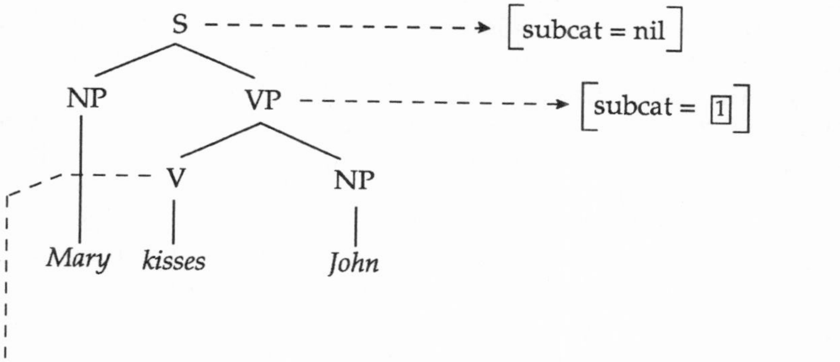

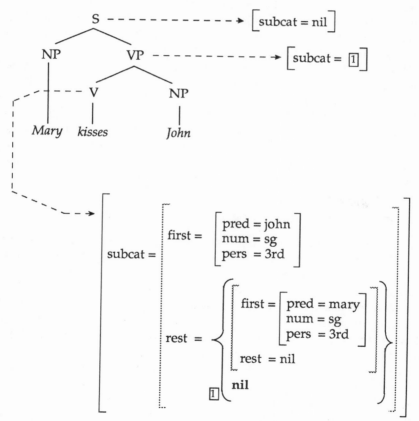

Figure 8 Incorrect subcategorization and the resulting ill-formed annotated constituent structure

Note that a theory that uses the hierarchical encoding does not run into the subcategorization problem found with the configurational encoding, since the list of the unsaturated arguments of a constituent is explicitly represented in the attribute-value element associated with that constituent. This means that additional devices are not required to account for subcategorization, in contrast to theories of grammar based on direct encoding. For example, only ill-formed annotated constituent structures such as the one depicted in Figure 8 correspond to subcategorization violations such as **Mary sleeps John.*

Grammars using hierarchical encoding possess one rather curious property, however: the information about the predicate-argument structure of the sentence is represented by the attribute-value element associated with the verb, rather than with the root S node that dominates it. This is because the attribute-value element of a daughter constituent does not automatically appear as the value of some attribute of the attribute-value structure associated with its mother, as in grammars that use a direct encoding of grammatical relations.

Whether this is a disadvantage or not depends on how annotated constituent structures are semantically interpreted, of course. It has become customary in attribute-value based theories to view the attribute-value element associated with the root S node as the 'feature structure' associated with the sentence as a whole, but nothing forces us to adopt this. In any case, an extra attribute, say *semantics*, can be used to 'pass up' the value of the verb's *subcat* list to the S node of that clause, and ultimately to the node dominating the utterance.

4.4 Empirical Differences between the Encodings

The two types of encoding just discussed may appear to be notational variants of each other, but they can result in the adoption of analyses of the same linguistic phenomena that have radically different formal properties. Thus while it is not the case that the formal basis of attribute-value based theories of grammar determines the nature of the encoding of grammatical relations, there are important interactions between the formal basis of an attribute-value based theory and the particular substantive linguistic hypotheses that it contains. In the remainder of this chapter I discuss the Double Infinitive Construction in Dutch, and show how the choice of argument encoding affects the types of analyses of it that are possible within the attribute-value framework developed in Chapter 3.

One of the celebrated analyses of attribute-value grammar is the analysis of the Dutch Cross-Serial Dependencies presented in Bresnan,

Kaplan, Peters and Zaenen (1982) (hereafter BKPZ). This analysis showed that it was possible to provide an analysis of systematic discontinuity without resorting to transformational devices.

In this section I argue that the Dutch Cross-Serial Dependency construction is in fact an instance of a more general construction known as the Double Infinitive Construction (den Besten and Edmondson 1983), and show that the BKPZ analysis extends naturally to the whole of the Dutch Double Infinitive Construction. The extensibility of the BKPZ analysis to the Double Infinitive Construction as a whole suggests that the attribute-value devices employed in that analysis were correctly applied.

However, the implications of the Double Infinitive Construction analysis proposed here are not entirely supportive of LFG as currently formulated. Specifically, I show that when the BKPZ analysis is extended to cover the full range of the Double Infinitive Construction, a grammar using a direct encoding of grammatical relations must either violate the off-line parsability restriction, or employ more powerful devices for describing attribute-value structures than are provided by the language $\mathcal{A}$.

On the other hand, I provide a grammar based on the BKPZ analysis using a hierarchical encoding of grammatical relations which does not violate the off-line parsability restriction. This grammar is expressed in the grammar format developed in chapter 3, and thus uses only the devices for describing attribute-value structures provided by the language $\mathcal{A}$. This shows that the use of the direct encoding of grammatical relations is an important aspect in the failure of the BKPZ analysis to both capture the full range of the Double Infinitive Construction of Dutch and require only constituent structures that satisfy the Off-line Parsability Constraint.

4.5 The Double Infinitive Construction in West Germanic

As den Besten and Edmondson (1983) point out, West Germanic languages (excepting English) generally exhibit a basic SOV word order in dependent clauses. According to Greenberg's Universal 16, in an SOV language an inflected auxiliary should follow, rather than precede, the main verb. In terms of phrase structure, this implies that an SOV language should have a left branching VP, rather than the right branching VP found in languages like in English.

West Frisian and Low German in fact exhibit left branching VPs, as shown in (9a) and (9b).

(9a) West Frisian[32]
dat er it boek [[[leze] kent] hat]
that he the book read can(PP[33]) has

(9b) Low German
dat er dat book [[[lezen] kunnt] hett]
that he the book read can(PP) has

However, the more widely spoken Continental West Germanic languages, High German and Dutch, do not behave as expected of SOV languages with this type of sentence. When a modal verb governing a main verb is itself the complement of *haben* 'to have', the future auxiliary *werden*, or a modal such as *sollen* 'should', the Double Infinitive Construction is used. This type of construction exhibits systematic variation across the whole of Continental West Germanic, absent in Frisian and Low German, and appearing in its 'full-blown' form in Dutch (den Besten and Edmondson 1983).

Consider the German equivalent of (9a), as shown in (9c).

(9c) High German
daß er das Buch [hat [[lesen] können]]
that he the book has read can(Inf)

In lieu of the expected past participle *gekonnt* only the infinitival form *können* appears. In addition to the anomalous form of the modal, (9c) also exhibits an unexpected order of elements. The finite auxiliary *hat* precedes rather than follows its complement, so the sentence ends in two infinitives (hence the name for the construction). In terms of the direction of branching, the top level of the VP is right branching, rather than left branching.

Finally, consider the corresponding Dutch example shown in (9d).

(9d) Dutch
dat hij het boek [heeft [kunnen [lezen]]]
that he the book has can(Inf) read

As in the German case, the modal is in infinitival, rather than participial form. Even though the verbal complex as a whole is still sentence final, the verbal complements of both *heeft* and *kunnen* appear to their right rather than left. That is, (9d) differs from (9c) in that the verbal elements in (9d) only exhibit right branching, while (9c) exhibits both left and right branching.

32 The data on West Frisian and Low German given here are from den Besten and Edmondson (1983).

33 The glosses *PP* and *Inf* indicate that the glossed forms are past participal and infinitival forms respectively.

Notice also that in both (9c) and (9d) the finite auxiliary is located between the main verb and its direct object, so that the main verb is not contiguous with its object. Any account of these constructions must explain the nature of this discontinuity.

The appearance of the Double Infinitive Construction also interacts with a variety of other syntactic phenomena, such as quantifier scope, clitic placement and the binding of reciprocal pronouns (Evers 1975, Zaenen 1979, Haegeman and van Riemsdijk 1986, Kroch and Santorini, to appear). Any complete account of this construction will have to explain these interactions. Neither of the two fragments presented in this chapter provides any account of these other phenomena, but attempt solely to describe the word order properties of the Double Infinitive Construction. There are three reasons for this.

First, my goal here is to show that a particular constellation of properties of a linguistic theory is untenable. To do this it suffices to show that such a theory is incapable of describing at least one aspect of the construction, for then this theory is incapable of describing all the relevant properties of this construction.

Second, there is considerable diversity among attribute-value based theories as to the treatment of phenomena such as quantifier scope, clitic placement and reciprocal binding, and moreover the analyses of these phenomena possible in attribute-value based theories of grammar are only weakly constrained by the attribute-value formalism. In conjunction with well-developed hypotheses about the principles governing quantifier scope, clitic placement and reciprocal binding, the data on these phenomena can provide powerful evidence to support or contradict a particular analysis of the Double Infinitive Construction, but in the absence of specific theories of these phenomena this data provides much less evidence for or against a particular analysis.

Third, I do not claim that the hierarchical encoding fragment presented later in this chapter is the correct analysis of the Double Infinitive Construction. Rather, all I claim is that it is a modified version of the BKPZ analysis that uses hierarchical encoding, and that in constrast to a direct encoding fragment, it does not require the use of constituent structures that violate the off-line parsability constraint to generate the examples of the Double Infinitive Construction discussed here. Thus even though the attribute-value framework only weakly constrains the substantive linguistic hypotheses of an attribute-value theory of grammar, the abstract properties of formalism do interact in interesting ways with particular linguistic analyses.

4.6 The Double Infinitive Construction in Dutch

In this section and the next I provide a series of descriptive generalizations to characterize the morphological and word order properties of the Double Infinitive Construction (DIC) in Dutch.

Firstly, in a verbal complex with only two verbal elements (i.e., modal or auxiliary and main verb) either order of elements is possible, as shown in (10).

(10a) dat hij dat wel begrijpen kan / kan begrijpen
that he that indeed understand can
'that he can in fact understand that'

(10b) dat hij gelachen heeft / heeft gelachen
that he laughed(PP) has
'that he has laughed'

(10c) dat hij het gekund heeft / heeft gekund
that he it can(PP) has
'that he can understand it'

When the verbal complex consists of three or more verbal elements, however, the order of all but the finite auxiliary is fixed in that a head always precedes its verbal complement,[34] irrespective of whether the finite verb is the perfect auxiliary, as in (11), or a modal, as in (12). On the other hand, the verbal complement of the finite auxiliary can appear either to the auxiliary's left or right. That is, while the 'top-level' structure may be either left or right branching, all lower structures must be strictly right branching.

(11a) dat hij het heeft kunnen zien
that he it has can see
'that he can see it'

(11b) * dat hij het heeft zien kunnen
that he it has see can

(11c) ?* dat hij het zien kunnen heeft
that he it see can has

(11d) * dat hij het zien heeft kunnen
that he it see has can

---

34 This differs from the descriptive generalization offered by den Besten and Edmondson (1983). They claimed that only strictly right-branching structures are possible, which would predict (11f) to be ungrammatical. It is possible that the difference in generalizations reflects a dialect split.

(11e) * dat hij het kunnen heeft zien
that he it can has see

(11f) dat hij het kunnen zien heeft
that he it can see has
'that he can see it'

(12a) dat men haar niet wilde laten gaan
that one her not wants let go
'that one doesn't want to let her go'

(12b) * dat men haar niet wilde gaan laten
that one her not wants go let

(12c) *? dat men haar niet gaan laten wilde
that one her not go let wants

(12d) * dat men haar niet gaan wilde laten
that one her not go wants let

(12e) * dat men haar niet laten wilde gaan
that one her not let wants go

(12f) dat men haar niet laten gaan wilde
that one her not let go wants
'that one doesn't want to let her go'

Also, only the infinitival forms of the modal verbs are 'true' modals, i.e., the participial forms cannot take another verb (or VP) as their complement. Thus we have the contrasts in (13a) and (13b), and (13c) and (13d). (13e) is ungrammatical because the complement of *kunnen* appears to its left, rather than to its right as required.

(13a) dat hij het boek heeft kunnen lezen
that he the book has can(Inf) read
'that he has been able to read the book'

(13b) * dat hij het boek heeft gekund lezen
can(PP)

(13c) dat hij het boek kunnen lezen heeft
that he the book can(Inf) read has
'that he has been able to read the book'

(13d) * dat hij het boek gekund lezen heeft
can(PP)

(13e) * dat hij het boek lezen kunnen heeft
that he the book read can(Inf) has

(13f) * dat hij het boek lezen gekund heeft
that he the book read can(PP) has

We can describe the contrasts in (13) by hypothesizing that 'true' modals (i.e., modals that subcategorize for a verbal complement rather than an NP complement) do not possess participial forms,[35] i.e., that their paradigm is defective.

4.7 Cross-Serial Dependencies in Dutch

Bresnan, Kaplan, Peters and Zaenen (1982) argue that Dutch cannot be strongly context free on the basis of a construction that appears in dependent clauses, examples of which are shown in (14). The construction is called the Cross Serial Dependency Construction (CSDC) because the verb-object dependencies cross each other, as indicated by the lines below each example.

(14a) dat Jan de kinderen zag zwemmen
that Jan the children saw swim

'that Jan saw the children swim'

(14b) dat Jan Piet de kinderen zag helpen zwemmen
that Jan Piet the children saw help swim

'that Jan saw Piet help the children swim'

(14c) dat Jan Piet Marie de kinderen zag helpen laten zwemmen
that Jan Piet Marie the children saw help let swim

'that Jan saw Piet help Marie let the children swim'

I claim that the construction shown in (14) is in fact the Double Infinitive Construction, the examples in (14) differing from those in (10) through (13) only in that the matrix verbs in (14) subcategorize for NP objects as well as a VP complement. That is, the verbs that appear in the Double Infinitive Construction examples are either modal verbs or subject control verbs, while the verbs that appear in the cross-serial dependency construction are either object raising, object control or causative verbs.

The verb complex in the cross-serial dependency construction is subject to exactly the same word order restriction that characterized

[35] This might be done by requiring that the lexical rule that generates participial forms not accept modal verbs as input.

the Double Infinitive Construction, namely that the top-level structure may be either left or right branching, but all lower structures are strictly right branching, as shown in (15) and (16).

(15a) dat Jan de kinderen zag zwemmen
that Jan the children saw swim
'that Jan saw the children swim'

(15b) dat Jan de kinderen zwemmen zag
that Jan the children swim saw
'that Jan saw the children swim'

(16a) dat Jan Piet de kinderen zag helpen zwemmen
that Jan Piet the children saw help swim
'that Jan saw Piet help the children swim'

(16b) * dat Jan Piet de kinderen zag zwemmen helpen
that Jan Piet the children saw swim help

(16c) * dat Jan Piet de kinderen zwemmen helpen zag
that Jan Piet the children swim help saw

(16d) * dat Jan Piet de kinderen zwemmen zag helpen
that Jan Piet the children swim saw help

(16e) * dat Jan Piet de kinderen helpen zag zwemmen
that Jan Piet the children help saw swim

(16f) dat Jan Piet de kinderen helpen zwemmen zag
that Jan Piet the children help swim saw
'that Jan saw Piet help the children swim'

Moreover, the verbs that appear in the Cross Serial Dependency Construction interact with the modal verbs that take part in the Double Infinitive Construction to form a mixed construction (i.e., with both modal Double Infinitive Construction verbs and Cross-Serial verbs in the same verb cluster) that again exhibits the same word order restrictions as the Double Infinitive Construction, as shown in (17).[36]

(17a) dat zij het kan zien bewegen
that she it can see move
'that she can see it move'

(17b) * dat zij het kan bewegen zien
that she it can move see

[36] Den Besten and Edmondson (1983, p. 190) report (17f) to be ungrammatical, and reach the generalization that modal, sensory and causative verbs require a right branching top level structure.

(17c) * dat zij het bewegen zien kan
that she it move can see

(17d) * dat zij het bewegen kan zien
that she it move can see

(17e) * dat zij het zien kan bewegen
that she it see can move

(17f) dat zij het zien bewegen kan
that she it see move can
'that she can see it move'

In summary, the Cross Serial Dependency Construction exhibits exactly the word-order properties one would expect of object-raising or object-control verbs appearing in the Double Infinitive Construction. As I show below, the same set of syntactic rules can be used to generate both constructions, lending further support to the hypothesis that they are in fact instances of the same construction. On the other hand, if one were to assume that the Cross Serial Dependency Construction and the Double Infinitive Construction are not instances of the same construction, we would not only have to provide separate accounts of each construction and the 'mixed' construction shown in (17), but also find some mechanism to prevent modal verbs from appearing in the Cross Serial Dependency Construction and object raising or object control verbs from appearing in the Double Infinitive Construction.

4.8 The BKPZ Analysis of Cross Serial Dependencies

BKPZ analyze Dutch Cross Serial Dependency constructions such as (18) (=14c) as the multi-clausal structure shown in Figures 9 and 10.

(18) dat Jan Piet Marie de kinderen zag helpen laten zwemmen
that Jan Piet Marie the children saw help let swim

'that Jan saw Piet help Marie let the children swim'

To simplify the depiction of the annotated constituent structure that corresponds to (18), its constituent structure is depicted in Figure 9 and its attribute-value structure is depicted separately in Figure 10. Each syntactic constituent in Figure 9 is subscripted: this subscript is used in Figure 10 to identify the attribute-value element associated with this constituent.

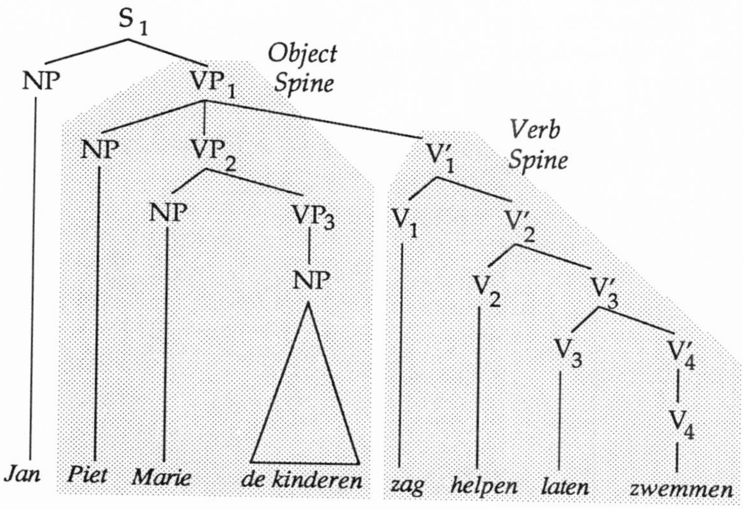

Figure 9 The constituent structure of (17) generated by
the BKPZ analysis

$$
\begin{array}{l}
\left.
\begin{array}{l}
S_1 \\
VP_1 \\
V'_1 \\
V_1
\end{array}
\right[
\begin{array}{l}
\text{subj} \ = \left[\text{pred} = \text{jan}\right] \\
\text{pred} \ = \text{see} \\
\text{obj} \ = \boxed{1}\left[\text{pred} = \text{piet}\right] \\[2mm]
\left.
\begin{array}{l}
VP_2 \\
V'_2 \\
V_2
\end{array}
\right[
\text{vcomp} = \left[
\begin{array}{l}
\text{subj} \ = \boxed{1} \\
\text{pred} \ = \text{help} \\
\text{obj} \ = \boxed{2}\left[\text{pred} = \text{marie}\right] \\[2mm]
\left.
\begin{array}{l}
VP_3 \\
V'_3 \\
V_3
\end{array}
\right[
\text{vcomp} = \left[
\begin{array}{l}
\text{subj} \ = \boxed{2} \\
\text{pred} \ = \text{let} \\
\text{obj} \ = \boxed{3}\left[\text{pred} = \text{children}\right] \\[2mm]
\text{vcomp} = \begin{array}{l} \\ V'_4 \\ V_4 \end{array}\left[
\begin{array}{l}
\text{pred} \ = \text{swim} \\
\text{subj} \ = \boxed{3}
\end{array}\right]
\end{array}\right]
\end{array}\right]
\end{array}\right]
\end{array}
$$

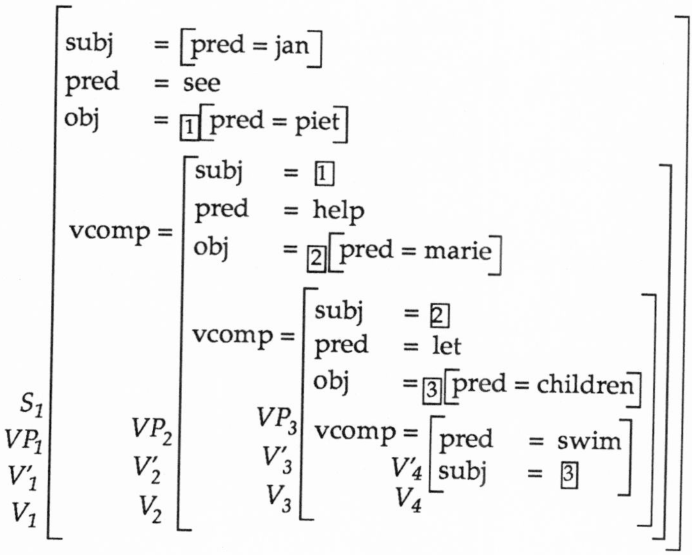

Figure 10 The attribute-value structure of (17) generated by

Bresnan *et al.* (1982, p. 615) argue that the constituent structure shown in Figure 9 is correct, and support their position by showing that such structures permit a simple description of constituent conjunction in the CSDC. Since I do not challenge the constituent structures assigned by Bresnan *et al.* (1982), I will not review this material here.[37]

The key to the BKPZ grammar is that two discontinuous constituents, one located in the 'object spine' and the other located in the 'verb spine' of Figure 9, are associated with the same attribute-value element. This association is required by virtue of a series of attribute-value equations that appear in the syntactic rules. Each recursive level of constituent structure embedding[38] is required to correspond to a recursive level of VCOMP embedding in the attribute-value structure, so, for example, VP_2 and V'_2 are required to be associated with the same attribute-value element.

Informally, the attribute-value formulae in the syntactic rules force a 'lock-step' behaviour in the attribute-value elements associated with the constituents of the two spines, even though these constituents are discontinuous.

The syntactic rules (in LFG format) that require this are given in display (19).

(19a)	S	→	NP (↑ SUBJ) = ↓	VP ↑ = ↓	
(19b)	VP	→	(NP) (↑ OBJ) = ↓	(VP) (↑ VCOMP) = ↓	(V′) ↑ = ↓
(19c)	V′	→	V ↑ = ↓	(V′) (↑ VCOMP) = ↓	

These LFG rules can be regarded as abbreviations for syntactic rules of the form developed in chapter 3. The most complex rule in (19), (19b), abbreviates the rules in (20).

(20a) VP → NP VP V′ $\quad x = x_3 \wedge$
$x(\mathrm{obj}) = x_1 \wedge$
$x(\mathrm{vcomp}) = x_2.$

(20b) VP → NP V′ $\quad x(\mathrm{obj}) = x_1 \wedge$
$x = x_2.$

---

[37] Steedman (1985), working within the categorial grammar framework, adopts a different theory of conjunction, and assigns constituent structures to the CSDC examples radically different to those proposed by Bresnan *et. al.* (1982).

[38] The VP nodes are the recursive nodes of the 'object spine' and the V′ nodes are the recursive nodes of the 'verb spine'.

(20c) VP → NP VP $x(\text{obj}) = x_1 \wedge$
$x(\text{vcomp}) = x_2$.

(20d) VP → VP V′ $x = x_2 \wedge$
$x(\text{vcomp}) = x_1$.

(20e) VP → NP $x(\text{obj}) = x_1$.

(20f) VP → VP $x(\text{vcomp}) = x_1$.

(20g) VP → V′ $x = x_1$.

Finally, the BKPZ lexicon is given in (21). Note that the attribute-value equations associated with the verbs *laten*, etc., which identify the matrix object's attribute-value structure with the embedded subject's attribute-value structure, are of the same type as those associated with object control verbs, so BKPZ in effect analyse the matrix verbs of the cross-serial dependency construction as object control verbs.

(21a) *zwemmen* V (↑ PRED) = 'swim< (↑ SUBJ) >'

(21b) *laten*, etc. V (↑PRED)='let<(↑SUBJ),(↑OBJ),(↑VCOMP)>'
(↑ VCOMP SUBJ) = (↑ OBJ)

(21c) *kinderen* N (↑ PRED) = 'children'

These lexical entries can be translated into the format for lexical entries presented in chapter 3 as follows. (I use the 'existential technique' for accounting for subcategorization discussed above, since this is the technique used by LFG.) The second equation in *laten*'s lexical entry (22b) forces the feature structure associated with its object to be equal to the feature structure of its complement's subject: this is the standard equation associated with an Object Control verb in an attribute-value grammar that uses a direct encoding of grammatical relations.

(22a) *zwemmen* V $x(\text{pred}) = \text{swim} \wedge$
$\sim\exists x(\text{obj}) \wedge \sim\exists x(\text{vcomp})$.

(22b) *laten*, etc. V $x(\text{pred}) = \text{cause} \wedge$
$x(\text{vcomp})(\text{subj}) = x(\text{obj}) \wedge$
$\exists x(\text{obj}) \wedge \exists x(\text{vcomp})$.

4.9 The BKPZ Analysis and the Double Infinitive Construction

Interestingly, if we analyse the Double Infinitive Construction matrix verbs as Subject Raising or Subject Control verbs the BKPZ grammar generates[39] the grammatical Double Infinitive Construction examples in (10) through (13) and the mixed examples in (17) without modification. The appropriate lexical entries (in LFG format) are given in (23).

(23a) *lezen* V (↑ PRED) = 'read< (↑ SUBJ) , (↑ OBJ) >'

(23b) *heeft*, etc. V (↑ PRED) = 'perf (↑ SUBJ)< (↑ VCOMP) >'
(↑ VCOMP SUBJ) = (↑ SUBJ)

(23c) *hij* N (↑ PRED) = 'PRO

The lexical entry for *kunnen* can be translated into standard attribute-value format as in (24).

(24) *heeft*, etc. V x(pred) = perf ∧
x(vcomp)(subj) = x(subj) ∧
~∃x(obj) ∧ ∃x(vcomp).

The grammar rules given by BKPZ, together with the new lexical entries, generate an analysis of (25) (= 9d) as shown in Figures 11 and 12.

(25) dat hij het boek [heeft [kunnen [lezen]]]
that he the book has can(Inf) read
'that he has been able to read the book'

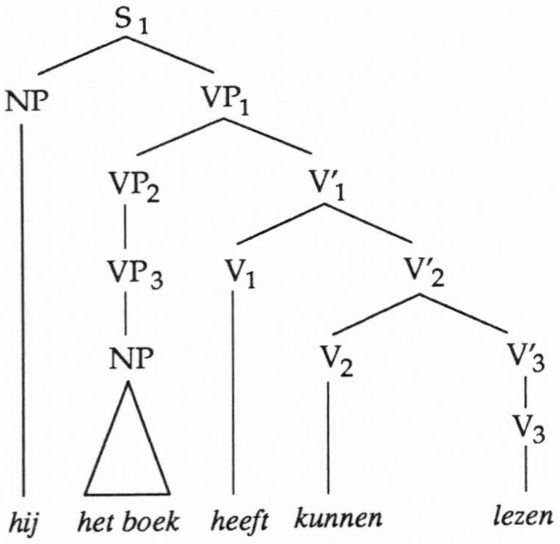

Figure 11 The constituent structure of (9d) generated by the modified grammar

---

[39] This ignores the off-line parsability restriction on syntactic structures discussed in Chapter 3 and later in this chapter.

$$
\begin{array}{r} S_1 \\ VP_1 \\ V'_1 \\ V_1 \end{array}
\left[\begin{array}{lll}
\text{subj} & = & \boxed{1}\left[\text{pred} = \text{pro}\right] \\
\text{pred} & = & \text{perf} \\
\text{vcomp} = & \begin{array}{r} VP_2 \\ V'_2 \\ V_2 \end{array} & \left[\begin{array}{lll}
\text{subj} & = & \boxed{1} \\
\text{pred} & = & \text{able} \\
\text{vcomp} = & \begin{array}{r} VP_3 \\ V'_3 \; V_3 \end{array} & \left[\begin{array}{lll}
\text{subj} & = & \boxed{1} \\
\text{obj} & = & \left[\text{pred} = \text{book}\right] \\
\text{pred} & = & \text{read}
\end{array}\right]
\end{array}\right]
\end{array}\right]
$$

Figure 12 The attribute-value structure of (9d) generated by the modified grammar

Thus the BKPZ fragment can be extended by simply adding the appropriate lexical entries to generate the entire range of Double Infinitive Construction phenomena in Dutch, even though it was designed only to generate the cross-serial dependency constructions.

This is a confirmation that the application of the formal devices made available by the attribute-value formalism used in the BKPZ analysis were in fact correctly applied. In particular, the technique of merging the attribute-value structures from two different spines generalizes correctly to the case where verbs other than Object Control verbs appear in the verb spine.

4.10 Overgeneration and the BKPZ Analysis

In sections 4.6 and 4.7 I noted that both the Double Infinitive Construction and the cross-serial dependency constructions allowed the finite, top-level verbal element to appear either to the left or to the right of the other verbal elements. An interesting question, then, is to determine what modifications need to be made to the BKPZ grammar in order to generate these left-branching constructions.

The answer, somewhat surprisingly, is: none, the BKPZ grammar as formulated generates these top-level left-branching constructions. Figure 13 contains the constituent structure of (26) that corresponds to the top-level left-branching version of the cross-serial dependency construction (14c), the attribute-value structure of (26) is the same as the one we gave to (14c), i.e., that shown in Figure 10.

(26) dat Jan Piet Marie de kinderen helpen laten zwemmem zag
that Jan Piet Marie the children help let swim saw
'that Jan saw Piet help Marie let the children swim'

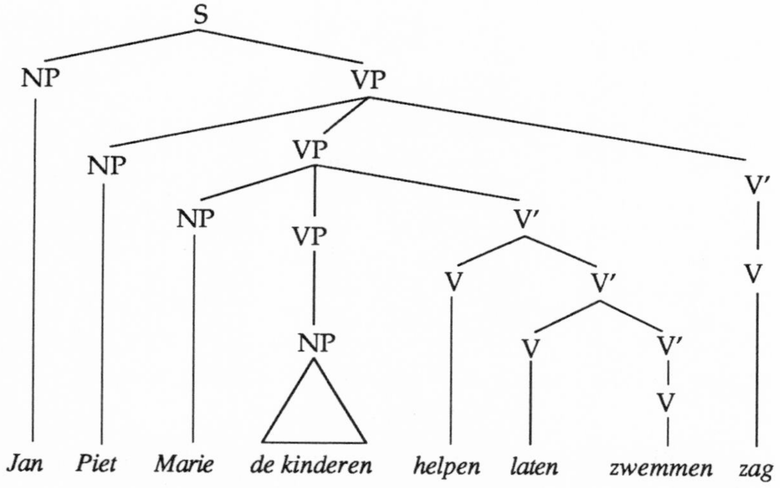

Figure 13 The constituent structure of (26)

The BKPZ grammar thus generates the left-branching top-level Double Infinitive Construction structures identified in section 4.6.

However, the BKPZ analysis generates some of the ungrammatical examples given in sections 4.6 and 4.7 as well. For example, the ungrammatical cross-serial dependency construction example shown in (27) is the yield of the constituent structure in Figure 14 and the attribute-value structure in Figure 10 that are generated by the BKPZ grammar given above.

The reason for this overgeneration is simple: nothing in the BKPZ grammar forces all verbal constituents to be dominated by the top-level V′ node, so at any stage verbal elements may be dominated by a lower VP node. This means that in effect the BKPZ grammar generates verbal elements in a left-branching sequence of right-branching structures of verbal elements, clearly overgenerating.[40]

Thus the BKPZ grammar suffers from the same deficiency that BKPZ claimed any CFG for these constructions must, ie. the BKPZ grammar does not "generate all and only the correct structural descriptions for Dutch" (BKPZ p. 622), and it is not the case that "the general well-formedness conditions on attribute-value structures will

[40] Interestingly, the German DIC example (10c) is not among the overgenerated structures of the BKPZ grammar: in fact the context-free skeleton from the BKPZ grammar cannot generate the correct structural description for (10c). This implies that syntactic rules other than those in (20) will be needed to generate the DIC in German.

eliminate those trees in which the depth of branching on the left and right is mismatched" (p. 625).

(27) * dat Jan Piet Marie de kinderen laten zwemmen zag helpen
that Jan Piet Marie the children let swim saw help

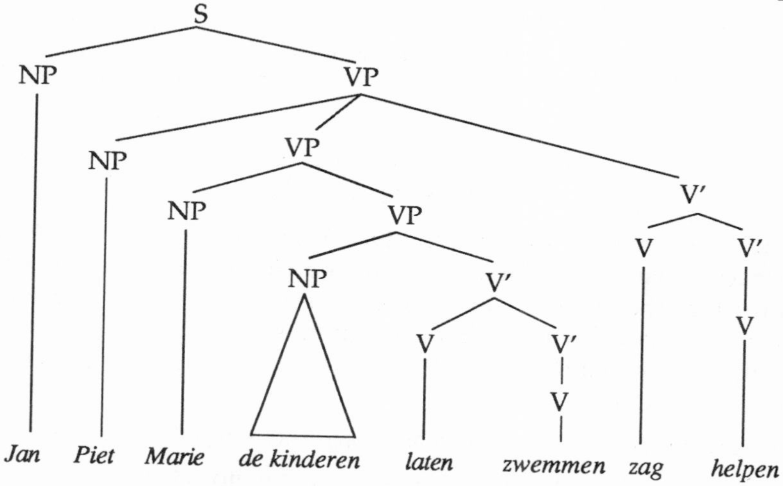

Figure 14 The constituent structure of (27)

However, it is quite straightforward to modify the BKPZ grammar so that only the correct constituent structures are admitted. For example, one can use a diacritic feature (encoded as the value of the attribute *inverted* of the attribute-value element associated with a constituent) to indicate whether that constituent structure appears in a left or a right branching structure; i.e., whether it appears as the V′ complement daughter of a VP constituent or a V′ constituent respectively. Verbs that require a right-branching complement, namely the infinitival Double Infinitive Construction and Cross Serial Dependency Construction verbs, will require that their complement have this diacritic feature, thus requiring that their V′ complements be daughters of V′, as required.

In (28) an attribute-value equation has been added to the V′ rule so that if that V′ has a V′ daughter then the value of the attribute *inverted* of the attribute-value element associated with that daughter must be '+'. Similarly, an attribute-value equation has been added to the VP rule so that if it has a V′ head then the value of the attribute *inverted* of the attribute-value element associated with that daughter must be '–'. These two additional equations (shown in bold for emphasis) ensure that the value of the attribute *inverted* of the attribute-value element corresponding to a V′ constituent is '+' if and only if that constituent appears in a right-branching structure.

(28)	S →	NP (↑ SUBJ) = ↓	VP ↑ = ↓	
	VP →	(NP) (↑ OBJ) = ↓	(VP) (↑ VCOMP) = ↓	(V′) ↑ = ↓ **(↑ INVERTED) = –**
	V′ →	V ↑ = ↓	(V′) (↑ VCOMP) = ↓ **(↓ INVERTED) = +**	

The lexical entries for the infinitival forms of the Double Infinitive Construction verbs contain an additional attribute-value equation that requires that the value of the attribute *inverted* of the attribute-value element associated with their complement be '+', as shown in (29). This effectively requires that their complement appear in a right-branching structure.

(29a)	*zwemmen*	V	(↑ PRED) = 'swim<(↑ SUBJ)>'
(29b)	*lezen*	V	(↑ PRED) = 'read<(↑ SUBJ) , (↑ OBJ)>'
(29c)	*laten*, etc.	V	(↑ PRED) = 'let<(↑ SUBJ),(↑ OBJ),(↑VCOMP)>' (↑ VCOMP SUBJ) = (↑ OBJ) **(↑ VCOMP INVERTED) = +**
(29d)	*kunnen*, etc.	V	(↑ PRED) = 'able (↑ SUBJ) <(↑ VCOMP)>' (↑ VCOMP SUBJ) = (↑ SUBJ) **(↑ VCOMP INVERTED) = +**
(29e)	*heeft, kan* etc.	V	(↑ PRED) = 'perf (↑ SUBJ) <(↑ VCOMP)>' (↑ VCOMP SUBJ) = (↑ SUBJ)

The syntactic rules of (28) and lexical entries of (29) now associates the attribute-value structure depicted in Figure 16 with the constituent structure shown in Figure 15. In this sentence the verbs *helpen* and *laten* require that their complement be right branching; i.e, that the attribute-value structure of their complement satisfy the equation 'inverted=+'.

The revised grammar shown in (28) and (29) does not generate the ungrammatical sentence (27), because the verb *helpen* requires its complement be part of a right branching structure, i.e., that the value of the attribute *inverted* of the attribute-value element associated with that complement be '+', yet the syntactic rule used to expand that complement (the VP rule) requires that the value of the attribute *inverted* be '–'. These requirements are unsatisfiable, and hence the example is not generated by the revised grammar. Figure 17 depicts the constituent structure that corresponds to (27), and Figure 18 depicts the corresponding ill-formed attribute-value structure.

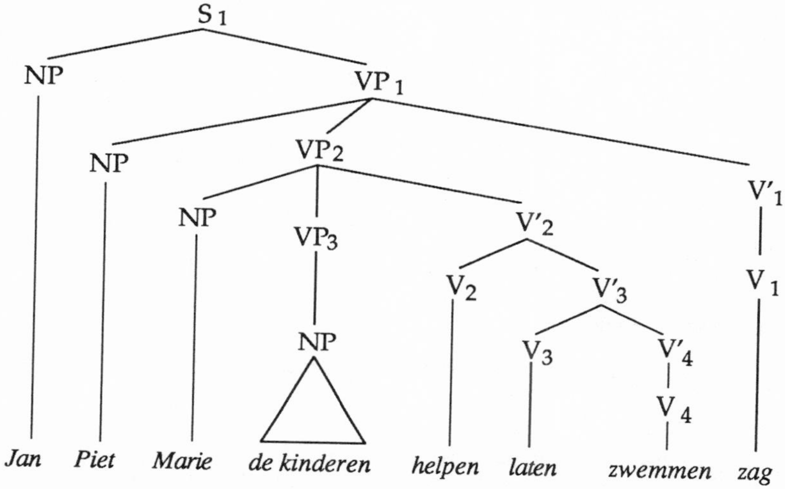

Figure 15 The constituent structure of (26)

$$
\begin{bmatrix}
\text{subj} & = & [\text{pred} = \text{jan}] \\
\text{inverted} & = & - \\
\text{pred} & = & \text{see} \\
\text{obj} & = & \boxed{1}[\text{pred} = \text{piet}] \\
\\
\text{vcomp} & = &
\begin{bmatrix}
\text{subj} & = & \boxed{1} \\
\text{inverted} & = & + \\
\text{pred} & = & \text{help} \\
\text{obj} & = & \boxed{2}[\text{pred} = \text{marie}] \\
\\
\text{vcomp} & = &
\begin{bmatrix}
\text{subj} & = & \boxed{2} \\
\text{inverted} & = & + \\
\text{pred} & = & \text{let} \\
\text{obj} & = & \boxed{3}[\text{pred} = \text{children}] \\
\text{vcomp} & = &
\begin{bmatrix}
\text{subj} & = & \boxed{3} \\
\text{inverted} & = & + \\
\text{pred} & = & \text{swim}
\end{bmatrix}
\end{bmatrix}
\end{bmatrix}
\end{bmatrix}
$$

S_1 VP_1 V'_1 V_1 VP_2 V'_2 V_2 VP_3 V'_3 V_3 V'_4 V_4

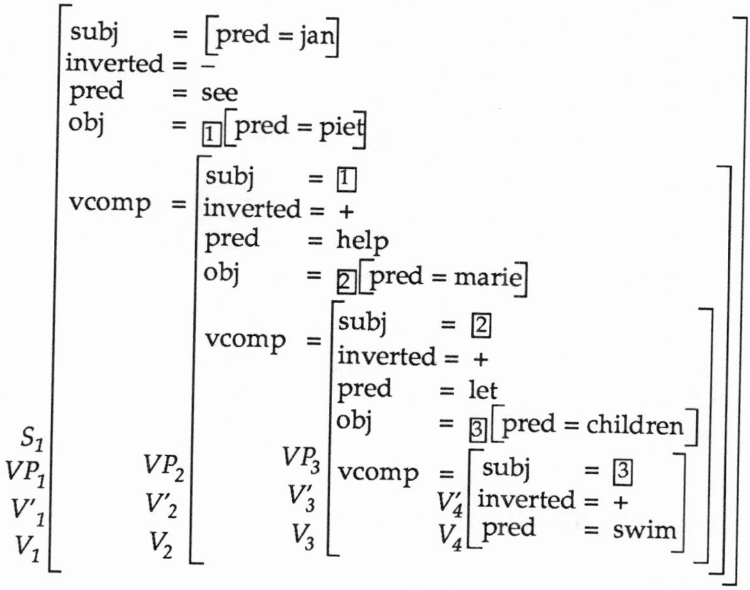

Figure 16 The attribute-value structure of (26)

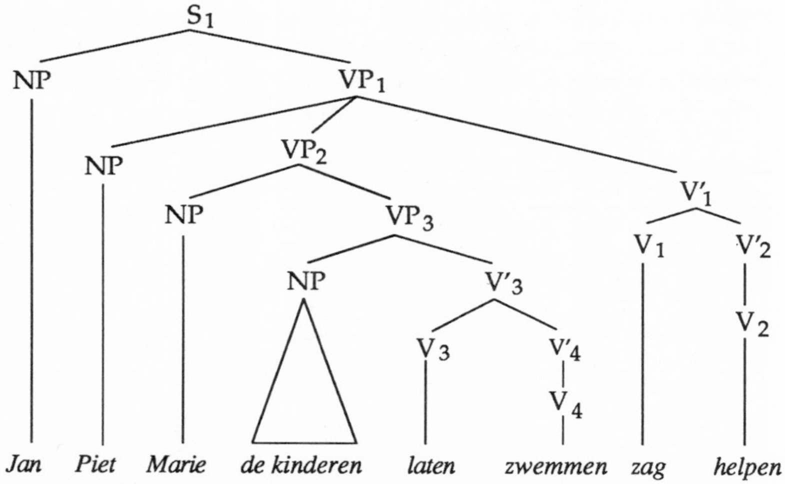

Figure 17 The constituent structure of (27)

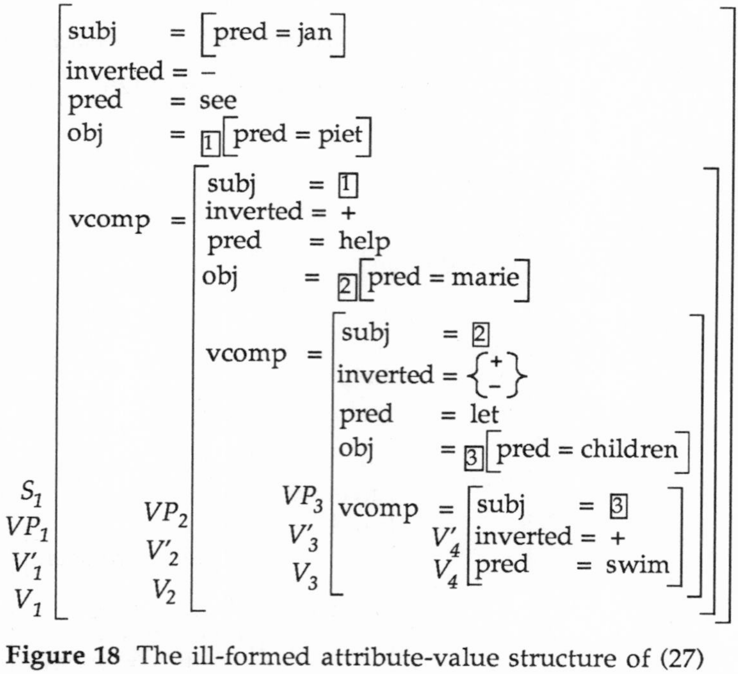

Figure 18 The ill-formed attribute-value structure of (27)

To summarize the results so far, it appears that the BKPZ grammar is in fact capable of being extended to cover the whole range of Double

Infinitive Construction constructions, as well as capturing the correct word order dependencies of Dutch.

4.11 The Double Infinitive Construction and Off-Line Parsability

In the presentation of the theory of LFG Kaplan and Bresnan (1982) place strong restrictions on what they call "vacuous" constituent structures by adopting the off-line parsability constraint discussed in the last chapter. This constraint prohibits 'empty' constituent structure nodes and non-branching exhaustive dominance constituent chains of the form $A \to^* A$. This restriction is motivated on both linguistic and language-theoretic grounds.

From a linguistic perspective, Kaplan and Bresnan (1982) claim that these restrictions prohibit the constituent structure from encoding hierarchical or other relationships that in their view should be represented in the attribute-value structure.

As I showed in the last chapter, the off-line parsability constraint also reduces the computational complexity of attribute-value based theories of grammar markedly, making the universal parsing problem for such theories decidable. Thus there is a convergence of linguistic intuition and language-theoretic evidence supporting the Off-line Parsability Constraint.

It is therefore doubly unfortunate that many of the grammatical Double Infinitive Construction examples require constituent structures that violate this restriction by requiring a VP node to exhaustively dominate another VP node. For example, the grammatical example (30) (= 9d) requires such a constituent structure, as depicted in Figure 19.

(30) dat hij het boek [heeft [kunnen [lezen]]]
that he the book has can(Inf) read
'that he has been able to read the book'

The Off-line Parsability Constraint violation arises because the grammar in (28) requires that the level of syntactic embedding of each constituent correspond directly to the level of VCOMP embedding of the attribute-value element associated with that constituent. The NP *het boek* is the direct object of the verb *lezen*, and so both must be at the same level of VCOMP embedding; i.e., the attribute-value element associated with *het boek* must be the value of the OBJ attribute of the attribute-value element associated with the verb.

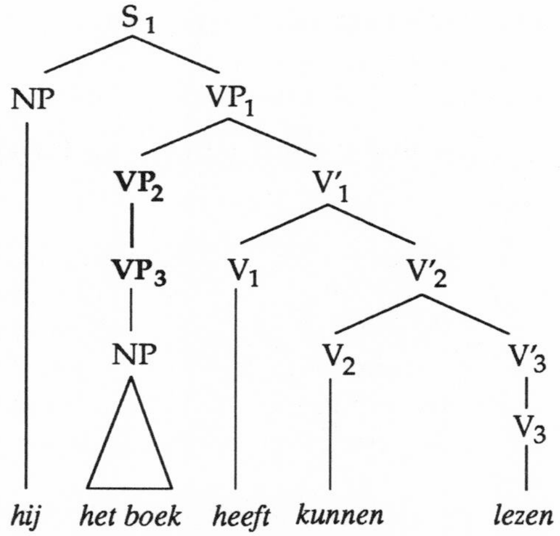

Figure 19 A constituent structure that violates Off-line Parsability

$$
\begin{array}{l}
S_1 \\
VP_1 \\
V'_1 \\
V_1
\end{array}
\left[
\begin{array}{l}
\text{subj} \quad = \quad \boxed{1}\big[\text{pred} = \text{pro}\big] \\
\text{pred} \quad = \quad \text{perf} \\[2mm]
\text{vcomp} =
\begin{array}{l}
VP_2 \\
V'_2 \\
V_2
\end{array}
\left[
\begin{array}{l}
\text{subj} \quad = \quad \boxed{1} \\
\text{pred} \quad = \quad \text{able} \\[2mm]
\text{vcomp} =
\begin{array}{l}
VP_3 \\
V'_3 \ V_3
\end{array}
\left[
\begin{array}{l}
\text{subj} = \boxed{1} \\
\text{obj} \quad = \big[\text{pred} = \text{book}\big] \\
\text{pred} = \text{read}
\end{array}
\right]
\end{array}
\right]
\end{array}
\right]
$$

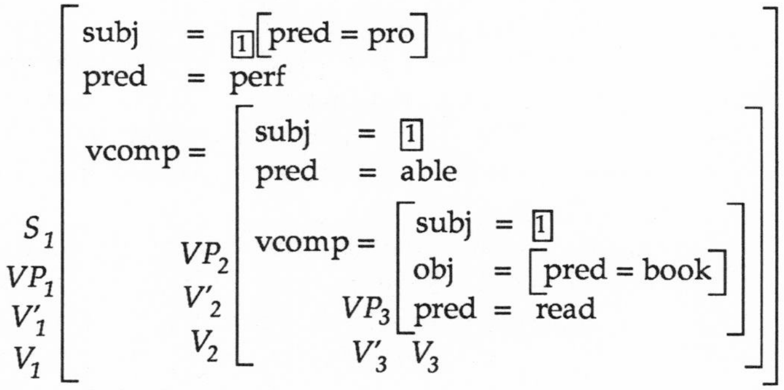

Figure 20 The attribute-value structure corresponding to Figure 19.

Since the structure is right-branching there are two spines, and the NP *het boek* is in a different spine to the V *lezen*. Furthermore, since all of the other verbs in the clause are Subject Raising or Subject Control verbs, *het boek* is the only object NP appearing in the clause, and hence the only NP in the object spine. In particular, because the VP constituent whose associated attribute-value element is required to be the same element associated with *kunnen* exhaustively dominates the VP that contains *het boek*, the constituent structure must violate the off-line parsability restriction. Nonetheless, it is necessary that all three VP constituents be present in the constituent structure, since if one were simply 'dropped', the attribute-value element associated with object NP would not appear at the correct level of VCOMP embedding.

Thus this non-branching dominance chain is required because of the 'lock-step' behaviour in the two spines discussed above. If the object NP *het boek* were immediately dominated by VP_2 the resulting structure would not violate the Off-line Parsability Restriction, but it would also result in an attribute-value structure that identified *het boek* as the object of *kunnen* rather than *lezen,* thus failing to satisfy the subcategorization requirements both verbs. Thus the BKPZ grammar, using a direct encoding of grammatical relations, when extended in the simple fashion proposed above to account for the Double Infinitive Construction as a whole, requires constituent structures that violate the Off-line Parsability restriction.

Moreover, there does not appear to be any simple way within the attribute-value framework developed in Chapter 3 of modifying the BKPZ analysis to avoid the off-line parsability violations without giving up the central idea behind this analysis: that a constituent from the 'object spine' is associated with the same attribute-value element as a constituent from the 'verbal spine' at the same level of clausal embedding.

4.12 A Hierarchical Encoding Analysis of the DIC

On the other hand, it turns out that when the basic idea behind the BKPZ grammar is implemented in a grammar using hierarchical encoding, no structures that violate the Off-line Parsability Constraint are required. I show this by presenting an attribute-value grammar that generates annotated constituent structures having the property that exactly the same substrings are identified as constituents as in the modified BKPZ analysis given in (28) and (29), yet the corresponding constituent structures do not violate the Off-line Parsability Constraint.

Requiring the constituent structures generated by this grammar to identify the same substrings as constituents as the BKPZ grammar makes this grammar more complex than is necessary to generate the strings of the well-formed DIC and CSDC examples. Nevertheless, doing so removes the possibility that a difference in constituency is responsible for the different properties of these grammars with respect to the Off-line Parsability Constraint.

The grammar developed in this section generates structures that have the same kind of double-spine structures as the BKPZ grammar does, and functions in essentially the same way: the same verbs are analysed as Object Control verbs or Subject Control verbs as in the BKPZ analysis. As mentioned above, the 'topology' of the constituent structures generated by this analysis are the same as those generated by the revised BKPZ grammar, i.e., there are two constituent structure 'spines', one containing the argument NPs and the other containing the verbal elements.

The significant difference between the two analyses is the nature of the attribute-value elements that the constituents in the 'object spine' are associated with. In the BKPZ grammar the constituent structure of the 'object spine' reflects the clausal structure of the construction as represented by the values of the VCOMP attributes, while in the grammar developed here the constituent structure of the 'object spine' reflects the argument structure of the whole verbal complex, as represented by the value of the *subcat* attribute.

In this grammar the order of the arguments under the *subcat* attribute is the opposite of the order of the earlier examples of configurational encoding: ie. the subject is the first element on the *subcat* list in the grammar given here, rather than the last (most deeply embedded) element as in the grammars above.

The grammar presented here is quite complex. Recall that my goal here is different to that of most linguistic research: I am not trying to motivate this analysis or its formulation, but only to point out its existence. A realistic linguistic theory that adopted this analysis would probably develop a more perspicuous notation for its presentation, and attempt to derive from independent principles many of the properties of the syntactic rules and the lexical entries that are simply stipulated here.

Nothing in the grammar presented here constructs in the annotated constituent structure a 'semantic representation' of a sentence as a whole, even though it would be fairly simple to extend the grammar to do so. There are two reasons why I did not extend the grammar in this manner.

First, as mentioned earlier, it is not clear that such a 'semantic representation' is needed for semantic interpretation of the annotated constituent structure. Clearly, all of the information necessary for semantic interpretation is already available in the annotated constituent structure itself.

Second, while in principle the addition of attribute-value equations to the lexical entries to require the presence of such a 'semantic representation' would not be difficult, it would unnecessarily complicate the already complex lexical entries and syntactic rules presented below.

The lexical entries of the grammar are presented in (31), and the syntactic rules in (32). I discuss each of the lexical entries in detail below.

(31a) *zwemmen* V x(pred) = swim $\wedge$
x(cat) = v $\wedge$
x(subcat)(first)(cat) = np $\wedge$
x(subcat)(rest) = nil.

(31b) *lezen* V x(pred) = read $\wedge$
x(cat) = v $\wedge$
x(subcat)(first)(cat) = np $\wedge$
x(subcat)(rest)(first)(cat) = np $\wedge$
x(subcat)(rest)(rest) = nil.

(31c) *kunnen* V x(pred) = able $\wedge$
x(cat) = v $\wedge$
x(subcat)(first)(cat) = v $\wedge$
x(subcat)(first)(inverted) = + $\wedge$
x(subcat)(rest) = x(subcat)(first)(subcat).

(31d) *zehen* V x(pred) = see $\wedge$
x(cat) = v $\wedge$
x(subcat)(first)(cat) = v $\wedge$
x(subcat)(first)(inverted) = + $\wedge$
x(subcat)(rest)(first)(cat) = np $\wedge$
x(subcat)(rest)(rest)=x(subcat)(first)(subcat).

(32a) S $\rightarrow$ NP VP x_1 = x_2(subcat)(first) $\wedge$
x_2(subcat)(rest) = nil $\wedge$
x(subcat) = nil.

(32b) VP $\rightarrow$ NP V′ x (subcat)(first) =x(subcat)(first)$\wedge$
x_2^2(subcat)(rest) = nil $\wedge$
x_2(subcat)(rest)(first) = x_1 $\wedge$
x_2(subcat)(rest)(rest) = nil.

(32c) VP $\rightarrow$ NP NP′ V′ x_3(subcat)(first) = x(subcat)(first) $\wedge$
x(subcat)(rest) = nil $\wedge$
x_3(subcat)(rest)(first) = x_1 $\wedge$
x_3(subcat)(rest)(rest) = x_2(subcat).

(32d) VP $\rightarrow$ V′ $x_1 = x$.

(32e) V′ $\rightarrow$ V V′ x_1(subcat)(first) = x_2 $\wedge$
x_1(subcat)(rest) = x $\wedge$
x(cat) = v$\wedge$
x(subcat)(first)(inverted) = +.

(32f) $V' \rightarrow V'\ V$ $\quad x_2(\text{subcat})(\text{first}) = x_1 \wedge$
$x_2(\text{subcat})(\text{rest}) = x \wedge$
$x(\text{cat}) = \text{v} \wedge$
$x(\text{subcat})(\text{first})(\text{inverted}) = -.$

(32g) $V' \rightarrow V$ $\quad x_1 = x.$

(32h) $NP' \rightarrow NP\ NP'$ $\quad x(\text{subcat})(\text{first}) = x_1 \wedge$
$x(\text{subcat})(\text{rest}) = x_2.$

(32i) $NP' \rightarrow NP$ $\quad x(\text{subcat})(\text{first}) = x_1 \wedge$
$x(\text{subcat})(\text{rest}) = \text{nil}.$

As is standard in grammars employing the hierarchical encoding of grammatical relations, the value of the *subcat* list of a constituent represents the list of unsaturated arguments of that category. The lexical entries for the intransitive verb *zwemmen* and the transitive verb *lezen* are straight-forward: these entries together with the syntactic rules (32a), (32b) and (32g) generate annotated constituent structure trees such as the one depicted in Figure 21.

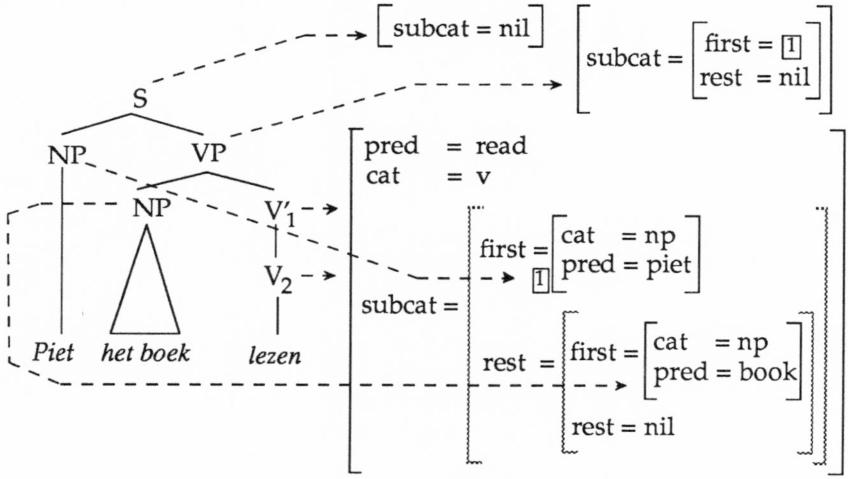

Figure 21 An annotated constituent structure generated by (31) and (32)

The attribute-value equations that manipulate the *subcat* lists associated with *kunnen* and *laten* are more complicated. The attribute-value equations in the lexical entries of the control and raising verbs of (31) ensure that the *subcat* list associated with each of these verbs includes as a sublist the *subcat* list associated with their complements. This 'inheritance' of argument structure is reminiscent of the way in which these verbs are analysed in the categorial framework by Steedman (1985) in terms of functional composition.

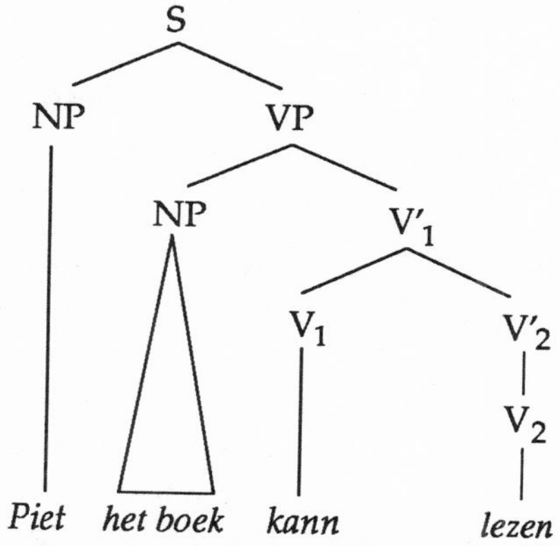

Figure 22 A constituent structure generated by (31) and (32)

$$VP\left[\text{subcat} = \begin{bmatrix} \text{first} = \boxed{3} \\ \text{rest} = \text{nil} \end{bmatrix}\right] \qquad V'_1\left[\begin{array}{ll} \text{cat} & = \text{v} \\ \text{subcat} = \boxed{1} \end{array}\right]$$

$$V_1\left[\begin{array}{ll} \text{cat} & = \text{v} \\ \text{pred} & = \text{can} \\ \text{subcat} = \begin{bmatrix} \text{first} = \boxed{1} \\ \text{rest} = \boxed{2} \end{bmatrix} \end{array}\right]$$

$$\begin{array}{l} \boxed{1} \\ V'_2 \\ V_2 \end{array}\left[\begin{array}{ll} \text{cat} & = \text{v} \\ \text{pred} & = \text{read} \\ \text{inverted} = + \\ \text{subcat} = \boxed{2}\begin{bmatrix} \text{first} = \boxed{3}\begin{bmatrix} \text{cat} = \text{np} \\ \text{pred} = \text{piet} \end{bmatrix} \\ \text{rest} = \begin{bmatrix} \text{first} = \begin{bmatrix} \text{cat} = \text{np} \\ \text{pred} = \text{book} \end{bmatrix} \\ \text{rest} = \text{nil} \end{bmatrix} \end{bmatrix} \end{array}\right]$$

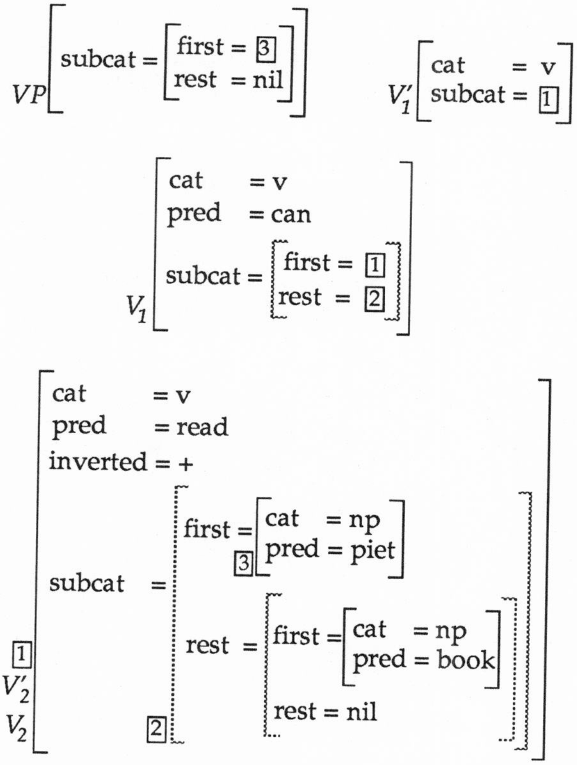

Figure 23 The attribute-value structure associated with Figure 22

The equations in (31c) require that the *rest* of the *subcat* list associated with *kunnen* must be the *subcat* list associated with the *first* element of *kunnen's subcat* list. Together with syntactic rule (32e) this will have the effect of requiring the *subcat* list associated with a V′ phrase such as *kunnen lezen* be equal to the *subcat* list associated with the V′ *lezen*. Thus the *subcat* list associated with *kunnen*'s complement will be the *subcat* list associated with the V′ phrase that *kunnen* heads, correctly reflecting the fact that the valence of a phrase like *kunnen lezen* is the same as the valence of *lezen* itself. Thus annotated constituent structures such as the ones depicted in Figures 22 and 23 are generated.

The lexical entries assigned to *laten, zehen* and other Cross Serial Dependency verbs differs from those assigned to modal verbs such as *kunnen* in that the *subcat* list associated with the V′ phrase headed by *laten* or *zehen* includes one more NP argument than does its V′ complement. That is, the *subcat* list associated with *zehen*'s complement will be the *rest* of the *subcat* list associated with the V′ phrase that *zehen* heads, correctly reflecting the fact that the valence of the V′ phrase *zehen lezen* is one greater than the valence of *lezen*. Thus annotated constituent structures such as the ones depicted in Figures 24 and 25 are generated.

Because the lexical entries for the DIC verbs and the CSDC verbs make no assumptions about the valence of (i.e., the *subcat* list associated with) the V′ complements they subcategorize for, the subcategorized complement of a DIC or CSDC verb can be a V′ that itself consists of another DIC or CSDC verb and its a V′ complement. The 'verb spine' of the constituent structure is constructed in this fashion.

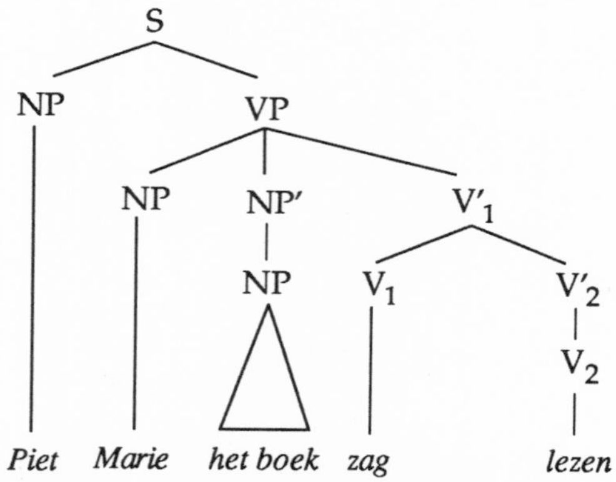

Figure 24 A constituent structure generated by (31) and (32)

$$VP\begin{bmatrix} \text{subcat} = \begin{bmatrix} \text{first} = \boxed{3} \\ \text{rest} = \text{nil} \end{bmatrix} \end{bmatrix} \qquad V'_1\begin{bmatrix} \text{cat} = \text{v} \\ \text{subcat} = \boxed{4} \end{bmatrix}$$

$$V_1\begin{bmatrix} \text{cat} = \text{v} \\ \text{pred} = \text{see} \\ \text{subcat} = \begin{bmatrix} \text{first} = \boxed{1} \\ \text{rest} = \boxed{4}\begin{bmatrix} \text{first} = \begin{bmatrix} \text{cat} = \text{np} \\ \text{pred} = \text{piet} \end{bmatrix} \\ \text{rest} = \boxed{2} \end{bmatrix} \end{bmatrix} \end{bmatrix}$$

$$\boxed{1}\, V'_2\, V_2\begin{bmatrix} \text{cat} = \text{v} \\ \text{pred} = \text{read} \\ \text{inverted} = + \\ \text{subcat} = \boxed{2}\begin{bmatrix} \text{first} = \boxed{3}\begin{bmatrix} \text{cat} = \text{np} \\ \text{pred} = \text{marie} \end{bmatrix} \\ \text{rest} = \begin{bmatrix} \text{first} = \begin{bmatrix} \text{cat} = \text{np} \\ \text{pred} = \text{book} \end{bmatrix} \\ \text{rest} = \text{nil} \end{bmatrix} \end{bmatrix} \end{bmatrix}$$

Figure 25 The attribute-value structure associated with Figure 24

Since modals, control verbs and normal transitive verbs are all represented as argument-taking verbs, some mechansim is needed to distinguish between them. This could be done by assigning the different classes of verbs to different constituent categories, but a neater way is to encode a constituent's category in its feature structure (under the attribute *cat*), which allows a predicate to subcategorize for the category of its complement.

In this fashion, the CSDC and DIC examples are straight-forwardly accounted for. Figure 26 shows the constituent structure associated with example (14c).

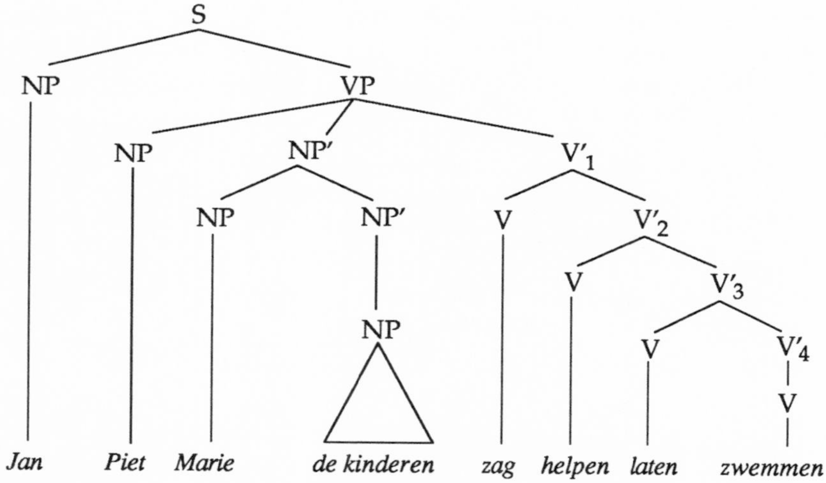

Figure 26 A constituent structure generated by the grammar of (32) and (31)

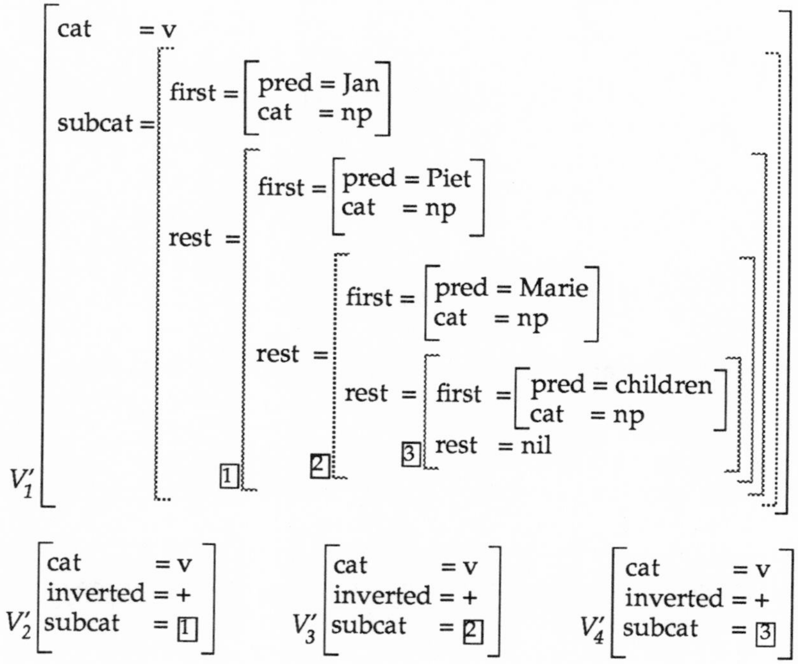

Figure 27 The attribute-value structure associated with Figure 26

Similarly, example (9d), repeated here as (33), which requires a constituent structure that violates the Off-line Parsability Constraint if generated by the grammar (28), is analysed as in Figure 28 and Figure 29 by the grammar of (32).

(33)   dat hij het boek [heeft [kunnen [lezen]]]
       that he the book has   can(Inf)   read
       'that he has been able to read the book'

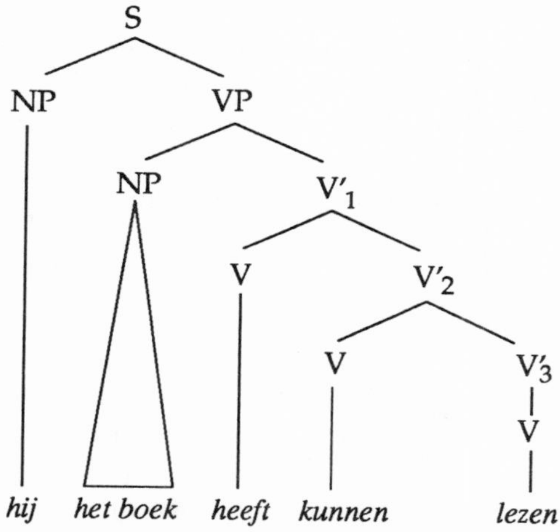

Figure 28 The constituent structure for (33)

$$
V'_1 \begin{bmatrix} \text{cat} & = \text{v} \\ \text{subcat} = \begin{bmatrix} \text{first} = \begin{bmatrix} \text{pred} = \text{pro} \\ \text{cat} & = \text{np} \end{bmatrix} \\ \text{rest} = \begin{bmatrix} \text{first} = \begin{bmatrix} \text{pred} = \text{book} \\ \text{cat} & = \text{np} \end{bmatrix} \\ \text{rest} = \text{nil} \end{bmatrix} \end{bmatrix} \boxed{1} \end{bmatrix}
$$

$$
V'_2 \begin{bmatrix} \text{cat} & = \text{v} \\ \text{inverted} = + \\ \text{subcat} & = \boxed{1} \end{bmatrix} \qquad V'_3 \begin{bmatrix} \text{cat} & = \text{v} \\ \text{inverted} = + \\ \text{subcat} & = \boxed{1} \end{bmatrix}
$$

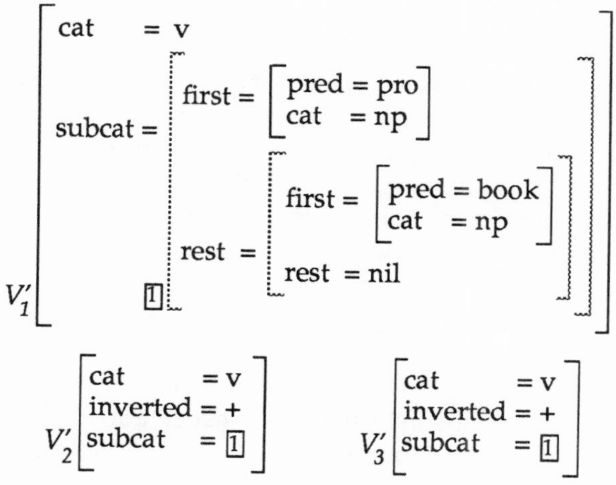

Figure 29 The attribute-value structure associated with Figure 28

Note that the *subcat* list associated with the V′ cluster *heeft kunnen lezen* in Figure 29 has the same structure as the *subcat* list associated with a 'normal' transitive verb such as *lezen*. The NP arguments shown in Figure 28 therefore occupy the same positions in the constituent structure that they would in a 'normal' transitive construction: thus the Off-line Parsability Constraint is not violated.

In conclusion, it is possible to adapt the extended BKPZ analysis of the Double Infinitive Construction to a grammar fragment that uses a hierarchical analysis of grammatical relations, and where the constituent structure of the 'object spine' is coupled to the argument structure (as reflected in the *subcat* list) of the construct as a whole. The resulting grammar fragment differs from the BKPZ grammar in that it does not require constituent structures that violate the off-line parsability constraint in order to generate examples such as the shown in (9d).

4.13 Conclusion

The formal basis of attribute-value based theories of grammar as developed in Chapter 3 only weakly determines the linguistic hypotheses about the nature of linguistic phenomena and their representation that form the content of substantive theories of language. In particular, the formal basis does not even determine the nature of the encoding of grammatical relations in an attribute-value based theory of grammar. I discussed two different ways in which grammatical relations might be encoded in an attribute-value based theory of grammar.

In the direct encoding of grammatical relations the grammatical relations are assigned names which are used as attributes in an attribute-value structure. In the hierarchical encoding the *subcat* list encodes the unsaturated arguments of a constituent. A grammar that uses the direct encoding of grammatical relations requires additional devices to account for subcategorization phenomena, while a grammar that uses the hierarchical encoding of grammartical relations needs no such devices.

I then demonstrated that there are subtle interactions between the formal basis of attribute-value theory, the nature of the encoding of grammatical relations employed by a particular theory, and the analyses of particular constructions that that theory adopts by showing the following constellation of properties to be untenable in an attribute-value based theory of the type introduced in Chapter 3.

(i) A direct encoding of grammatical relations,

(ii) An analysis of the Double Infinitive Construction in Dutch based on the analysis of Bresnan *et al.* (1982), and

(iii) The Off-line parsability constraint.

This particular constellation of properties characterizes LFG as it currently appears in the literature, so this result provides a motivation for an extension or revision to LFG as it is presently formulated, perhaps along the lines discussed in section 5.3.

Chapter 5

Conclusion

In this book I proposed a formalization of attribute-value structures, devised a language for their description and investigated the logic of that language. I then described one way in which this language can be used in an attribute-value based theory of grammar, and investigated interactions between particular substantive linguistic hypotheses and the formal devices of attribute-value grammar used for their expression.

There are two general conclusions to be drawn from this work.

First, one can indeed use logic as a tool to investigate the relationship between the formal basis of a theory of grammar, and how the 'knowledge of language' that grammars represent can be put to use. In this book this investigation was conducted at a relatively abstract level, removed from most substantive hypotheses about the nature of linguistic knowledge. The rationale for this approach was that it provided general results that pertain to the entire class of attribute-value based theories of grammar as defined in Chapter 3, independent of what specific hypotheses they might entail.

Second, the formal basis of attribute-value grammar may constrain substantive hypotheses about the nature of grammar only weakly, but the two are not completely independent. Specifically, I showed that there is an interaction between the representation of grammatical relations in an attribute-value based theory and the type of analysis that it can provide of phenomena such as the Double Infinitive Construction in Dutch.

This book also establishes several more specific results.

First, the successful treatment of negation and disjunction in Chapter 2 shows the importance of distinguishing between attribute-value structures (as linguistic entities) and the language for their description, as Kaplan and Bresnan (1982), Kasper and Rounds (1986) and Moshier and Rounds (1987) do. The relationship between attribute-value structures and the description language is exactly the same as the relationship between models and formulae in model-theoretic accounts of (logical) languages, which suggests that the relationship between a grammar and a linguistic structure in general might be fruitfully viewed in this way.

Second, the simple, classical interpretation of negation and disjunction was made possible by the adopting a 'structuralist perspective', instead of the 'informational perspective' of Kasper and Rounds (1986) and Moshier and Rounds (1987). That is, I assume there is a single linguistic structure that characterizes the utterance, rather than focussing on the changing informational states of the speaker/hearer and characterizing them by a sequence of linguistic structures. This suggests that it might be advantageous in general to view a linguistic structure as a complete object, and to locate the partiality in the system in the relationship between descriptions and linguistic structures, rather than in the structures themselves.

Third, the algorithms proposed in Chapters 2 and 3 operate solely on descriptions of attribute-value structures, rather than on attribute-value structures themselves. In particular, no use is made of the 'unification operation', showing that this operation is not an essential component of either the definition or the use (in the sense of processing) of an attribute-value grammar.

Fourth, by giving an account of the Dutch Double Infinitive Construction might in attribute-value based theories of grammar using a hierarchical encoding of grammatical relations, I showed in Chapter 4 that the key intuition of the Bresnan, Kaplan, Peters and Zaenen (1982) analysis of this construction can be expressed in other attribute-value based theories of grammar, even those that represent grammatical relations in a different way to LFG. This shows that the BKPZ analysis is not restricted to LFG, but it can (in principle at least) be adopted by any attribute-value based theory of grammar.

On a purely technical level, this book introduces several advances in the theory of attribute-value structures.

First, the treatment of attribute-value structures presented in Chapter 2 showed that the use of attributes as values does not involve a 'category error' (as was commonly suspected) but is in fact a principled generalization of the notion of attribute-value structure.

Second, the 'reduced forms' of Section 2.5.1 can be used to provide a simple characterization the set of attribute-models that satisfy a given description, yielding a tool for investigating the descriptive power of attribute-value languages. In particular, Corollary 12 of Section 2.5.4, which shows that any satisfiable wff is equivalent to a reduced form, leads directly to the characterization presented in Section 2.8 of a formula's models in terms of principal filters of subsumption equivalence classes of models.

Third, the Compactness Theorem of Section 2.6 establishes an important property of attribute-value description languages that may be of considerable value for future research in attribute-value systems. Within the context of this book, the Compactness Theorem and the Generalized Completeness Theorem that follows from it were important in establishing the completeness of the axiomatization of the acyclically valid wffs given in Section 2.7.3.

Fourth, the reduction of the language for describing attribute-value structures to the first-order quantifier-free languages with equality presented in Section 2.9 establishes an important connection between attribute-value systems and the predicate calculus: one which was exploited in Section 2.9.3 to determine the computational complexity of satisfiability of formulae from the language for describing attribute-value structures.

The results obtained (and the difficulties encountered) during the course of this book suggest various avenues along which this research might be profitably extended. I discuss several of these in the following sections.

5.1 Constraint Equations

At the purely technical level, the 'existential constraints' of Section 4.2.3, and the closely related 'constraint equations' of LFG, are in need of a principled treatment.[41] Such a treatment would be important for two reasons. First, such existential constraints appear not only in LFG, but also as components of theories outside of the attribute-value

[41] The account given by Kaplan and Bresnan (1982) in terms of 'minimal models' clearly does not extend to general case involving disjunctive descriptions, since the minimal model for a disjunctive description is not unique, as I showed in Section 2.8.

framework (such as the Case Filter and the Theta Criterion of GB), so formal results regarding these devices would bear on these theories as well. Second, a successful treatment of 'existential constraints' may require a nontrivial revision of the attribute-value framework developed here, since, as mentioned in Section 4.2.3, the boolean connectives in languages with these constraints are apparently non-compositional. Intuitively, because 'existential constraints' state requirements that every satisfying model must meet, and because the set of satisfying models is determined by the non-constraint equations of formula in which the constraint appears, it seems that 'existential constraints' are not descriptions of attribute-value structures (in the sense that formulae from the attribute-value language of Chapter 2 are), but rather express conditions that the attribute-value description itself must satisfy. It may be that techniques used in nonmonotonic logic, such as circumscription, can be usefully applied here (Genesereth and Nilsson 1987).

5.2 Implementation Issues

The efficient computational implementation of parsers for attribute-value grammars is of practical and even commercial importance for the development of natural language interfaces, as well as of theoretical importance regarding the neural implementation of language in the brain.

An implementation of Algorithm R of Section 2.5.4 as a formula rewriting system would probably not be efficient enough for practical use with moderately large grammar fragments on computer technology available today. However, it is likely that there are representations of attribute-value descriptions based on the reduced form representation of Section 2.5.1 that will allow more efficient processing. For example, if attention is restricted to conjunctions of positive and negative literals, then techniques similar to those used to implement unification can be used to represent and manipulate terms in a computationally inexpensive fashion.

These techniques do not appear to generalize to the disjunctive case, however. Given the $\mathcal{NP}$-completeness result of Section 2.9.3 (and assuming $\mathcal{P} \neq \mathcal{NP}$) there can be no general algorithm for determining the satisfiability of arbitrary descriptions of attribute-value structures in deterministic polynomial time. Nonetheless, it does seem possible to devise algorithms that are in practice efficient in a sufficiently wide range of cases to be computationally useful. Kasper (1987) shows that expansion to disjunctive normal form (and the exponential explosion in the size of formulae that this may involve) can often be delayed or avoided, and it is likely that his techniques generalize to the attribute-value description languages presented in this book. The logic of these languages presented in Section 2.3 may prove helpful in this investigation, since it can be used to derive new, sound equivalences that can be used in the reduction process. However, the logic provides only part of the answer: more work is needed to devise data structures to encode descriptions of attribute-value structures that have computationally attractive properties.

5.3 Regular Path Equations

At a more linguistic level, it would be interesting to see if the results presented in Chapter 4 regarding the incompatibility of the direct encoding of grammatical relations, the off-line parsability hypothesis, and the BKPZ analysis could be sharpened to yield a formal proof of this claim. This might involve developing formal tools that could be applied other aspects of the interaction between the formal basis of a linguistic theory, the substantive linguistic hypotheses it adopts, and the analyses of particular linguistic phenomena that it can express.

Conversely, it is possible that there are principled extensions to the attribute-value framework that would allow an attribute-value grammar to maintain the direct encoding of grammatical relations, the BKPZ analysis of the Dutch Cross-Serial Dependencies and the off-line parsability hypothesis. In Section 4.11 I claimed that the BKPZ analysis requires constituent structures that violate the off-line parsability constraint because that grammar requires the level of *f*–structure VCOMP embedding of an object NP to be equal to its level of *c*–structure VP embedding. If one extends the attribute-value framework along the lines proposed by Kaplan and Zaenen (in preparation) to include 'functional uncertainty' or 'regular path equations', then the strict 'lock-step' relationship between the levels of attribute-value structure and *c*–structure embedding can be relaxed and the need for constituent structures that violate the off-line parsability constraint avoided, as I discussed in Johnson (1986).

In a language for describing attribute-value structures in which attributes are distinguished from values, a wff of the form $\mathbf{x}(\mathbf{a}_1 \ldots \mathbf{a}_n) \approx \mathbf{x}'(\mathbf{a}_1' \ldots \mathbf{a}_m')$ is true of an attribute-value model if and only if the element that is the value obtained by following the sequence of attributes $\mathbf{a}_1, \ldots, \mathbf{a}_n$ from the element designated by $\mathbf{x}$ is also the element obtained by following the sequence of elements $\mathbf{a}_1', \ldots, \mathbf{a}_m'$ from the element designated by $\mathbf{x}'$. Such a language is extended to include 'functional uncertainty' or 'regular path equations' as follows: wffs are of the form $\mathbf{x}(\mathbf{r}) \approx \mathbf{x}'(\mathbf{r}')$, where $\mathbf{r}$ and $\mathbf{r}'$ are regular expressions over the set of attributes, and a wff $\mathbf{x}(\mathbf{r}) \approx \mathbf{x}'(\mathbf{r}')$ is true of an attribute-value model if and only if there are (possibly null) strings of attributes $\mathbf{a}_1 \ldots \mathbf{a}_n$ generated by $\mathbf{r}$ and $\mathbf{a}_1' \ldots \mathbf{a}_m'$ generated by $\mathbf{r}'$ such that $\mathbf{x}(\mathbf{a}_1 \ldots \mathbf{a}_n) \approx \mathbf{x}'(\mathbf{a}_1' \ldots \mathbf{a}_m')$ is true (in the former sense) of that attribute-value model.

It may be that the techniques used in this book to analyse attribute-value languages can be extended to the analysis of languages with 'regular path equations' as well. Specifically, one can formulate a notion of 'reduced form' for such a language (which have the property of always being satisfiable), and devise an equational calculus. However, as far as I know the completeness of any such equational calculus has not been demonstrated, and no algorithm for reducing arbitrary formulae to reduced form has been proven to terminate.[42]

5.4 Linguistic Properties of the Double Infinitive Construction

Returning to the linguistic level, a more detailed investigation of the BKPZ analysis of the Double Infinitive Construction is required. As I noted in Chapter 4, there is now a substantial literature detailing the interactions of the Double Infinitive Construction with other phenomena such as quantifier scope, clitic placement, WH-movement and anaphora. It would be interesting to confirm that the BKPZ analysis, within the context of fully developed theories of these phenomena, yields empirically correct predictions about their properties in the Double Infinitive Construction.

Along similar lines, it would be interesting to determine if the BKPZ analysis of the Double Infinitive Construction can be extended to account for the various different versions of this construction that appear in different Continental West-Germanic languages. As I remarked in Section 4.10, the syntactic rules given by BKPZ are incapable of generating some of the word orders exhibited in the High German version of the Double Infinitive Construction, but it is easy (if somewhat *ad hoc*) to devise a set of rules that do generate the desired orders. On the other hand, it may be somewhat more difficult to extend the BKPZ analysis to account for the version of the Double Infinitive Construction that appears in the Germanic dialect Züritüüsch (spoken in Zürich). Extrapolating slightly from the account given by Haegeman and van Riemsdijk (1986), it seems that the Züritüüsch Double Infinitive Construction satisfies the following three statements:

42 The chief difficulty arises from the possibility of cyclic models.

(i) A syntactically less embedded NP must precede a syntactically more embedded NP.

(ii) A syntactically less embedded V must precede a syntactically more embedded V.

(iii) All argument NPs of a verb must precede that verb.[43]

Thus examples such as those shown in (iv) through (vi) (= HvR 36e, 36f and 36g) are obtained.

(iv) das er wil sini chind medizin laa studiere
that he will his child medicine let study
'that he will let his child study medicine'

(v) das er wil sini chind laa medizin studiere
that he will his child let medicine study
'that he will let his child study medicine'

(vi) *das er wil laa sini chind medizin studiere
that he will let his child medicine study
'that he will let his child study medicine'

There does not seem to be a straight-forward extension of either the direct encoding or the hierarchical encoding versions of the BKPZ analysis that accounts for the word-order constraints listed in (i)–(iii). As far as I know, it is only possible to account for these constructions in a relatively complex and unintuitive fashion.[44] On the other hand, it is possible to give a relatively succinct account of these constructions within the Categorial Grammar framework developed by Steedman (1985), and it would be interesting to see if that analysis could be translated into the attribute-value framework. It is easy to represent the categories of Steedman's (1985) Categorial Grammar in an attribute-value framework as list structures similar to those used to encode the argument list of a category in the hierarchical encoding of grammatical relations. Unfortunately, Steedman's analysis makes crucial use of an operation called 'Forward Partial Combination', which does not appear to be directly encodable in an attribute-value framework. It would be interesting, then, to investigate further both Steedman's analysis of the Double Infinitive Construction and the

---

[43] I am assuming that verbs such as *laa* 'let' are object control verbs, following the corresponding analysis of Bresnan, Kaplan, Peters and Zaenen (1986) for Dutch; see section 4.8.

[44] By encoding grammatical relations using a modified version of a difference list, I have devised a grammar that generates precisely the word-order possibilities allowed by generalizations (i) - (iii). (A difference list is a data structure commonly used in Prolog programming). Thus there is an attribute-value grammar that generates exactly these word orders.

possibility of extending the attribute-value framework to allow Steedman's 'Forward Partial Combination' operation.[45]

5.5 Parsing as Deduction

Finally, the successful treatment of the logic of the language of attribute-value structures presented in Chapter 2 suggests that it might be useful to treat other linguistic structures in a similar way, permitting powerful logical tools to be brought to bear on questions of formal linguistics. In particular, it might be possible to develop a language for simultaneously describing both the constituent structure and the attribute-value components of attribute-value grammars. If a logic could be developed for such a language, then the processing involved in parsing could be viewed abstractly as a specialized kind of deduction (Pereira and Warren 1983).

In such a system a grammar of a language would be represented as a set of axioms, and the parsing operation viewed as a process of deriving logical consequences following from these and information about a specific utterance. This is attractive because it directly instantiates the intuition that a grammar represents contingent knowledge of a language, and that language processing is the use of that knowledge. This research program has in fact been carried out for Definite Clause Grammars, as described by Pereira and Warren (1983). Within the attribute-value approach to grammar, Rounds and Manaster-Ramer (1987) have recently proposed a logical formulation of Kay's (1979) Functional Unification Grammar in which constituent structure is represented as a component of attribute-value structure.

Significant problems in this area still remain to be solved. For example, the satisfiability problem for formulae from the language developed by Rounds and Manaster-Ramer (1987) is undecidable. Intuitively, this problem is undecidable for the same reason that the recognition problem for attribute-value grammars without the off-line parsability restriction is undecidable: no bound exists on the amount of 'structure' that can correspond to a given string.[46] Further,

---

45 One way of doing this would be to extend the language for describing attribute-value structures with an 'append' operation. The logical and computational properties of the resulting language are at this point unknown.

46 It is not clear what response is appropriate to this undecidability result. Earlier I claimed that showing the decidability of the universal recognition problem is an important part of demonstrating that the knowledge of language that a grammar represents can actually be put to use, but others can (and have) taken the contrary position, as I pointed out in Section 3.4.3. It may also be possible to restrict these languages in a way that makes the satisfiability problem for these languages decidable, perhaps along the lines proposed by Rounds (1986).

practical computational implementations for grammars written in such logics have yet to be devised. Nonetheless, the prospect of devising a language capable of expressing the 'generates' relationship between strings and linguistic structures and viewing the parsing operation as deduction in this language is one of the most exciting possibilities on the horizon today.

Bibliography

Aho, A. V., R. Sethi and J. D. Ullman. *Compilers, Principles, Techniques and Tools.* Addison-Wesley, Reading, Massachusetts. 1986.

Aho, A. V. and J. D. Ullman. *The Theory of Parsing, Translation and Compiling, Volume 1.* Prentice Hall, New Jersy. 1972.

Andrews, P. B. *An Introduction to Mathematical Logic and Type Theory: To Truth through Proof.* Academic Press, Orlando, Florida. 1986.

Besten, H. d. and J. A. Edmondson. The verbal complex in Continental West Germanic. In W. Abraham, editor, *On the formal syntax of the Westgermania,* pages 155–216, Benjamins, Amsterdam. 1983.

Bresnan, J. W, R. M. Kaplan, S. Peters and A. Zaenen. Cross-Serial Dependencies in Dutch. *Linguistic Inquiry,* 13, pages 613–635. 1982.

Chomsky, N. *Lectures on government and binding. (Studies in generative grammar 9.)* Foris, Dordrecht. 1981.

Chomsky, N. *Knowledge of Language, Its Nature, Origin and Use.* Praeger, New York. 1986.

Evers, A. *The Transformational cycle in Dutch and German.* Ph.D. dissertation, University of Utrecht. Distributed by Indiana University Linguistics Club. 1976.

Fitting, M. C. *Intuitionistic Logic, Model Theory and Forcing.* North Holland, Amsterdam. 1969.

Flickenger, D., C. Pollard and T. Wasow, Structure-Sharing in Lexical Representation, In *Proceedings of the 23h Annual Meeting,* pages 257–266, Association for Computational Linguistics, University of Chicago, Chicago, 1986.

Ford, M., J. Bresnan and R. M. Kaplan. A Competence-based Theory of Syntactic Closure. In J. Bresnan, editor, *The Mental Representation of Grammatical Relations,* pages 727–796, The MIT Press, Cambridge, Mass. 1982.

Gallier, J. H. *Logic for Computer Science,* Harper and Row, New York. 1986.

Garey, M. R. and D. S. Johnson. *Computers and Intractability, A Guide to the Theory of NP–Completeness.* W. H. Freeman and Company, New York. 1979.

Gazdar, G., E. Klein, G. K. Pullum and I. A. Sag. *Generalized Phrase Structure Grammar.* Harvard University Press, Cambridge, Mass. 1982.

Gorn, S. Explicit Definitions and Linguistic Dominoes. In J. Hart and S. Takasu, editors, *Systems and Computer Science.* University of Toronto Press, Toronto, Canada. 1965.

Grimshaw, J. On the Representation of Romance Reflexive Clitics. In J. Bresnan, editor, *The Mental Representation of Grammatical Relations,* pages 87–148, The MIT Press, Cambridge, Mass. 1982.

Haegeman, L. and H. v. Riemsdijk. Verb projection raising, scope and the typology of verb movement rules. *Linguistic Inquiry* 17, pages 417–466. 1986.

Hopcroft, J. E. and J. D. Ullman. *Introduction to Automata Theory, Languages and Computation,* Addison-Wesley, Reading, Mass. 1979.

Johnson, M. The LFG Treatment of Discontinuity and the Double Infinitive Construction in Dutch, in *Proceedings of the West Coast Conference on Formal Linguistics,* Stanford Linguistics Association, 1986.

Kaplan, R. and J. Bresnan, Lexical-functional grammar, a formal system for grammatical representation. In J. Bresnan, editor, *The Mental Representation of Grammatical Relations,* pages 173–281, The MIT Press, Cambridge, Mass. 1982.

Karttunen, L. Features and Values. In *Proceedings of Coling 1984,* Association for Computational Linguistics, Stanford, 1984.

Karttunen, L. *Radical Lexicalism.* CSLI Report 68. CSLI, Stanford University, California, 1986.

Kasper, R. T. *Feature Structures: A Logical Theory with Application to Language Analysis.* Ph.D. thesis, University of Michigan, Ann Arbor, Michigan, 1987.

Kasper, R. T. and W. C. Rounds, A logical semantics for feature structures. In *Proceedings of the 24th Annual Meeting,* pages 257–266, Association for Computational Linguistics, Columbia University, New York, 1986.

Kay, M. Functional Grammar. In *Proceedings of the Fifth Annual Meeting of the Berkeley Linguistics Society,* Berkeley Linguistics Society, Berkeley, California. 1979.

Knuth, D. E. *The Art of Computer Programming, Volume 1.* Addison-Wesley, Reading, Massachusetts. 1973.

Kroch, A. S. and B. Santorini. The Derived Consituent Structure of the West Germanic Verb Raising Construction. In R. Freiden, editor, *Proceedings of the Princeton Workshop on Comparative Grammar.* The MIT Press, Cambridge, Massachusetts. To appear.

Levelt, W. J. M. *Formal Grammars in Linguistics and Psycholinguistics.* 3 vols. Mouton, The Hague. 1974.

Marcus, M. *A Theory of Syntactic Recognition for Natural Language.* The MIT Press, Cambridge, Massachusetts. 1980.

Mathews, R. Are the sentences of a language a recursive set? *Synthese* 40, pages 209–224. 1979.

Minsky, M. *Computation, Finite and Infinite Machines.* Prentice Hall, New Jersy. 1967.

Moshier, M. D. and W. C. Rounds, A logic for partially specified data structures, In *ACM Symposium on the Principles of Programming Languages,* Association for Computing Machinery, Munich, Germany, 1987.

Nelson, G. and Oppen, D. C. Fast Decision Procedures based on Congruence Closure. *J.ACM* 27.2, pages 245–57. 1980.

Oppen, D. C. Reasoning about Recursively Defined Data Structures. *J.ACM* 27.3, pages 403–411. 1980.

Pereira, F. C. N. Grammars and Logics of Partial Information. In *Proceedings of the International Conference on Logic Programming,* Melbourne, Australia, 1987.

Pereira, F. C. N. and S. M. Shieber. The semantics of grammar formalisms seen as computer languages. In *Proceedings of Coling 1984*, pages 123–129, Association for Computational Linguistics, Stanford, 1984.

Pereira, F. C. N. and D. Warren. Parsing as Deduction. In *Proceedings of the 21st Annual Meeting*, pages 137–144, Association for Computational Linguistics, MIT, Massachusetts. 1987.

Pinker, S., A Theory of the Acquisition of Lexical Interpretive Grammars. In J. Bresnan, editor, *The Mental Representation of Grammatical Relations*, pages 655–726, The MIT Press, Cambridge, Mass. 1982.

Pollard, C. and I. A. Sag, *Information-based Syntax and Semantics.* CSLI Lecture Notes Series, Chicago University Press, Chicago, 1987.

Putnam, H. Some issues in the theory of grammar. In *Proceedings of Symposia on Applied Mathematics*, vol. 12. American Mathematical Society. 1961.

Rounds, W. C. and R. Kasper. A complete logical calculus for record structures representing linguistic information. In *Symposium on Logic in Computer Science*, IEEE Computer Society. 1986.

Rounds, W. C. and A. Manaster-Ramer. A logical version of functional grammar. In *Proceedings of the 25th Annual Meeting*, pages 89–96, Association for Computational Linguistics, Stanford University, California. 1987.

Sag, I. A. and C. Pollard, *HPSG, An Informal Synopsis*, CSLI Report 79, CSLI, Stanford University, California. 1987.

Shieber, S. M. *An Introduction to Unification-based Approaches to Grammar.* CSLI Lecture Notes Series, Chicago University Press, Chicago, 1986.

Stabler, E. P. Jr. Berwick and Weinberg on linguistics and computational psychology. *Cognition* 17, pages 155-179. 1984.

Steedman, M. Dependency and coordination in the grammar of Dutch and English. *Language* 61, pages 523–568. 1985.

Zaenen, A. Infinitival Complements in Dutch. In *Papers from the 15th Regional Meeting of the Chicago Linguistic Society*, pages 378–389. The Chicago Linguistic Society, Chicago. 1979.

Index

CSLI Publications

Reports

The following titles have been published in the CSLI Reports series. These reports may be obtained from CSLI Publications, Ventura Hall, Stanford University, Stanford, CA 94305-4115.

The Situation in Logic–I Jon Barwise CSLI–84–2 ($*2.00*)

Coordination and How to Distinguish Categories Ivan Sag, Gerald Gazdar, Thomas Wasow, and Steven Weisler CSLI–84–3 ($*3.50*)

Belief and Incompleteness Kurt Konolige CSLI–84–4 ($*4.50*)

Equality, Types, Modules and Generics for Logic Programming Joseph Goguen and José Meseguer CSLI–84–5 ($*2.50*)

Lessons from Bolzano Johan van Benthem CSLI–84–6 ($*1.50*)

Self-propagating Search: A Unified Theory of Memory Pentti Kanerva CSLI–84–7 ($*9.00*)

Reflection and Semantics in LISP Brian Cantwell Smith CSLI–84–8 ($*2.50*)

The Implementation of Procedurally Reflective Languages Jim des Rivières and Brian Cantwell Smith CSLI–84–9 ($*3.00*)

Parameterized Programming Joseph Goguen CSLI–84–10 ($*3.50*)

Morphological Constraints on Scandinavian Tone Accent Meg Withgott and Per-Kristian Halvorsen CSLI–84–11 ($*2.50*)

Partiality and Nonmonotonicity in Classical Logic Johan van Benthem CSLI–84–12 ($*2.00*)

Shifting Situations and Shaken Attitudes Jon Barwise and John Perry CSLI–84–13 ($*4.50*)

Aspectual Classes in Situation Semantics Robin Cooper CSLI–85–14-C ($*4.00*)

Completeness of Many-Sorted Equational Logic Joseph Goguen and José Meseguer CSLI–84–15 ($*2.50*)

Moving the Semantic Fulcrum Terry Winograd CSLI–84–17 ($*1.50*)

On the Mathematical Properties of Linguistic Theories C. Raymond Perrault CSLI–84–18 ($*3.00*)

A Simple and Efficient Implementation of Higher-order Functions in LISP Michael P. Georgeff and Stephen F.Bodnar CSLI–84–19 ($*4.50*)

On the Axiomatization of "if-then-else" Irène Guessarian and José Meseguer CSLI–85–20 ($*3.00*)

The Situation in Logic–II: Conditionals and Conditional Information Jon Barwise CSLI–84–21 ($*3.00*)

Principles of OBJ2 Kokichi Futatsugi, Joseph A. Goguen, Jean-Pierre Jouannaud, and José Meseguer CSLI–85–22 ($*2.00*)

Querying Logical Databases Moshe Vardi CSLI–85–23 ($*1.50*)

Computationally Relevant Properties of Natural Languages and Their Grammar Gerald Gazdar and Geoff Pullum CSLI–85–24 ($*3.50*)

An Internal Semantics for Modal Logic: Preliminary Report Ronald Fagin and Moshe Vardi CSLI–85–25 ($*2.00*)

The Situation in Logic–III: Situations, Sets and the Axiom of Foundation Jon Barwise CSLI–85–26 ($*2.50*)

Semantic Automata Johan van Benthem CSLI–85–27 ($*2.50*)

Restrictive and Non-Restrictive Modification Peter Sells CSLI–85–28 ($*3.00*)

Institutions: Abstract Model Theory for Computer Science J. A. Goguen and R. M. Burstall CSLI–85–30 ($*4.50*)

A Formal Theory of Knowledge and Action Robert C. Moore CSLI–85–31 ($*5.50*)

Finite State Morphology: A Review of Koskenniemi (1983) Gerald Gazdar CSLI–85–32 ($*1.50*)

The Role of Logic in Artificial Intelligence Robert C. Moore CSLI–85–33 ($*2.00*)

Applicability of Indexed Grammars to Natural Languages Gerald Gazdar CSLI–85–34 ($*2.00*)

Commonsense Summer: Final Report Jerry R. Hobbs, et al CSLI–85–35 ($*12.00*)

Limits of Correctness in Computers Brian Cantwell Smith CSLI–85–36 ($*2.50*)

On the Coherence and Structure of Discourse Jerry R. Hobbs CSLI–85–37 ($*3.00*)

The Coherence of Incoherent Discourse Jerry R. Hobbs and Michael H. Agar CSLI–85–38 ($*2.50*)

The Structures of Discourse Structure Barbara Grosz and Candace L. Sidner CSLI–85–39 ($*4.50*)

A Complete, Type-free "Second-order" Logic and Its Philosophical Foundations Christopher Menzel CSLI–86–40 ($*4.50*)

Possible-world Semantics for Autoepistemic Logic Robert C. Moore CSLI–85–41 ($*2.00*)

Deduction with Many-Sorted Rewrite José Meseguer and Joseph A. Goguen CSLI–85–42 ($*1.50*)

On Some Formal Properties of Metarules Hans Uszkoreit and Stanley Peters CSLI–85–43 ($*1.50*)

Language, Mind, and Information John Perry CSLI–85–44 ($*2.00*)

Constraints on Order Hans Uszkoreit CSLI–86–46 ($*3.00*)

Linear Precedence in Discontinuous Constituents: Complex Fronting in German Hans Uszkoreit CSLI–86–47 ($*2.50*)

A Compilation of Papers on Unification-Based Grammar Formalisms, Parts I and II Stuart M. Shieber, Fernando C.N. Pereira, Lauri Karttunen, and Martin Kay CSLI–86–48 ($*10.00*)

An Algorithm for Generating Quantifier Scopings Jerry R. Hobbs and Stuart M. Shieber CSLI–86–49 ($*2.50*)

Verbs of Change, Causation, and Time Dorit Abusch CSLI–86–50 ($*2.00*)

Noun-Phrase Interpretation Mats Rooth CSLI–86–51 ($*2.00*)

Noun Phrases, Generalized Quantifiers and Anaphora Jon Barwise CSLI–86–52 ($*2.50*)

Circumstantial Attitudes and Benevolent Cognition John Perry CSLI–86–53 ($*1.50*)

A Study in the Foundations of Programming Methodology: Specifications, Institutions, Charters and Parchments Joseph A. Goguen and R. M. Burstall CSLI–86–54 ($*2.50*)

Quantifiers in Formal and Natural Languages Dag Westerståhl CSLI–86–55 ($*7.50*)

Intentionality, Information, and Matter Ivan Blair CSLI–86–56 ($*3.00*)

Graphs and Grammars William Marsh CSLI–86–57 ($*2.00*)

Computer Aids for Comparative Dictionaries Mark Johnson CSLI–86–58 ($*2.00*)

The Relevance of Computational Linguistics Lauri Karttunen CSLI–86–59 ($*2.50*)

Grammatical Hierarchy and Linear Precedence Ivan A. Sag CSLI–86–60 ($*3.50*)

D-PATR: A Development Environment for Unification-Based Grammars Lauri Karttunen CSLI–86–61 (*$4.00*)

A Sheaf-Theoretic Model of Concurrency Luís F. Monteiro and Fernando C. N. Pereira CSLI–86–62 (*$3.00*)

Discourse, Anaphora and Parsing Mark Johnson and Ewan Klein CSLI–86–63 (*$2.00*)

Tarski on Truth and Logical Consequence John Etchemendy CSLI–86–64 (*$3.50*)

The LFG Treatment of Discontinuity and the Double Infinitive Construction in Dutch Mark Johnson CSLI–86–65 (*$2.50*)

Categorial Unification Grammars Hans Uszkoreit CSLI–86–66 (*$2.50*)

Generalized Quantifiers and Plurals Godehard Link CSLI–86–67 (*$2.00*)

Radical Lexicalism Lauri Karttunen CSLI–86–68 (*$2.50*)

Understanding Computers and Cognition: Four Reviews and a Response Mark Stefik, Editor CSLI–87–70 (*$3.50*)

The Correspondence Continuum Brian Cantwell Smith CSLI–87–71 (*$4.00*)

The Role of Propositional Objects of Belief in Action David J. Israel CSLI–87–72 (*$2.50*)

From Worlds to Situations John Perry CSLI–87–73 (*$2.00*)

Two Replies Jon Barwise CSLI–87–74 (*$3.00*)

Semantics of Clocks Brian Cantwell Smith CSLI–87–75 (*$2.50*)

Varieties of Self-Reference Brian Cantwell Smith CSLI–87–76 (*Forthcoming*)

The Parts of Perception Alexander Pentland CSLI–87–77 (*$4.00*)

Topic, Pronoun, and Agreement in Chicheŵa Joan Bresnan and S. A. Mchombo CSLI–87–78 (*$5.00*)

HPSG: An Informal Synopsis Carl Pollard and Ivan A. Sag CSLI–87–79 (*$4.50*)

The Situated Processing of Situated Language Susan Stucky CSLI–87–80 (*Forthcoming*)

Muir: A Tool for Language Design Terry Winograd CSLI–87–81 (*$2.50*)

Final Algebras, Cosemicomputable Algebras, and Degrees of Unsolvability Lawrence S. Moss, José Meseguer, and Joseph A. Goguen CSLI–87–82 (*$3.00*)

The Synthesis of Digital Machines with Provable Epistemic Properties Stanley J. Rosenschein and Leslie Pack Kaelbling CSLI–87–83 (*$3.50*)

Formal Theories of Knowledge in AI and Robotics Stanley J. Rosenschein CSLI–87–84 (*$1.50*)

An Architecture for Intelligent Reactive Systems Leslie Pack Kaelbling CSLI–87–85 (*$2.00*)

Order-Sorted Unification José Meseguer, Joseph A. Goguen, and Gert Smolka CSLI–87–86 (*$2.50*)

Modular Algebraic Specification of Some Basic Geometrical Constructions Joseph A. Goguen CSLI–87–87 (*$2.50*)

Persistence, Intention and Commitment Phil Cohen and Hector Levesque CSLI–87–88 (*$3.50*)

Rational Interaction as the Basis for Communication Phil Cohen and Hector Levesque CSLI–87–89 ()

An Application of Default Logic to Speech Act Theory C. Raymond Perrault CSLI–87–90 (*$2.50*)

Models and Equality for Logical Programming Joseph A. Goguen and José Meseguer CSLI–87–91 (*$3.00*)

Order-Sorted Algebra Solves the Constructor-Selector, Mulitple Representation and Coercion Problems Joseph A. Goguen and José Meseguer CSLI–87–92 (*$2.00*)

Extensions and Foundations for Object-Oriented Programming Joseph A. Goguen and José Meseguer CSLI–87–93 ($*3.50*)

L3 Reference Manual: Version 2.19 William Poser CSLI–87–94 ($*2.50*)

Change, Process and Events Carol E. Cleland CSLI–88–95 ($*4.00*)

One, None, a Hundred Thousand Specification Languages Joseph A. Goguen CSLI–87–96 ($*2.00*)

Constituent Coordination in HPSG Derek Proudian and David Goddeau CSLI–87–97 ($*1.50*)

A Language/Action Perspective on the Design of Cooperative Work Terry Winograd CSLI–87–98 ($*2.50*)

Implicature and Definite Reference Jerry R. Hobbs CSLI–87–99 ($*1.50*)

Thinking Machines: Can There be? Are we? Terry Winograd CSLI–87–100 ($*2.50*)

Situation Semantics and Semantic Interpretation in Constraint-based Grammars Per-Kristian Halvorsen CSLI–87–101 ($*1.50*)

Category Structures Gerald Gazdar, Geoffrey K. Pullum, Robert Carpenter, Ewan Klein, Thomas E. Hukari, Robert D. Levine CSLI–87–102 ($*3.00*)

Cognitive Theories of Emotion Ronald Alan Nash CSLI–87–103 ($*2.50*)

Toward an Architecture for Resource-bounded Agents Martha E. Pollack, David J. Israel, and Michael E. Bratman CSLI–87–104 ($*2.00*)

On the Relation Between Default and Autoepistemic Logic Kurt Konolige CSLI–87–105 ($*3.00*)

Three Responses to Situation Theory Terry Winograd CSLI–87–106 ($*2.50*)

Subjects and Complements in HPSG Robert Borsley CSLI–87–107 ($*2.50*)

Tools for Morphological Analysis Mary Dalrymple, Ronald M. Kaplan, Lauri Karttunen, Kimmo Koskenniemi, Sami Shaio, Michael Wescoat CSLI–87–108 ($*10.00*)

Cognitive Significance and New Theories of Reference John Perry CSLI–87–109 ($*2.00*)

Fourth Year Report of the Situated Language Research Program CSLI–87–111 (*free*)

Bare Plurals, Naked Relatives, and Their Kin Dietmar Zaefferer CSLI–87–112 ($*2.50*)

Events and "Logical Form" Stephen Neale CSLI–88–113 ($*2.00*)

Backwards Anaphora and Discourse Structure: Some Considerations Peter Sells CSLI–87–114 ($*2.50*)

Toward a Linking Theory of Relation Changing Rules in LFG Lori Levin CSLI–87–115 ($*4.00*)

Fuzzy Logic L. A. Zadeh CSLI–88–116 ($*2.50*)

Dispositional Logic and Commonsense Reasoning L. A. Zadeh CSLI–88–117 ($*2.00*)

Intention and Personal Policies Michael Bratman CSLI–88–118 ($*2.00*)

Propositional Attitudes and Russellian Propositions Robert C. Moore CSLI–88–119 ($*2.50*)

Unification and Agreement Michael Barlow CSLI–88–120 ($*2.50*)

Extended Categorial Grammar Suson Yoo and Kiyong Lee CSLI–88–121 ($*4.00*)

The Situation in Logic—IV: On the Model Theory of Common Knowledge Jon Barwise CSLI–88–122 ($*2.00*)

Unaccusative Verbs in Dutch and the Syntax-Semantics Interface Annie Zaenen CSLI–88–123 ($*3.00*)

What Is Unification? A Categorical View of Substitution, Equation and Solution Joseph A. Goguen CSLI–88–124 ($*3.50*)

Types and Tokens in Linguistics Sylvain Bromberger CSLI–88–125 (*$3.00*)

Determination, Uniformity, and Relevance: Normative Criteria for Generalization and Reasoning by Analogy Todd Davies CSLI–88–126 (*$4.50*)

Modal Subordination and Pronominal Anaphora in Discourse Craige Roberts CSLI–88–127 (*$4.50*)

The Prince and the Phone Booth: Reporting Puzzling Beliefs Mark Crimmins and John Perry CSLI–88–128 (*$3.50*)

Set Values for Unification-Based Grammar Formalisms and Logic Programming William Rounds CSLI–88–129 (*$4.00*)

Fifth Year Report of the Situated Language Research Program CSLI–88–130 (*free*)

Locative Inversion in Chicheŵa: A Case Study of Factorization in Grammar Joan Bresnan and Jonni M. Kanerva CSLI–88–131 (*$5.00*)

An Information-Based Theory of Agreement Carl Pollard and Ivan A. Sag CSLI–88–132 (*$4.00*)

Lecture Notes

The titles in this series are distributed by the University of Chicago Press and may be purchased in academic or university bookstores or ordered directly from the distributor at 5801 Ellis Avenue, Chicago, Illinois 60637.

A Manual of Intensional Logic Johan van Benthem, second edition. Lecture Notes No. 1

Emotions and Focus Helen Fay Nissenbaum. Lecture Notes No. 2

Lectures on Contemporary Syntactic Theories Peter Sells. Lecture Notes No. 3

An Introduction to Unification-Based Approaches to Grammar Stuart M. Shieber. Lecture Notes No. 4

The Semantics of Destructive Lisp Ian A. Mason. Lecture Notes No. 5

An Essay on Facts Ken Olson. Lecture Notes No. 6

Logics of Time and Computation Robert Goldblatt. Lecture Notes No. 7

Word Order and Constituent Structure in German Hans Uszkoreit. Lecture Notes No. 8

Color and Color Perception: A Study in Anthropocentric Realism David Russel Hilbert. Lecture Notes No. 9

Prolog and Natural-Language Analysis Fernando C. N. Pereira and Stuart M. Shieber. Lecture Notes No. 10

Working Papers in Grammatical Theory and Discourse Structure: Interactions of Morphology, Syntax, and Discourse M. Iida, S. Wechsler, and D. Zec (Eds.) with an Introduction by Joan Bresnan. Lecture Notes No. 11

Natural Language Processing in the 1980s: A Bibliography Gerald Gazdar, Alex Franz, Karen Osborne, and Roger Evans. Lecture Notes No. 12

Information-Based Syntax and Semantics Carl Pollard and Ivan Sag. Lecture Notes No. 13

Non-Well-Founded Sets Peter Aczel. Lecture Notes No. 14

Partiality, Truth and Persistence Tore Langholm. Lecture Notes No. 15

Attribute-Value Logic and the Theory of Grammar Mark Johnson. Lecture Notes No. 16

Mark Johnson is assistant professor in cognitive and linguistic sciences at Brown University. He was a Fairchild postdoctoral fellow at the Massachusetts Institute of Technology during the 1987-88 academic year.